CO-ATX-679

African-American Odyssey

African-American Odyssey

The Stewarts, 1853–1963

Albert S. Broussard

UNIVERSITY PRESS OF KANSAS

© 1998 by the University Press of Kansas

All rights reserved

Photo insert provided by courtesy of the Moorland-Spingarn Research Center, Howard University

Published by the University Press of Kansas (Lawrence, Kansas 66049), which was organized by the Kansas Board of Regents and is operated and funded by Emporia State University, Fort Hays State University, Kansas State University, Pittsburg State University, the University of Kansas, and Wichita State University

Library of Congress Cataloging-in-Publication Data

Broussard, Albert S.

African-American odyssey : the Stewarts, 1853-1963 / Albert S. Broussard.

p.   cm.

Includes index.

ISBN 0-7006-0916-4 (cloth : alk. paper)

1. Stewart, T. McCants (Thomas McCants), 1854?-1923. 2. Afro-Americans—Biography. 3. Stewart, T. McCants (Thomas McCants), 1854?-1923—Family. 4. Stewart family. 5. Afro-American families—History. I. Title.

E185.97.S844 1998

973'.0496073'0092—dc21

[b]   98-23811

British Library Cataloguing in Publication Data is available.

Printed in the United States of America

10 9 8 7 6 5 4 3 2 1

The paper used in this publication meets the minimum requirements of the American National Standard for Permanence of Paper for Printed Library Materials Z39.48-1984.

For my mother,

Margaret Broussard,

and for Valerie and Matthew,

with love

Contents

❖ ❖ ❖ ❖ ❖ ❖ ❖

Acknowledgments

❖ ❖ ❖ ❖ ❖ ❖ ❖

All books, to some degree, are collaborative projects, and this one is no exception. Numerous scholars, colleagues, librarians, archivists, and friends have contributed to the completion of this book. Donald J. Pisani read an early draft of the manuscript, offered numerous suggestions, and urged me to place the lives of the Stewart family and their descendants into the broader context of western and American history. August Meier, George C. Wright, Donald A. Ritchie, and Robert A. Calvert each read several chapters, and I have profited from their comments. Quintard Taylor read my chapters on McCants and Carlotta Stewart, and shared with me his unrivaled knowledge of African-Americans in the Pacific Northwest. Patricia Nelson Limerick, through her encouragement and scholarship, helped me to conceptualize the West in a broader context by arguing that Hawaii and Alaska should be viewed also as part of the West. Larry Yarak read my material on T. McCants Stewart's residence in Africa and made numerous suggestions. Carleton Mabee permitted me to read his extensive notes on African-Americans in New York. Darlene Clark Hine, a friend and critic, deserves a special note of gratitude, for she encouraged me at every stage of my research and writing. Gretchen Lemke-Santangelo read the entire manuscript, and her incisive and careful critique has made this a much better book.

I am indebted, as well, to many librarians and archivists who provided assistance. I wish to especially thank William O. Harris and Henry I. Mac-Adam, archivists at the Princeton Theological Seminary, for their assistance during a most enjoyable research visit. The entire staff at the Moorland-Spingarn Research Center, especially Esme Bhan, was always helpful, and allowed me to read the restricted San Quentin prison files in the Stewart-Flippin Papers. Librarians and archivists at the New York Public Library, California State Archives, Oregon Historical Society, Schomburg Center for Research in Black Culture, Columbia University Archives and Special Collections, Amistad Research Center, New York State Historical Association,

Nebraska Historical Society, Hampton University Archives, Tuskegee University, Cincinnati Historical Society, Wilberforce University, British Library, College of Charleston's Special Collections, Charleston Library Society, South Carolina Historical Society, Library of Congress Manuscripts Division, Medical College of Pennsylvania, and Enid Baa Library, St. Thomas, Virgin Islands, assisted my research at various stages, answered my inquiries, and directed me to new sources. Mary S. Judd, archivist at the Punahou School in Hawaii, provided me with material on Carlotta Stewart's years at Punahou, and Alicia Hartsell's assistance at the Kauai Historical Society was invaluable. Warren S. Nishimoto allowed me to read the transcripts of African-Americans in Hawaii at the University of Hawaii's Center for Oral History and placed the entire collection of oral interviews at my disposal.

This book is considerably richer in detail because several descendants of the Stewarts granted me personal interviews. They include Katherine Stewart Flippin and Beryl E. Kean, both granddaughters of T. McCants Stewart, Judge Franklin W. Morton, Jr., and his wife Gwen. Judge Morton, the grandson of Dr. Verina Morton-Jones, invited me to his homes in Sarasota, Florida, and West Chester, Pennsylvania, and permitted me to read the Morton family papers in his possession. He also embraced me as a friend and confidant.

The National Endowment for the Humanities awarded me a Travel to Collections Grant, and Texas A & M University provided several Mini-Grants to assist my research. Julia Kirk Blackwelder, my department head and colleague, granted me release time for one semester in order to revise the manuscript. Judy Mattson, my word processor, assisted me in preparing the final draft of the manuscript.

Most of all, I am indebted to my editors and family. Michael Briggs, editor-in-chief at the University Press of Kansas, supported this book from its inception. I owe a special note of gratitude, however, to Nancy Scott Jackson, acquisitions editor, for her consistent encouragement and enthusiasm; to Carol Estes, my copy editor, and to Melinda Wirkus, senior production editor. My family, who tolerated my travel, writing, and mood swings during the course of this study, deserves a medal, though this acknowledgment will have to suffice. Mary L. Broussard, my wife, supported my work at every stage. Matthew and Valerie, my son and daughter, asked only that I travel less often. Finally, my mother, Margaret Broussard, who saw this story unfold, has applauded me every step of the way.

Introduction

❖   ❖   ❖   ❖   ❖   ❖   ❖

Family history remains one of the most exciting areas of historical inquiry, and the past several decades have witnessed considerable scholarship in this area. These studies have enriched our understanding of such diverse issues as gender relations, class, patriarchy, occupational roles in both the household and workplace, relationships between siblings, divergent expectations for boys and girls, and values transmission within the family. However, most of them deal with white families. Many of these books were written during the explosion in women's studies and social history in the 1970s and 1980s. Richard Buel, Jr., and Joy Day Buel's compelling study of Mary Fish and her descendants exemplifies the best of this scholarship. A poignant account of an eighteenth-century white woman and her family, the Buels traced this remarkable woman from 1736 in Stonington, Connecticut, through the era of the American Revolution and its aftermath, illuminating, in careful and vivid detail, Mary Fish's public and private spheres.[1]

The rich scholarly literature on women during the nineteenth and twentieth centuries has also informed and shaped our understanding of the American family. Suzanne Lebsock's study of free white women, in Petersburg, Virginia, for example, demonstrates how women attempted to gain power and autonomy in a predominantly male society and gave meaning to their lives through work and reform.[2] The work by Jacqueline Dowd Hall on the world of the southern cotton mill worker is particularly useful in recreating the day-to-day joys and travails of white female laborers in the Carolinas.[3] William H. Chafe's *The American Woman: Her Changing Social, Economic, and Political Role, 1920-1970* is effective in discussing the idea of a woman's "proper place" in American society and the impact that World War II had on the role of women and the family.[4] Carl N. Degler's study, *At Odds: Women and the Family in America from the Revolution to the Present*, is sweeping in its scope and breadth and one of the most important books ever written on the American family. Tracing the status of American women and the family over more than two centuries, Degler explains how the roles of women in society, as well as their relationships within the family unit, changed over time.[5]

Yet neither the wealth of scholarship on white families nor the phenomenal success of Alex Haley's best-selling book *Roots: The Saga of an American Family* produced a comparable increase in books on African-American families.[6] Those few studies that did appear focused on the slave family and the antebellum free black family, with few exceptions. And while dozens of excellent books on the role of African-American women have appeared in the past twenty years, histories of African-American families are still in critically short supply, and few discuss more than a single generation or evaluate the struggles of black families in numerous geographic locations. Only Jacqueline Jones's study of African-American women from slavery to the present, *Labor of Love, Labor of Sorrow: Black Women, Work, and the Family from Slavery to the Present*, attempts to analyze the struggles that black women faced over three centuries. But even Jones's excellent study has its limitations, for it is essentially a book about the struggles of black women against white oppression rather than a history of the black family.[7]

Similarly, Sarah Lawrence-Lightfoot's excellent study, *I've Known Rivers: Lives of Loss and Liberation*, which examines the lives of six prominent African-Americans and illuminates the creative ways in which they have coped with their careers, personal struggles, and race in American society, belongs to the genre of African-American story-telling rather than family biography. Nor does the highly popular *Having Our Say: The Delany Sisters' First Hundred Years*, based on the lives of two African-American women, Sarah and Elizabeth Delany, examine the careers and struggles of an African-American family in a comprehensive manner.

Herbert Gutman's important study, *The Black Family in Slavery and Freedom, 1750-1925*, remains the most ambitious and original study on black families to date, and a model for scholars. Gutman challenged the long-held view that slavery had destroyed the African-American family as well as the idea that post-Civil War black families were weak and disorganized. He argued, moreover, that even though the "Afro-American household changed its shape between 1880-1930, at all times, and in all settings, the typical black household had in it two parents and was not unorganized and disorganized." Previous scholars, such as E. Franklin Frazier and Gilbert Osofsky, as well as Daniel Patrick Moynihan, a public official who wrote an influential report on the African-American family in 1965, lacked the empirical evidence, Gutman wrote, for their claims that the heritage of slavery made twentieth-century black family life unstable and disorganized.[8]

Gutman's important book notwithstanding, we still know painfully little about how the majority of African-American families, irrespective of class, educational level, or region, persevered from the end of Reconstruction to the present.[9] Scholarship on African-American families in the West, especially the Pacific Coast and Rocky Mountain states, has been particularly neglected. My book, *African-American Odyssey: The Stewarts, 1853-1963*, attempts to reconstruct the lives of a prominent African-American family and to place these men and women within the context of both their local communities and significant events in American history from 1850 through the 1960s. At times, this has proven a daunting task, for the Stewarts and their descendants lived in many diverse locales, including South Carolina, New Jersey, New York, Oregon, California, Nebraska, Ohio, Liberia, London, Hawaii, and the Virgin Islands. However, my research indicates that it is possible to reconstruct black family history even in such remote locations as Hawaii and the U.S. Virgin Islands, where only a small number of African-Americans have migrated and established communities.

The Stewarts were not an ordinary African-American family. Rather, they were part of what urban historians have called the "black elite," those whom Willard B. Gatewood has labeled "aristocrats of color."[10] These terms, which I have used interchangeably throughout this study, are appropriate, for the Stewarts perceived themselves as an elite within their communities and were also viewed as leaders. Indeed, the Stewarts were expected to occupy leadership roles, since they were among the most highly educated African-Americans in their community. Unlike most black laborers, who worked at unskilled jobs and did not attend college, the Stewarts were employed in the professions, and every member of the family across three generations was college educated. They, like the majority of white middle-class Americans, believed that an informed, educated citizenry was best equipped to lead their community as well as American society.

But the Stewarts were not remarkable simply because they were educated and worked at professional jobs. They were remarkable and their lives merit study because their collective struggles illustrate the numerous obstacles that were repeatedly placed in the path of African-Americans of all classes in order to enforce second-class citizenship. The Stewarts rejected this characterization of African-Americans as racially inferior. They turned

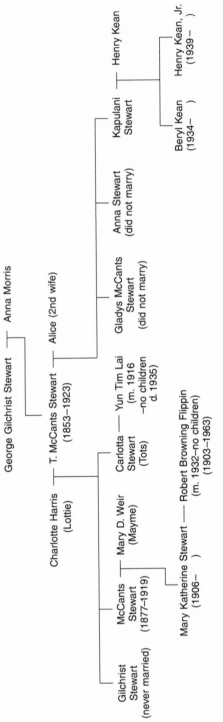

Thomas McCants Stewart family tree.

this racist dogma on its head and argued, through their words as well as their deeds, that American society, not African-Americans, was sick and in need of repair. The Stewarts believed, too, that they had been blessed as a family. Thus one of their missions in life was to improve the condition of the race and to make life better for African-Americans less fortunate than themselves. They believed that they were obligated to serve as role models, to provide leadership to their communities, and to transmit their values of mission and racial activism from one generation to the next.

T. McCants Stewart was the pivotal figure in the Stewart family. Born a free man in Charleston, South Carolina, in 1853, Thomas McCants Stewart (he never used "Thomas," even in formal correspondence) grew up during the Civil War and Reconstruction. By the early 1880s, he was recognized nationally as an important African-American spokesman. Indeed, between 1880 and 1898, Stewart, through his association with such prominent leaders as Booker T. Washington and T. Thomas Fortune, was transformed into a national leader. He, like Washington and his followers, advocated self-help, moral reform, industrial education, and racial pride. Yet Stewart was also a black nationalist who emigrated to Liberia in 1883 and again in 1906. Moreover, like the most militant black leaders of his era, Stewart was an uncompromising champion of racial equality, and his ideas were regularly published in the nation's leading black newspapers and periodicals.

T. McCants Stewart's life is examined in the first five chapters of this book. Chapters one through three reconstruct Stewart's formative years in Charleston, South Carolina, his undergraduate education at Howard University and the University of South Carolina, his professional training at the Princeton Theological Seminary, and his rise to race leadership in New York City and Brooklyn. Stewart was also considered one of the leading black political thinkers of his day and probably the most influential African-American to embrace the Democratic party during the late nineteenth century. Through analysis of his correspondence with President Grover Cleveland and others, I have attempted to explain why this prominent African-American leader felt that black voters would be better served by the Democrats, despite the party's abysmal record on civil rights.

Chapter four examines Stewart's thinking about race over the course of his long life, his association with prominent black thinkers, and his efforts through both local and national organizations to promote a lively discourse in the African-American community. Here, I have tried to place Stewart's views in the context of the ideas of prominent African-American thinkers of his generation but also to illustrate how Stewart's perspective differed from theirs. Stewart's views on Africa, in particular, are given considerable attention. He promoted emigration to Africa, wrote numerous articles on Africa's economic development, and served as an associate justice of the Liberian Supreme Court.[11]

Chapter five evaluates the final two decades of T. McCants Stewart's long career, as he traveled to Hawaii, Liberia, and the U.S. Virgin Islands to escape the racism he believed had become even more prevalent in the United States. Through archival and legal records, and through newspapers in Hawaii and the Virgin Islands, I have carefully tracked Stewart's movements during these years and examined how his views changed over the course of his lifetime.

I have also attempted to portray Stewart and his family in the private sphere. A domineering husband and father, Stewart was a feared and respected patriarch within his family. He impressed upon his children at a very early age that they were obligated to establish important careers and to carry on the family's tradition of service to the race.

Chapters six through eight examine the lives of Stewart's children from his first marriage, McCants, Gilchrist, and Carlotta, and assess their professional careers as well as their leadership in their respective communities. I have also evaluated the relationship of Stewart's children, largely through their letters, to each other and to their father. Although none rose to the stature of their father, each achieved a measure of success as a leader and professional. I argue that they were pioneers, both in their decision to break free from their father's control and in their decision to stake out new territory and pursue fresh opportunities. Carlotta lived in the territory of Hawaii for more than five decades, and she in particular was widely respected and admired as a teacher and administrator in the Hawaiian schools. Through archival research, personal interviews, and recent scholarship in family history, I have tried to discern what it was like for an African-American woman to live in a society with only a minuscule black population prior to World War II. Finally, I have situated Carlotta's career in the context of Hawaiian history during the early 1900s but also evaluated her life in reference to black middle-class womanhood, particularly the ideology of work, community service, and reform.

Chapter nine examines the lives and careers of Katherine Stewart Flippin, granddaughter of T. McCants Stewart, and her husband Robert Flippin. In addition to representing the joining of two elite African-American families, their lives also illustrate how a direct descendant of T. McCants Stewart, Katherine Stewart, and her husband, Robert Flippin, continued a tradition of racial activism and community leadership through the 1930s and beyond World War II. Like T. McCants Stewart's children, who found it liberating to break away from the grasp of a domineering father, Robert Flippin also moved to San Francisco to make his own way. Within a decade, he was recognized as one of the most important leaders in San Francisco's African-American community. During World War II, as tens of thousands of black migrants moved to West Coast cities to work in the wartime defense industries, Robert, a prominent social worker, served as a bridge between the white and black communities. After World War II Flippin served as an important racial spokesman in San Francisco and as the first African-American parole officer at San Quentin prison. Here, he dedicated himself to building the prison chapter of Alcoholics Anonymous and counseling gay inmates.

African-American Odyssey represents both a frustrating story and a triumphant saga. The Stewarts' personal struggles recapitulate the lives and feelings of millions of black men and women forced to cope with a pernicious system of racial prejudice on a daily basis. Yet their story also reveals the resiliency of African-Americans, the importance of family, religion, and local community institutions, and the creative approaches that black men and women developed to maintain some modicum of dignity as they raised their families, established careers, and provided service and leadership to their communities. The third generation's activism reveals, too, that in the 1950s and 1960s, black elite families in the far West believed strongly in the values of racial uplift and community service.

Studying the lives of the Stewarts over three generations enriches our understanding of family history, African-American leadership, class, and gender. The Stewarts' experiences typify many of the frustrations and anxieties that families of all races and nationalities felt during the nineteenth and twentieth centuries, although African-American families felt these anxieties more keenly. Black families like the Stewarts (and Flippins) were concerned with educating their children, providing a decent standard of living for their families, and establishing their careers. But they were equally concerned with instilling the proper moral and religious values in their children, taking active leadership roles in their communities, and providing service to African-Americans less fortunate than themselves. Thus, the lives of the Stewarts not only mirror the lives of many black middle-class families.

They also illuminate the felt necessities, aspirations, and desires of a large segment of the white middle class. White Americans, too, were anxious about establishing their careers, supporting their families, educating their children, buying homes, and saving for their futures. But the Stewarts were more than simply middle-class Americans. They were "aristocrats of color" who believed sincerely that it was their duty and mission as a family to provide leadership and service for the betterment of the race. This characteristic, above all others, makes them distinctive.

Part One

❖ ❖ ❖ ❖ ❖ ❖ ❖ ❖ ❖ ❖ ❖ ❖ ❖ ❖ ❖

The Mission of the Talented Tenth

1

Humble Beginnings

❖ ❖ ❖ ❖ ❖ ❖ ❖ ❖ ❖ ❖ ❖ ❖ ❖ ❖ ❖

Antebellem Charleston was the cultural and intellectual capital of South Carolina, a city that had contributed enormously to education, commerce, and science in the Palmetto state. But its beginnings two centuries earlier were inauspicious. Initially a trading post, Charleston had attracted only 700 settlers by 1680, and in that year the original site at Albemarle Point was abandoned in favor of a new location between the Ashley and Cooper rivers. Even so, this frontier community of English, Dutch, French, and Scottish immigrants neither prospered nor grew during its formative decades. Instead, Charleston experienced a series of misfortunes not uncommon to city dwellers in the American colonies. In 1697 a smallpox epidemic swept through the town killing between 200 and 300 people. Most of the fatalities were Native Americans, who, according to a contemporary account, remained "unburied, lying upon the ground for the vultures to devour." The following year brought another tragedy. An earthquake struck, and the fire that followed destroyed a third of the city. In September 1699, as the town was rebuilding, a yellow fever epidemic killed almost half of the members of the legislative assembly and an undetermined number of others. To compound this disaster—and a sure sign that Providence was not in the Charlestonians' corner, a hurricane hit the town during the middle of the epidemic.[1]

Given these circumstances, and the threat of attack by both the Native Americans and the Spanish, who occupied present-day Florida, Charleston's population grew slowly until the eighteenth century. Then, a sharp rise in trade, particularly in furs, timber, foodstuffs, and naval stores, and

THE CITY OF
CHARLESTON
SOUTH CAROLINA.

PUBLISHED BY J. H. COLTON & Co. N°172 WILLIAM ST NEW YORK
1859

the development of rice as a commercial staple stimulated significant economic and demographic growth in Charleston and throughout the colony. Indeed, rice cultivation, perhaps more than any single factor, ushered in a new era for South Carolina, for it became the colony's chief export and accelerated the ascendancy of the planter class to power. Rice culture also stimulated an increased demand for African slaves, and by the early 1700s slaves outnumbered white settlers throughout the colony. On the eve of the American Revolution, African slaves comprised nearly 60 percent of South Carolina's population, an illustration of the colony's utter dependence on slave labor.[2]

A small number of free blacks also resided in colonial Charleston. These individuals had accompanied the early white settlers who came from Barbados, where mulattoes composed an intermediate class between slaves and whites. In 1790, less than 600 free blacks lived in Charleston, but their numbers increased rapidly following the American Revolution, a pattern that was evident throughout most of the former colonies. By 1830, Charleston's free black community had increased to 2,107, and by 1850 it had risen to 3,441. Although the city's free black population declined by approximately 200 between 1850 and 1860, the 3,237 free blacks in Charleston in 1860 represented 8 percent of the city's total population and exceeded the population of every town in the state but Columbia.[3]

The presence of an expanding free black population in the midst of a sizable slave community did not strike most Charlestonians as desirable. South Carolinians had made several unsuccessful attempts to restrict the size of its free black population in the wake of slave revolts and conspiracies such as the 1739 Stono uprising and the Denmark Vesey conspiracy in 1822.[4] These reforms, however, did little to slow the growth of either South Carolina's free black population or its large slave community. Charleston, in particular, became densely populated with slaves as well as free blacks. In 1860, over 17,000 blacks lived in Charleston, 81 percent of whom were slaves.[5]

In the 1850s, the free black community in Charleston was one of the most dynamic in the South. It resembled, in many respects, the free black community in New Orleans, where the majority of the free Negro men worked in the skilled trades. There, writes John W. Blassingame, free black men were employed in a wide spectrum of occupations. Their ranks included architects, bookbinders, engineers, carpenters, cabinetmakers, and blacksmiths. Indeed, the ratio of skilled to unskilled laborers among free blacks in New Orleans was even higher than that among the Irish and German immigrants. Of the 1,792 free black males recorded in the 1850 census, only 9.9 percent were listed as unskilled laborers.[6]

Free black Charlestonians also achieved remarkable economic progress in spite of numerous obstacles, not the least of which were racial discrimination and competition with slave labor. Although Charleston's free blacks performed the customary menial tasks of unskilled labor, they, too, gained prominence as artisans, semiskilled laborers, teamsters, seamen, and small businessmen. As historian Ira Berlin notes, "In Charleston, a declining city which could boast neither the new industry nor the booming commerce of Richmond, three-quarters of the free Negro men worked at skilled trades in 1860." In sharp contrast, only one-third of free blacks in Richmond worked in the skilled trades. These black artisans in Charleston "controlled a large share of the work in some prominent trades and dominated others outright." For example, 75 percent of the millwrights and 40 percent of the city's tailors were free blacks. Indeed, free blacks were among the most skilled laborers in the city, surpassed only by Southern-born whites and German immigrants.[7]

Despite their skills, some free blacks were paid less than whites for comparable work. Nor did free black females fare as well economically as their male counterparts, for their employment opportunities were restricted largely to domestic service and menial labor. Free black women in Charleston also lagged behind their counterparts in a southern city like Petersburg, Virginia, where free black females composed nearly 46 percent of Petersburg's free black property owners in 1860.[8] Charleston also contained a large class of impoverished and uneducated blacks who lived predominately on the city's east side. Notwithstanding the large percentage of skilled blacks in antebellum Charleston, less than a quarter of the city's free blacks owned property in 1860, and fewer still owned slaves. Yet Charleston's free black elite, or "brown aristocrats," as historians Michael P. Johnson and James L. Roark called them, were far more likely to own both slaves and real estate. Prominent free black artisans such as William McKinlay and James M. Johnson amassed greater wealth than most white Charlestonians.[9] Thus class divisions and social stratification within the black community, as well as freedom, were based in large measure on skin color. Throughout the South, mulattoes were more likely than dark-skinned blacks to be manumitted. Light skin and the patronage of prominent whites often determined the opportunities available for free blacks, not only within the marketplace but also in their own communities.[10]

Charleston's dynamic free black community established numerous institutions that not only served as bulwarks against segregation and exclusion but also conferred status and recognition in a society that perceived blacks, slave or free, as an inferior caste. Independent black churches had filled this role in many cities, but Charleston's white leadership suppressed the growth of separate black churches, with few exceptions. Instead, a number of denominations, including the Episcopalians, Presbyterians, Methodists, and Baptists, worked to convert African-Americans. But black Charlestonians grew increasingly dissatisfied with the policies of predominantly white churches and desired their own autonomous churches. In 1818, the newly consecrated Methodist bishop Morris Brown organized the African Church, an affiliate of the African Methodist Episcopal Church in Philadelphia, after more than three-fourths of Charleston's black Methodists withdrew from the white Methodist Church. The charismatic Brown, a galvanizing force in Charleston's black community, attracted a wide following, and membership in the African Church (AME) grew rapidly, perhaps too rapidly for the tranquility of local whites: The church enrolled more than 4,000 members by 1822, slaves as well as free blacks. Its remarkable growth, however, was shortlived. The Charleston city council ordered it closed in 1822 after it was implicated in the Denmark Vesey insurrection. The AME Church did not return to Charleston until 1865.[11]

Fortunately, free black Charlestonians had much better success maintaining their secular organizations. The development of several important benevolent and fraternal organizations, including the Brown Fellowship Society and the Humane Brotherhood, illustrated African-Americans' intense desire to create and maintain their own benevolent societies as well as the significance of skin color and class in Charleston's black community. Organized in 1790 by five "Free Brown men," the Brown Fellowship Society created an exclusive organization where free mulattoes of similar social and economic status intermingled. Membership, which included the leading mulattoes in Charleston, was restricted to fifty mulattoes. Each member paid an initiation fee of $50 and monthly dues, both of which were beyond the means of most working-class Charlestonians, black or white. The society's benevolent work was also impressive. If a member was too sick to work, the organization provided a small monetary payment. It also paid the funeral and burial expenses of its members and an annual stipend of $60 in the event that a member's widow and orphans became indigent. The society also provided financial support for "up to five poor colored orphans or adults."[12]

Respectable dark men in Charleston who felt slighted by the exclusivity of the Brown Fellowship Society organized the Humane Brotherhood in 1843. A sort of poor cousin to the Brown Fellowship Society, the Humane Brotherhood adopted many of its rival's policies. Membership, for example, was limited to thirty-five "respectable Free Dark Men," although some mulattoes were listed on the organization's membership rolls. (The Brown Fellowship Society had made no such exception.) The brotherhood also provided sick benefits and burial expenses, as well as a modest annuity of $12 for widows and orphans of deceased members. The brotherhood maintained a cemetery for its members, located beside the burial ground of its higher-status mulatto counterpart, although separated by a "sturdy fence." Ironically, free mulattoes and "free dark men" may have come closer in death than in society, for the two groups generally, write Michael P. Johnson and James Roark, "did not socialize with one another, and they rarely married one another."[13]

This urban milieu of race, class, culture, commerce, and bondage, dominated economically by planters and merchants who tolerated a small though influential class of free mulattoes and a larger group of free blacks, was the setting for Thomas McCants Stewart's formative years. Antebellum Charleston also shaped Stewart's character, values, and worldview. Thomas McCants Stewart was born to George Gilchrist Stewart and Anna Morris Stewart on December 28, 1853.[14] Little is known about his early years in Charleston or the backgrounds of his parents, although he insisted that they were free blacks. Indeed, both George Stewart and Anna Morris Stewart are listed in the 1860 population schedules and in the tax schedules of free blacks in Charleston during the nineteenth century. The tax assessor was careful to list a George and Ann Stuart who resided on Laurel Street in the capitation tax book for free blacks in 1852, 1855, and 1857. (George Stewart is listed separately in 1851.) The capitation tax was a poll tax imposed on the state's entire free black population between 1756 and 1865. The tax was initially set at $2 per person by the general assembly, but it escalated to $2.75 in 1858, $3 in 1860, $6.75 in 1863, and $10 in 1864. White males paid a separate capitation tax until 1788, when it was abolished. After that date, only free blacks were subject to the tax, which was "collected as part of the state's general tax, which was principally a levy on land and slaves."[15]

George and Anna Stewart were also listed intermittently in the Charleston city directories. George Stewart appears in the 1859 city directory, and both George and Anna paid their $10 capitation tax in 1863.[16] The Stewarts continued to reside in Charleston through the early 1870s, generally at the same address or in close proximity, for they were recorded in the 1870 manuscript census returns and in the Charleston city directory for 1873. But unlike many of Charleston's free blacks, some of whom became substantial property holders, the Stewarts apparently never owned property, although George Stewart worked as a skilled artisan (blacksmith) and Anna as a dressmaker.[17]

Young Stewart, who was known as T. McCants rather than Thomas, wrote very little about his father. Anna Morris Stewart, his mother, played a more prominent role in her son's early years. Stewart not only admired his mother, he venerated her. "My mother is a woman of strong intellect, noble soul, generous nature, and great energy. I owe all I am to my mother," Stewart wrote.[18] The absence or inattention of his father may explain, in part, Stewart's early maturity and his desire to assist his mother financially at such a young age. There was little time for idleness or frivolous activities in his childhood. Rather, his family circumstances, perhaps typical for free blacks in many urban locales, and the urgency of the times prompted Stewart to mature more rapidly than he might have otherwise in a more stable and financially secure household.

Although Stewart remained devoted to his mother, he slowly began to separate himself from her after 1865. As a young black man in post–Civil War Charleston, he was expected to prepare himself for the numerous challenges that the city's large black community would face during Reconstruction. He was also expected to make his own way, which meant that he must educate himself, contribute to the economic support of his family, and think about his future. Stewart had begun attending school at the age of five, though only a small percentage of free blacks in Charleston attended school during the 1850s. Indeed, antebellum Charleston had one of the lowest percentages of free blacks attending school (5.44 percent) of any southern city. In sharp contrast, nearly three-fourths (70.65 percent) of school-aged white children attended school.[19]

It is unclear, however, who provided Stewart's formative educational instruction, since Charleston, like most southern cities, had no public schools for free blacks. Yet black Charlestonians, stubbornly determined to educate their own, had established private schools in a variety of settings including benevolent societies, churches, and private homes, and Stewart may have attended one of these. The Charleston Negro School, started by Alexander Garden and operating as early as 1743, was "one of the earliest colonial efforts to recognize and develop the potentialities of Negroes for Enlightment."[20] It closed in 1765. Charleston's Brown Fellowship Society maintained schools for black children in 1790, the year of its founding, and the Minor's Moralist Society, which was established in 1803, provided education for the black indigent and orphans. Charleston's Coming Street School, which was taught by a white schoolmaster though managed by a black board of trustees, also educated black children. Despite a South Carolina law requiring the presence of whites in classes conducted for free blacks, at least fifteen schools were run by free African-Americans between 1800 and 1860 without interference from local or state authorities. Thus it appears, as Leonard P. Curry concludes, that by 1850 most of the formal instruction black children received in Charleston and in most urban areas of the nation was provided by black teachers.[21]

It is also possible that Stewart's parents hired a private tutor to educate their son, though this practice was more common among Charleston's black elite, of which Stewart's family was not a member. The Morris Street School, a private school established for free blacks, was attended by several of Stewart's childhood friends, including Francis and Archibald Grimké and Thomas Miller. It also educated a small though elite segment of Charleston's black community following emancipation, but it is not clear that Stewart attended this institution. It is more likely that he received some rudimentary education in his Sunday school, a common source of educational training for blacks of all ages. As a young boy, Stewart attended the Centenary Methodist Episcopal Church in Charleston, and black Methodists had by that time, already made important strides in providing education to their members throughout the nation. Regardless of how T. McCants Stewart received his formal schooling, he had made sufficient progress by the late 1860s to attend the Avery Normal Institute in Charleston.[22]

Charleston's free black community, with strong independent institutions that predated the Civil War, produced a new generation of black leaders, who, confronting the limits of freedom, embraced racial uplift and worked zealously to prepare African-Americans for the future. This spirit was behind the creation of the Avery Normal Institute. Founded in 1865 by the American Missionary Association (AMA), Avery was the most ambitious effort undertaken in the post-Civil War period to provide preparatory training for black Charlestonians. Francis L. Cardozo, a prominent member of Charleston's free black community, was instrumental in Avery's early success.[23]

It is not certain precisely when Stewart attended Avery or if he enrolled in the primary, intermediate, or grammar department. Nor is it possible to reconstruct the courses that he completed. However, the school's primary mission, wrote the AMA, "aims to fit its graduates to be competent teachers." Black teachers were in critically short supply during Reconstruction, due to the unprecedented demand for an education by blacks of all ages in South Carolina and throughout the South. Moreover, former slaves in many southern states, including South Carolina, seized the initiative by raising funds, running for political office, passing bills to support schools, and insisting on free public education. In so doing, according to James D. Anderson, they "laid the first foundation for universal public education in the South."[24]

Stewart's tenure at Avery must have been relatively brief, for he was not included among the school's early graduates. He took considerable pride, however, in the fact that he had attended the prestigious school and that his sister Cecilia graduated from Avery in 1877, then attended the State Normal School of Massachusetts and became a teacher. But instead of becoming a teacher himself, Stewart left the school in 1869 to enroll at Howard University.[25]

Residing in the nation's capital during the early 1870s must have been more exciting in some respects for young Stewart than his formative years in South Carolina. Like his native Charleston, the District of Columbia also had a sizable black community as well as an established black elite composed of well-to-do mulattoes and prestigious black families, most of whom had been free born. But Washington, D.C., was also the seat of both the national government and a politically active black leadership circle. Stewart could observe firsthand how an eminent black leader such as Frederick Douglass or the black senator Hiram R. Revels worked with the Grant administration to secure civil rights and an economic foothold for African-Americans.[26] Both the District of Columbia and Howard University were also in a state of transition during the 1870s, although moving on parallel courses. Each was attempting to improve the plight of freedmen, who now swelled the ranks of Washington's black community.

Founded in 1867 by General Oliver Otis Howard, director of the Freedmen's Bureau, Howard University attempted to train a new generation of black leaders during the post–Civil War era. To a large extent, it succeeded. By 1910 the black scholar W. E. B. Du Bois included Howard among the first tier of black colleges in his pioneering study that classified thirty-two black institutions of higher learning. Yet Howard University did not achieve academic acclaim immediately, and during its formative decades it struggled to gain legitimacy. Howard University, writes Rayford W. Logan, "was a university in name only," for many students who attended the university during its early decades were not prepared academically for the rigors of college work. Nonetheless, the school contained a normal and preparatory department, and the original charter also established a medical school.[27]

Since he was separated for the first time from his family, Stewart's years at Howard were characterized by uncertainty, loneliness, and an occasional episode of immaturity. Only fifteen years old when he arrived on Howard's campus in the fall of 1869, his residence in the nation's capital also marked the first time he had lived outside of South Carolina. But he was apparently an able and conscientious student, although in one instance Stewart was brought before the faculty at Howard "on the charges of Disobedience of orders." He was exonerated, however, by General Howard, the president of the university. "I gained the victory," Stewart boasted to his mother, in one of the few letters between mother and son that has survived.[28] Stewart's attendance at Howard also revealed a willingness to take risks and a determination to improve his status through education, both habits that he learned very early in life.

Although Howard University had not yet achieved academic acclaim, some of the nation's future black leaders also matriculated during Stewart's tenure. Among his classmates were George Washington Williams, the future black historian and diplomat, and Hugh H. Browne, who later gained acclaim as an educator. An undetermined number of black South Carolinians also attended Howard during these years, providing friendship, emotional support, and a connection with Stewart's past. On at least one occasion, a fellow black South Carolinian, Alonzo Clifton McClennan, visited Stewart in the nation's capital. McClennan was the second black student admitted to the United States Naval Academy in September 1873, following the lead of another black South Carolinian, James H. Conyers, who preceded him by one year. The extent of Stewart's relationship with McClennan is unknown. However, the black midshipman was careful to note in his journal that

"McCants Stewart, who was then at Howard, was notified of my coming and I stopped over with him and in the morning took the train to Annapolis."[29]

Despite the presence of other black South Carolinians Stewart remained homesick and emotionally disconnected from the university. He wrote his mother in the spring of 1871 to inquire about her health, which had not been good, and to reassure her that he had no immediate plans to get married, although he had considerable interest in girls. "Tell Aunt Martha," wrote Stewart, "that I have not as yet seen the damsel whom I shall lead to the marriage altar!! It is true, I smile with the girls, and perhaps *flirt* with them, but can't talk about the married life." Stewart also appeared disturbed over the news that his sister Cecilia was leaving school, for reasons that remain unclear. He expressed, moreover, some fond boyhood memories of Charleston and was troubled over his mother's financial status. "Have you freed yourself from debt?" he inquired.[30] Stewart's query into his mother's financial affairs provides another illustration of his early maturity and reveals that he took a keen interest in his family's financial affairs, even as a relatively young boy. Two years later, Stewart was still concerned with his mother's finances. He vowed to help her after graduation, but in the interim sent her $2, a small though important gesture of his concern.[31]

Stewart was also troubled over the quality of academic instruction at Howard, a sign of his mounting ambition, and he wanted to attend a more challenging and prestigious university closer to home. "There are a very few students who are satisfied with the university. Our instruction is now poor and our advantage meager," he informed his mother. He decided to leave Howard at the conclusion of the 1873 academic semester and attend the University of South Carolina at Columbia. Stewart tried to assure his mother that his decision had not been made in haste. "I can not in a letter, mother, give you an idea of this Institution as it now is a wreck of its former self. It has gone down." He urged her to "read Mr. [Francis L.] Cardozo's letter." Cardozo thinks, Stewart continued, that "*This University is in a bad way.*" Stewart also believed that "the whole South Carolina delegation would probably leave at the end of this school year." And while he would have preferred to graduate from a "good Institution like Harvard," he stated that because of his mother's bad health, he could not stay in school for four or five additional years. "I must go into life and help you," he concluded.[32]

Although Stewart never specified the nature of his mother's illness, he was deeply concerned with her welfare. After his father's death in 1879, he probably felt an even stronger obligation to assist his mother financially and emotionally, for he was now the man in the family. Stewart's sharp criticism of Howard University was probably predicated in large measure on his desire to return to South Carolina. He had chosen to pursue law at the University of South Carolina and was confident he could "graduate from there in due course of time." Stewart also expressed in his correspondence a sense of urgency in moving forward in his career and taking advantage of some of the opportunities that were available to blacks during Reconstruction.[33]

The ambitious young student's dissatisfaction with the intellectual environment at Howard University did not prevent him from taking part in community affairs in Washington or developing leadership skills. As early as 1870, Stewart published an article in the Washington *New National Era*, a black newspaper, entitled "Our Country." Whether Stewart contributed the article at the urging of the paper's editors, J. Sella Martin and Frederick Douglass, or took the initiative himself is uncertain. What is most impressive is Stewart's age: he was only sixteen years old when he wrote it.[34]

Stewart began the article with a long commentary on the founding of the American colonies, describing the progress and travails of the original settlers. Yet he was quick to note that the settlers had often disregarded the rights of certain groups in their zeal to satisfy their economic interests. America, Stewart wrote, had not lived up to her promise to serve as a refuge for the oppressed. But, Stewart argued, it was still possible to fulfill this obligation: "If we maintain just, high and noble institutions, despise the wrong and love the right, fear God and obey his injunctions, our country will be abundantly blest by Him, who holds in his hands the destinies of nations." On the other hand, "If we despise the teachings of the great, I Am, and follow the dictates of the Evil One, America will lose its present greatness, sink into obscurity, and leave nothing to tell of its glory save the pen of the historian."[35]

Finally, Stewart was adamant that it was the responsibility of his generation to set the nation on its proper course. "May it be the aim of the people of the present generation to hand down to posterity a Government stable and uncorrupted," he wrote. Thus Stewart saw his own mission to uplift African-Americans as part of a larger mission for black leaders of his generation: to make America a more humane and democratic society. This was a formidable challenge for a young boy of sixteen.[36]

The article, though written in clear and lucid prose, reads like a sermon rather than a commentary on the fate of the nation, and it presages Stewart's career as a minister. It also reflects the influence that religion had played in his formal education. It is noteworthy, too, that at such an early age Stewart had begun to think of the nation's destiny and could express these ideas cogently.

Stewart enrolled in the University of South Carolina in 1874. The state-supported university, located in Columbia, was an exciting opportunity for Stewart and a small contingent of black students. It was unique among public institutions of higher learning in the South because it admitted black as well as white students. It was no coincidence that the integration of this formerly segregated institution had occurred in the wake of the 1868 congressional elections, for the new legislature was overwhelmingly Republican and over half of the delegates were black. South Carolina's new constitution required that all publicly funded schools, colleges, and universities be open to all students, without regard to race and color. As a consequence, the University of South Carolina admitted its first black student in 1873, one year before Stewart enrolled. The integration of this southern university prompted some white students to withdraw from the institution and a number of white faculty to resign in protest.[37]

Stewart's academic preparation at Avery and Howard had been sufficient to permit him to enroll at the University of South Carolina with advanced standing as a junior. As he had indicated to his mother, several of his former classmates also enrolled in the university, perhaps at his suggestion. By 1876, wrote Daniel Walker Hollis in his history of the University of South Carolina, these students were part of "the most heterogeneous student body ever assembled."

Many of the university's black students, who included William D. Crum, Joseph W. Morris, and Thomas E. Miller, would later assume important leadership roles on both the state and national levels. Crum, for example, who gained the admiration of Booker T. Washington, became a respected physician and was appointed collector of the Port of Charleston by President Theodore Roosevelt. Morris served as president of Allen University, and Miller became president of the Agricultural and Mechanical College in Orangeburg.[38] Thus in Columbia Stewart had the opportunity to interact with some of the most capable black students in the state of South Carolina.

T. McCants Stewart was considerably happier in Columbia than in Washington, D.C. He proved a capable and meticulous student and selected law and mathematics as his major areas of concentration. He also polished his skills as an orator. At a memorial service for Senator Charles Sumner in 1874, Stewart, the only junior on the campus, delivered a well-received oration on "Robespierre." His presentation led a reporter from the Columbia *Daily Herald* to write, "Those who think the colored man an inferior . . . should have witnessed the exhibition last night."[39] There is no evidence that Stewart was required to correct any academic deficiencies through the university's preparatory department like many of his black counterparts. At Howard University he had stood, wrote G. F. Richings, "at the head of his class," distinguishing himself in foreign languages, belles lettres, and public speaking. While at Howard he also found time to lecture occasionally for small fees on the topics of the day in both Washington, D.C., and Virginia, a practice that he would continue throughout his life to promote his ideas and supplement his income. In December 1875, having mastered his academic subjects at the University of South Carolina, Stewart graduated with B.A. and L.L.B. degrees.[40]

In 1876, during his residence in Columbia, Stewart married Charlotte Pearl Harris. Lottie Harris, as she was known to close friends, was accustomed to the duties of a minister's wife, since her father, Reverend W. D. Harris, was a Methodist minister himself and the brother of C. R. Harris, a professor at Livingstone College in North Carolina and a bishop in the AME Zion church.[41] Reverend Harris had provided unusual opportunities for his two daughters, Lottie and Verina, and Lottie did not disappoint her parents. She enrolled in Wilberforce University between 1870 and 1872 in an era when few women attended college.

In the 1870s, Wilberforce University was a challenging college for a student of any race to attend, particularly a young black woman. The bucolic university, located in Xenia, Ohio, which had gained considerable fame as a summer health resort, had opened its doors in 1856. By 1860 Wilberforce's annual enrollment exceeded 200 students. The Civil War halted both student demand and the school's ability to attract financial support, however, and Wilberforce was forced to close its doors in June 1862.[42]

The college's savior appeared in the form of Bishop Daniel A. Payne, one of the original incorporators of the school and the first black college president in the United States. In 1863, Payne secured funding and the support of the AME church and purchased the school for $10,000. During Payne's thirteen years as president (1863-1876), Wilberforce once again achieved academic respectability and attracted a steady base of financial support.

He refused to be deterred from his mission by temporary setbacks, such as a mysterious fire that burned down Shorter Hall, the main building on the campus. Racial violence and suspicious fires had long been common occurrences for many black schools and colleges. As early as 1858, just two years after its incorporation, local whites and the Democratic press, upset over the growing number of black students and residents in Xenia, campaigned to close Wilberforce and attempted to prevent the respected black leader John Mercer Langston from delivering a speech there. Despite the threats, Langston delivered the speech without incident.[43]

Whether Bishop Payne influenced Reverend W. D. Harris's decision to send his daughter to this black institution during its formative years cannot be known with certainty. Payne perceived education, wrote Paul R. Griffin, "primarily as a means to enhance Christian piety," a point that would have carried considerable weight with Lottie's father. With Payne serving as president, the curriculum emphasized a classical education, considerable religious instruction, and an appreciation for hard work. "Our aim is to make Christian scholars not merely book worms, but workers, educated workers with God for man," wrote Bishop Payne. Not surprisingly, Lottie's courses included natural history, rhetoric, French, elocution, penmanship, orthography (spelling), and deportment, which was particularly important at a Christian school where one's conduct and academic achievement were inseparable. Aside from bad penmanship, which her written correspondence strongly attests to, Lottie's grades were consistently above average, though not outstanding. She excelled in deportment, rhetoric, orthography, and French. In the spring of 1871, the administrators of Wilberforce thought so highly of Lottie Harris that she was permitted to attend a school conference with several of her classmates in Pittsburgh, Pennsylvania. In 1872 Lottie Harris graduated from Wilberforce University, receiving her degree from the scientific department, one of five degree-granting departments at the university. Four of her classmates who also received degrees in 1872 took the more traditional route and graduated from the theological department, clearly Wilberforce's academic strength.[44]

Following her graduation in 1872, Lottie Harris taught school for a time. She also taught piano and organ at Claflin University in Orangeburg, South Carolina, shortly after her marriage to T. McCants Stewart.[45] In a word, Stewart had married "up," for Lottie Harris's family background was far more prominent than his own. That Stewart married a member of a socially prominent black family was not surprising; it was the expected behavior of an aspiring black leader. The black elite generally shared the values and expectations of their spouses, and these unions also enhanced the reputation of both husband and wife by giving them immediate status within the black leadership class and visibility in a wider and more prestigious social circle.[46]

Lottie's sister, Verina Morton-Jones, became a prominent "clubwoman," one of the cofounders of the National Urban League and the Brooklyn chapter of the NAACP, a suffragette, settlement-house worker, and an active member of the National Association of Colored Women and the colored YWCA in Brooklyn. Lottie Stewart, on the other hand, took little interest in club work, politics, women's equality, or civil rights.[47] Instead, she quickly learned to submerge her own career ambitions in favor of her husband's. Consequently, Lottie suspended her professional career temporarily when the Stewarts moved to New York, became a full-time housewife, and raised her three children. Lottie tolerated her husband's frequent absences from home as well as the painful separation from her family in South Carolina. As she wrote many years later, "When a girl marries, her husband has to be mother and father to her to keep her from missing her mother."[48] The start of her own family eroded some of the isolation that she felt, however, and evoked a desire to set down roots. In 1877, Lottie Stewart bore McCants, her first child. Two years later, a second son, Gilchrist, was born, and in 1881 she gave birth to a daughter, Carlotta. T. McCants Stewart now faced the difficult task of juggling a promising career, a wife, and three children.[49]

Black South Carolinians, irrespective of their education or class, faced tremendous challenges during Reconstruction. For African-Americans, the eradication of slavery and the conclusion of the Civil War signaled the dawning of a new era; white southerners, however, did not loosen their grip on white supremacy willingly. Rather, they had to be coerced by an occupying army of Union troops and convinced by Republican politicians, who held many state offices, that the freedmen were entitled to the full range of civil liberties that white South Carolinians enjoyed. White resentment manifested itself throughout the state in indiscriminate violence against African-Americans, whippings, and race riots. The idea of black freedom was so repugnant to most whites in the South that they began almost immediately after the war to write a new body of laws that attempted to reassert white authority by defining and classifying the social, economic, and legal status of the freedmen. These laws, passed in South Carolina and in the majority of ex-Confederate states, were known as the Black Codes.[50]

Even putting the best face on these restrictive statutes, their purpose was to control the black population. "If the Codes did not reestablish slavery, as some northern critics charged, neither did they recognize the former slaves as free men and women, entitled to equal protection under the law," wrote Leon Litwack. Although the Black Codes granted the freedmen civil and legal rights, including the right to marry, to own property, and to sue or be sued in a court of law, most of the codes, including South Carolina's, restricted African-Americans to agricultural or domestic labor, prohibited competition with white artisans or businessmen, and compelled blacks to work or risk being arrested and charged with vagrancy. The restrictive South Carolina code threatened the long-established position of many free black artisans who had assumed commanding positions in the skilled trades in Charleston prior to the Civil War.[51]

A Republican-controlled Congress, convinced that white Southerners were attempting to reestablish slavery under a different guise, overturned the Black Codes in South Carolina and throughout the South. With the purpose of granting blacks equal protection under the law, Congress passed the Civil Rights Act of 1866. Many of its provisions were embodied in the Fourteenth Amendment (1868), which granted blacks citizenship rights. As George Tindall wrote, "the provisions of the black codes were thus superseded, and the work of establishing a new subordinate caste for Negroes had to follow somewhat more subtle methods once the Radicals were ousted from power in the state." However, this "new subordinate caste" was not established immediately, for African-Americans enjoyed a brief interlude of freedom. They celebrated their new-found civil rights by voting in large numbers, electing their own to numerous local and statewide offices, attending political conventions, establishing schools and homes for orphans and the aged, and attempting to acquire the requisite tools to become responsible citizens.[52]

T. McCants Stewart joined the small though expanding circle of blacks who had obtained college degrees during Reconstruction. He was eager, on the one hand, to take his place among South Carolina's black leadership class. On the other, he was not entirely certain how to begin. He was aware that the Redeemers, white Southern Democrats, had regained political power in South Carolina following the disputed 1876 presidential election and restored white supremacy. But Stewart, full of youthful optimism, struck out as if few limits had been placed on his ambition. With little to guide him except instinct and determination, Stewart moved to Sumter, South Carolina. There he practiced law briefly before accepting a teaching position in mathematics at the State Agricultural and Mechanical School in Orangeburg between 1877 and 1878. Yet Stewart had no intention of spending the remainder of his life in the classroom. Unlike his sister Cecilia or many African-American teachers, he felt no moral fervor to excel in the classroom. For him, teaching was simply a means to an end. Thus, when the opportunity presented itself, Stewart also joined the new law firm of black South Carolina congressman Robert Brown Elliott.[53]

Elliott, Stewart's senior by almost ten years, had been elected to Congress in 1868. His Orangeburg law firm included Stewart and David Augustus Straker, a native of the Barbados and a graduate of Howard University Law School.[54] Stewart's association with Elliott and Straker was an important step in both his legal career and his path toward becoming a respected black leader. It is unclear why Elliott, a prominent black figure in South Carolina politics, allowed Stewart, a young man with little experience in either law or politics, to join his prestigious law firm. Stewart's degree from the University of South Carolina may have convinced Elliott that he was a potentially important black leader in the state and someone whose friendship and loyalty he should cultivate. At any rate, this association gave Stewart instant stature and briefly catapulted him into the limelight. The law firm of Elliott, Stewart, and Straker, which the Cleveland *Gazette* later called the "first colored law firm in the United States," dissolved at the end of Reconstruction, and Stewart as well as his legal partners were forced to seek new challenges.[55]

Stewart took another important step toward joining South Carolina's black leadership circle when he became a minister in the African Methodist Episcopal Church (AME). In October 1877, approximately two years after he had received his college degree, Stewart was licensed to preach by the Quarterly Conference of the Lewisville Circuit of the AME Church in Orangeburg. The young black leader's religious calling ultimately led him to apply for admission to the prestigious Princeton Theological Seminary. It is highly probably that Stewart knew of the seminary's reputation for admitting black students, and this fact, as well as the seminary's national stature, were pivotal factors in his decision to apply for admission. It was also no coincidence that Stewart decided to move north shortly following the collapse of Reconstruction in South Carolina, which led to diminished economic and political opportunities for African-Americans and markedly increased racial violence. He was accepted at Princeton, perhaps to his surprise, and he began his formal theological training in 1878.[56]

Stewart's stint at Princeton Theological Seminary was unique in two respects. It marked the first time that he had received formal religious training and the first time he lived in a northern state. He had been transferred in May 1878 to the New Jersey Conference of the AME Church and he served as an assistant at the AME Church of Princeton. (Stewart had personally requested the transfer to the New Jersey Conference in order to attend the seminary.)

By the late nineteenth century, only a few black students attended the seminary. As early as 1825, Theodore Sedgwick Wright, a free black born in Providence, Rhode Island, and raised in New York, attended the school and reportedly became, in 1828, the first black student to graduate from it. Wright would later become a prominent Presbyterian minister in New York and one of the leading black abolitionists of his era. He served, for example, on the executive committees of the American Anti-Slavery Society and the American and Foreign Anti-Slavery Society and was a leading figure in the Underground Railroad.[57]

Hugh M. Browne, who later became a close friend of Stewart's, and Francis Grimké were also black graduates of Princeton Theological Seminary. Browne, like Stewart, had attended Howard University before enrolling at the seminary, where he graduated in 1878. Browne went on to study philosophy for two years at Edinburgh University in Scotland and take advanced training in languages in Germany. It is reasonable to assume that Stewart met Browne at the seminary, although Browne graduated from the seminary in 1878, the year that Stewart arrived. Or the two men may have become acquainted when Stewart attended Howard University between 1869 and 1873. The two men later developed a close friendship.[58]

Francis James Grimké was unquestionably the most distinguished African-American to attend Princeton Theological Seminary during the nineteenth century. Born a slave in Charleston, South Carolina, in 1850 to Henry Grimké, a prominent white planter, and Nancy Weston, a slave, Francis Grimké had a privileged upbringing. Francis, his youngest brother John, and Archibald, who would later graduate from the Harvard University Law School and serve as the American consul to the Dominican Republic, were emancipated during the Civil War and began long careers of public service. After attending the Morris Street School, a private school established for Charleston's free blacks, Francis and Archibald enrolled in Lincoln University in 1866. Francis graduated at the top of his class in 1870. While Archibald pursued a legal career, Francis enrolled in the Princeton Theological Seminary in 1875 and graduated in 1878, the year that T. McCants Stewart arrived. Grimké was a brilliant student who excelled in all of his subjects. Dr. A. A. Hodge, one of the world's leading authorities on theology, described Francis Grimké as one of the most able students he taught. Today, a color portrait of Grimké hangs in Stuart Hall on the campus.[59]

Stewart's admission to Princeton Theological Seminary was another indication that his education at Avery, Howard, and the University of South Carolina had prepared him to compete with some of the most gifted students in the nation. The academic training at the seminary was more rigorous than Stewart had encountered heretofore, but he appears to have met the challenge satisfactorily. His Princeton register of alumni activities reveals that he took a post-graduate course in philosophy under Professor James McCosh, the president of Princeton College, but it does not indicate any additional course work. It is possible that Stewart, having already secured a college degree and already a Methodist minister, was interested only in additional training or in affiliating with a prestigious northern religious seminary rather than in obtaining a graduate degree in theology. In fact, it was quite common in the nineteenth century for undergraduate and graduate students to attend the seminary for a limited time without the intention of completing their formal programs, since the seminary issued only a certificate, rather than a diploma, until World War I. Whatever his intentions, Stewart terminated his enrollment at the seminary in May 1880 before completing the requirements for his degree. That same month, he was ordained by the African Methodist Episcopal Church.[60]

By 1880, T. McCants Stewart had come a long way from his boyhood years in Charleston. He had made considerable progress toward joining the leadership circle of black South Carolinians and was confident that he would eventually take his place on the national stage as well. By the time he left the seminary, Stewart was a mature, well-educated man with a sense of purpose and a bright future before him. His mission was not only to advance his professional career but also to help advance his race. He believed that middle-class black leaders should not pursue status and material gains as ends in themselves but should work to uplift the race. The progress and future of African-Americans would depend in part, he argued, on how unselfishly he and his fellow "colored aristocrats" performed their obligation and the degree to which they succeeded in opening doors for blacks less fortunate than themselves.[61]

Stewart's formative years also reveal the pattern of restlessness and mobility that continued throughout his life. He had also been bold and assertive as a young man in his attempt to stake out new opportunities, a characteristic that he would later instill in each of his children. Indeed, Stewart had shown little reluctance to take risks in order to advance his education or professional career. By the age of twenty-six, this well-traveled young man had resided in Charleston, Sumter, Orangeburg, and Columbia, South Carolina, and in Washington, D.C., and Princeton, New Jersey. Yet T. McCants Stewart would continue to seek new challenges and opportunities to fulfill his personal ambitions as well as his mission to uplift his race.

2

A National Leader Emerges

❖ ❖ ❖ ❖ ❖ ❖ ❖ ❖ ❖ ❖ ❖ ❖ ❖ ❖ ❖

The period from 1880 to 1885 represented an important era in T. McCants Stewart's career, for it was during these years that Stewart emerged as a national leader. Like many black southerners who left the South during the aftermath of Reconstruction in search of greater economic and political opportunities, Stewart also moved north in 1880. His formal training at Princeton Theological Seminary had prepared him to serve as pastor of a Methodist church, provided that he could find a position. After completing his studies at the seminary, Stewart relocated to New York, where he became pastor of the Bethel AME Church. Here, he forged a reputation as a respected minister, emigrationist, writer, and racial activist. It was also during these years that Stewart gradually developed his ideas on black nationalism and the role that African-American leaders like himself should play in helping Africa to Christianize its people and to develop its vast natural resources. Moving to New York also gave Stewart an opportunity to test his ideas and intellect against other blacks in leadership positions.[1]

In 1880 New York City was an exciting place for a black South Carolinian to work. Although Stewart had lived in Charleston and Washington, D.C., two major urban centers, the size, diversity of ethnic and racial groups, and sophistication of New York must have seemed overwhelming initially. New York was a major financial, cultural, and commercial center, and with 1,206,299 residents, America's largest metropolis. Yet only 19,663 blacks lived in the city, only 1.6 percent of the total population.[2]

Stewart's decision to settle in New York was logical in light of his desire to become an important black leader and to fulfill his mission to uplift the

African-American race. During the antebellum era the city contained one of the most politically active black communities in the nation. The first black newspaper, *Freedom's Journal,* was established there and the city's black community included an active group of abolitionists, such as David Ruggles, who organized a vigilance committee to assist runaway slaves, and Theodore Wright, who served on the executive committees of several prominent antislavery societies. The antebellum black community also established schools, such as the African Free School, which educated free blacks, and numerous literary societies, many of which were organized by black women.[3] This tradition of reform and political activism apparently excited Stewart, who felt challenged by the quality of black leadership and the challenges of this northern metropolis.

But for all of its promise and opportunity, New York at the turn of the century was no "crystal stair" for African-Americans. The majority of black New Yorkers, whose population had increased to 38,616 by 1900, worked in unskilled, menial, or service jobs. Black workers also competed with a large population of foreign-born white immigrants, even in service jobs such as catering, where African-Americans had made substantial progress before the Civil War. Black New Yorkers also lived in the poorest sections of town, which were often overcrowded and centers of vice and crime. Overcrowding and poverty took their toll in many ways, not the least of which was a high rate of infectious diseases and high black mortality. "Of all the peoples in New York City," notes historian Gilbert Osofsky, "foreign-born as well as natives, Negroes had, proportionally, the highest mortality rates."[4]

By the time that T. McCants Stewart and his wife arrived in New York in 1880, the once bustling Five Points district, located in the sixth ward, where many black families had resided before the Civil War, was overwhelmingly Irish, the result of the large Irish immigration between 1830 and 1860 and the corresponding shifts in residential and business patterns. "In a few years there will not be a [black] family living on the East Side of our city, that part known as Stagg Town, where the colored people lived years ago," wrote the New York *Freeman* in 1887. The majority of blacks moved to the north and west of Five Points, including Greenwich Village. Here in the twelfth ward the Bethel AME Church was located.[5]

Founded in 1819, Bethel AME was located on Sullivan Street in Greenwich Village in a section called "Little Africa." A reporter for the New York *Sun* described the church in 1882 as "a plain, garbled building without tower or steeple and on the outside it looks somewhat old and neglected. It is made of brick and the front is painted a sort of grayish blue. A marble tablet, set in the front wall, says that it was the first African Methodist Church in the city." This claim, was inaccurate, however, for "Mother Zion," the African Methodist Episcopal Zion Church was organized in 1796. Following the appointment of Bethel's Reverend William F. Dickerson as a bishop to South Carolina, Stewart was chosen to be pastor of this prestigious church.[6]

The black church in New York City had a long tradition as an agency of racial uplift. During the nineteenth century, black ministers such as Theodore S. Wright, Samuel Cornish, Henry Highland Garnet, and Charles Ray had frequently taken center stage in pushing for the abolition of slavery and racial equality. Reverend Adam Clayton Powell, Sr., pastor of the Abyssinian Baptist Church, the largest black church in New York City with more than 10,000 members, extended this tradition into the twentieth century. Stewart was not only aware of this proud history, but he also attempted to place his ministry within the larger tradition of racial uplift and black protest in New York.[7]

Reverend Stewart, at twenty-six years of age, was a popular and dedicated pastor, who very capably managed the church's affairs. His congregation of approximately 1,000 members was interracial, though predominately African-American, and blacks controlled the affairs of the church. During his ministry, Stewart added 200 members to the church and raised approximately $25,000, of which $7,000 was on Bethel's bonded debt. A conscientious guardian of church resources, Stewart also renegotiated the church's annual rate of interest (from 6 percent to 5 percent). Indeed, fund-raising commanded as much of his time as saving souls. Although Stewart had no formal experience as a fund-raiser, he succeeded in raising money for Christian education, to assist the poor, and for home and foreign missions.[8]

Stewart was also active in Bethel AME's social welfare project, which labored to establish a black YMCA branch in New York. That project was not completed until 1901, in large measure through the financial assistance of the white philanthropist George Foster Peabody. That Stewart and New York's black leadership attempted to establish a segregated YMCA branch within a northern city with few segregation laws reveals their desire to control the direction of their own community institutions and at the same time acknowledges that segregated institutions operated openly in many northern cities. Citing the success of their churches, lodges, fraternal societies, and mutual aid societies, which were strong and autonomous black institutions, Stewart and most African-American leaders insisted that blacks control and lead these organizations.

Although he had served a small black church in South Carolina and served as an assistant pastor of a Methodist church in Princeton, New Jersey, his pastorate at Bethel was Stewart's first experience managing a large congregation in an urban area. The young minister was responsible for renovating the entire church property, and under his leadership Bethel AME would never succumb to the factional disputes and infighting that paralyzed many black and some white churches during this era. For his services, Stewart received an annual salary of $1,500, of which $300 was allocated specifically for lodging. Though not extravagant, Stewart's salary was almost three times larger than that of Reverend George Washington Williams, the black pastor of the Twelfth Baptist Church in Boston, himself a rising black leader. This steady and predictable income placed Stewart squarely in New York's black middle class, and it permitted him the free time to become a racial activist.[9]

T. McCants Stewart also supported the work of his black and white ministerial colleagues in New York, which increased his visibility and the prestige of his congregation. In November 1881, for example, Reverend Stewart and a group of distinguished New Yorkers, including Reverend J. D. Fulton and Samuel Morley, a member of British Parliament visiting the United States, attended a meeting at the Academy of Music in New York with more than 2,000 people of all races. The purpose of the meeting was to discuss the role of the Talented Tenth. The keynote address, delivered by Reverend Fulton, was "The Uplift of the Men of Color." Stewart, who was building a network of friends and associates in New York's black and white communities, was also invited to participate in a celebration in honor of Henry Highland Garnet, who had been appointed as U.S. minister to Liberia.[10]

Garnet, who had held the pastorate at Shiloh Presbyterian Church for twenty-five years, was one of the most revered and respected black ministers in the nation. This former slave who had escaped from bondage had caused a stir in 1843 when his address "To the Slaves of the United States of America" at the National Negro Convention in Buffalo, New York, urged slaves to take up arms against their white oppressors. "Rather die freemen," Garnet thundered, "than live to be slaves." The convention delegates rejected the address by one vote. In his later years, Garnet toned down his rhetoric considerably, and in June 1881, President James A. Garfield appointed him minister to

Liberia, a traditional reward to black leaders for their loyalty to the Republican party. Regrettably, Garnet died just three months after his arrival in Monrovia.

Participating in these activities was important for Stewart because they allowed him to make new contacts in both the black and white communities. These formal affairs also permitted Stewart to interact with some of the most distinguished African-Americans in the nation and to measure his talent, intelligence, speaking ability, and organizational skill against them.[11]

Serving as pastor of the Bethel AME Church also gave Stewart the freedom to pursue many related interests. Stewart chose to become an activist, essentially a new role for him, but a role that he would have to relish if he expected to become a creditable black spokesman. In July 1880, he was one of four black leaders who petitioned New York governor Alonzo B. Cornell on behalf of Chastine Cox, a black New Yorker convicted of murder. The black petitioners, who included John D. Bagwell, editor of the Washington, D.C., *Exodus*, John J. Freeman, editor of the *Progressive American*, and W. H. Russell, pastor of the Rutherford Methodist Episcopal Church, assailed the governor for his refusal to receive them and to answer their petition: "We reafectfully [sic] submit that we are astounded at such treatment from a human being, particularly a professed Republican who claims to represent an advanced civilization. We would not expect worse treatment from a Roman governor two thousand years ago."[12]

The petition illustrates how rapidly Stewart became part of a leadership circle in New York City. Although he had resided in New York for only a few months, Stewart had already made some important contacts in New York's black community. Moreover, to support his convictions Stewart was willing to risk confronting a high-ranking political figure, even at this early stage of his career. A cautious black leader clearly would not have taken this route.

Stewart was also increasingly willing to use his pulpit to demand equal rights and the elimination of segregation laws. Thus Stewart had few if any reservations about attacking segregation laws in Florida after the distinguished AME bishop Daniel A. Payne was ejected from a railroad car for refusing to sit in the Jim Crow section. Stewart was outraged. Not only had one of the most respected men in the AME church been ousted from a southern railroad car, but Payne was seventy-one years of age, and his removal from the train resulted in a five-mile trek in the scorching sun to Jacksonville, Florida, his destination.[13]

This affront touched a particularly raw nerve in young Stewart, for he considered Payne, a fellow South Carolinian, his mentor. Stewart decided to put the incident in the national spotlight. He urged Payne to sue the railroad company, and he challenged all members of the AME church to raise money in support of Payne's anticipated legal fees. When Payne decided not to pursue the matter, Stewart nonetheless urged blacks to boycott Jim Crow railroad cars. But this action was easier advocated than accomplished. In the 1880s, railroads were the chief mode of long-distance transportation, and most southern states segregated their coaches, either by law or by custom. Segregation laws in the South were also multiplying at this time, and they were often enforced with terrorism and violence.[14]

T. McCants Stewart had hardly established a foothold in New York when he decided in November 1882 to resign his post as pastor of the Bethel AME Church and accept a position as the Charles Sumner Professor of Belles Lettres at Liberia College in Monrovia.[15] Stewart's decision to leave New York after less than three years to teach in Africa was surprising, for there is no evidence that he had expressed interest in African affairs.

What prompted Stewart, then, to interrupt a promising career as a minister in New York and move to Liberia? Perhaps Stewart's years at the Avery Institute had instilled in him the belief that teaching would be his mission in life, but up to now he had shown almost no inclination to fulfill that calling. If Stewart were hell-bent on teaching, why had he not moved back to the South and taught at a black college? What was the attraction of Liberia? And who, if anyone, had persuaded Stewart to seek this new challenge? These questions cannot be answered easily, although many factors appear to have influenced Stewart's decision.

Liberia had attracted nearly 14,000 black Americans by 1883, and the vast majority had settled in this African nation under the auspices of the American Colonization Society. Founded in 1817, the American Colonization Society attempted to resettle free blacks and former slaves in Liberia, a country established specifically as a refuge for these individuals. That the American Colonization Society had selected Liberia for this pioneering venture was no coincidence. White reformers in Great Britain had founded a city for ex-slaves in Sierra Leone, which was adjacent to Liberia, in 1787. Although the American Colonization Society attracted a number of influential white supporters, including the Kentucky congressman Henry Clay and John Randolph of Roanoke, Virginia, the organization came under sharp attack from northern free blacks. These leaders, which included

James Forten, a prominent black abolitionist, and Richard Allen, the first bishop consecrated in the African Methodist Episcopal Church and a prominent African-American leader in Philadelphia, argued that colonization was an ill-conceived and nefarious scheme to benefit the slaveholding interests and to rid the nation of free blacks. By 1830, the American Colonization Society had settled less than 1,500 blacks in the colony, and the majority of free African-Americans, despite their hardships in America, were opposed to emigrating to Africa.[16] Thus Stewart would be operating in an environment where black Americans had settled for over six decades, but with mixed success and generally surrounded by controversy.

Seldom did black settlers or leaders travel to Liberia alone, and T. McCants Stewart was no exception. He was accompanied by Hugh H. Browne, another prominent black minister and educator. Browne, who was born in Washington, D.C., had graduated from Howard University and the Princeton Theological Seminary in 1878 before succeeding Henry Highland Garnet as pastor of the Shiloh Presbyterian Church in New York. Browne resigned his ministry in November 1882 and was appointed the Charles Hodge Professor of Intellectual and Moral Philosophy at Liberia College. It is reasonable to assume that Stewart and Browne collaborated in making their decision to go to Liberia. Their paths may have crossed at Howard University and later at the Princeton Theological Seminary, but most certainly, Stewart and Browne had come into contact as pastors of two of the most prominent churches in New York. In fact, the rapport that these two ministers had established by 1882 was a pivotal factor in their decision to undertake this venture jointly.[17]

In deciding to undertake this journey, Stewart and Browne were accepting the challenge of Edward Wilmot Blyden, who urged American blacks to move to Liberia and help develop the resources of the young republic. Blyden, president of Liberia College, had encouraged black leaders throughout the world to join him in developing a strong liberal arts curriculum in the college. "The instruments of culture which we shall employ in the College," stated Blyden, "will be chiefly the classics and Mathematics."[18] In attempting to strengthen the curriculum Blyden was attempting to strengthen the government of Liberia "through a better system of education," argues historian Hollis Lynch. The addition of Stewart and Browne to the faculty of Liberia College could shape the college's curriculum for future generations of students and attract a large following of African students. It was also an important triumph for Blyden personally, for it gave his work greater respectability and brought immediate visibility to the college.[19]

In early January 1883, T. McCants Stewart preached his final sermon before a packed congregation at the Bethel AME Church. "The closing remarks of Mr. Stewart were very sad and affecting, especially his reference to his departure from this country, to his new field of labor," reported the New York *Globe*.[20] Stewart had apparently won over his congregation during his short time in New York, and he chose to inform them at length about the task before him. He also read numerous letters of encouragement from friends and prominent religious leaders. "If the Lord Jesus has summoned you to the African field, I say go, and may He be your counsellor, your Guide, and your Glorious Commander," wrote Bishop Daniel A. Payne. Bishop Alexander Wayman offered similar encouragement. Stewart's old friend and legal colleague David Augustus Straker, now dean of law at Allen University in Columbia, South Carolina, was not as enthusiastic as either Payne or Wayman: "I am undecided as to the wisdom of your case except as the path of duty directs you."[21]

James McCosh, president of Princeton College and one of Stewart's academic mentors when he studied at the Princeton Theological Seminary, was also present for Stewart's final sermon. McCosh spoke highly of his former pupil. "I am here," stated McCosh, "to bear testimony to the capability of the colored race to receive great education. They have a capacity for indefinite improvement. I do not believe, however, that the North or the South can elevate the Negro alone; it must be done by themselves." Stewart was probably moved by the attention and praise that he and Browne received and particularly impressed that a man of McCosh's distinction would endorse his proposed work in Liberia.[22]

Although supporters of the venture far outnumbered the critics, Stewart noted that "some people" had discouraged them. Even so, Stewart and Browne were adamant that they had made the right decision. "Our desire to be at work in Liberia," Stewart wrote, "grows with our growth and strengthens with our strength. That the Negro must develop a Nationality, a civilization somewhere, before he will be able to stand erect among the races and nations of the earth, becomes clearer and clearer to us as we travel and observe, and read and reflect. We feel that our brethren have a great work in America, but ours is to where Ethiopia shall soon stretch forth her hand unto God."[23]

Stewarts' comments illustrate his evolving nationalism as well as his attitude toward the progress and the degree of civilization that Africans had attained. These remarks also reflect the role he believed American blacks should play in developing the African continent. Like many Americans, both white and black, Stewart believed that African cultures were backward in relation to Western civilization. His work in Liberia would, in his view, raise the level of civilization in Africa so that Africans could compete more effectively with other nations. (Stewart's reference to Ethiopia stretching "forth her hand unto God" would be adopted as a slogan by Marcus Garvey more than three decades later.) Thus, educating a backward nation and bringing it in touch with Christianity appear to have been Stewart's primary motivations for moving to Liberia. At the same time, however, Stewart nust have recognized that his work in Africa would benefit his career. He would be able to boast that he had not only traveled abroad but also that his work as a "race leader" had extended to the shores of Africa.[24]

Imbued with confidence that their work in Liberia would serve the needs of Liberia College, the Republic of Liberia, and their careers, Stewart and Browne sailed from New York to Monrovia in July 1883. This voyage, Stewart's first trip outside the United States, allowed him to see the European continent for the first time. In a letter to the New York *Globe,* a black weekly, he described his journey aboard ship and his impressions of the Netherlands. Rejoicing that he had seen firsthand the famous Dutch windmills and that his experience with European customs was uneventful, Stewart observed that "the Dutch have certainly spent millions of dollars on what Americans call 'internal improvement.' The sand banks that act as sea walls are wonderful. What labor! What expense! And as we passed through the country, we see canals everywhere. The cities—Amsterdam, the Hague, Rotterdam—are covered with canals, just as New York City is with street car tracks; we do not exaggerate. It is wonderful."[25]

Although Stewart had no facility with Dutch and referred to it as a "horrid language," he took ample advantage of his time in the Netherlands by visiting museums, cathedrals, and art galleries and observing the customs of the people. He described Amsterdam as one of the cleanest cities he had ever visited, for "even the sidewalks are bright and inviting. They wash them often." Stewart also marveled at the economic contribution of Dutch women: "The women seem to do a great part of the manual labor. They push and unload boats, carry great burdens on their shoulders and on their heads, and do other things that city women would not touch in America."

Stewart, now firmly entrenched in the black elite of New York City, had clearly forgotten that black women performed many of these tasks in American cities including Charleston, South Carolina, his hometown.[26]

When Stewart and Browne arrived in 1883, Liberians were attempting to harness the nation's resources and simultaneously to develop its educational system. Liberia College, the brainchild of the Massachusetts Colonization Society, had opened its doors two decades earlier, in 1862. Unfortunately, it was hampered by an awkward administrative structure. The society had established a separate fund-raising unit, the Trustees of Donations for Education in Liberia (TDEL), and administrative decisions were made by three boards: a Liberian board of trustees and two American boards, one in Boston and one in New York, that controlled the selection of faculty and the college's finances.[27]

In 1880, three years before Stewart and Browne arrived, Liberia's political leaders had appointed Edward Blyden president of Liberia College in an attempt to bring stability to their fledgling system of higher education. A native of St. Thomas, Virgin Islands, and an ordained Presbyterian clergyman, Blyden had emigrated to Liberia in 1850. His intellect was quickly recognized as an asset to the Liberian Republic, and Blyden was appointed to a series of important political posts. He served, for example, as the Liberian educational commissioner to Great Britain and the United States, the Liberian secretary of state, the Liberian ambassador to the Court of St. James, and professor of classics at Liberia College. As president, Blyden hoped to "make the college a place of learning for Africa and the race." Thus Liberia College's curriculum included courses in the classics, Greek, Latin and Arabic languages, ancient and European history, and mathematics. Blyden also permitted women to enroll in the college and appointed Jennie E. Davis, who had emigrated to Liberia from the United States, to head the Female Department. Blyden required that students devote part of their time to manual labor, a requirement that reflected the influence of Samuel Chapman Armstrong, founder and president of Hampton Institute, on the African leader. Moreover, Blyden was both suspicious and critical of white Protestant missionaries. He believed that a college in West Africa should be organized by a Christian government run by blacks and that the faculty of Liberia College should consist of African instructors.[28]

Rather than evolving into a center of learning under Blyden's leadership, however, Liberia College became "one of the battle grounds for the Negro-mulatto conflict in Liberia." But Blyden had inherited an institution with a troubled past. The trustees of the college, who were based in Boston, closed it entirely between 1876 and 1877 on the grounds "that it had failed to be of practical utility for the purpose of education in the Republic."[29] By 1881, there were only twenty-seven students in the Preparatory Department and only eight enrolled in the college. The college had difficulty attracting professors as well as students, and fund-raising, as evidenced by the college's deteriorating physical plant, had not succeeded either. Similarly, Blyden's criticism of white Protestant missionaries was hypocritical, for he openly solicited funds from these organizations in the United States to run Liberia College. Blyden's belief that Liberia College should consist solely of African professors was also flawed. The African leader had toured the United States in 1882 for the expressed purpose of recruiting black students and professors to work on behalf of Liberia College. T. McCants Stewart, Hugh H. Browne, and Jennie Davis were three African-Americans who answered this call.[30] This was exactly the situation in August 1883, when Stewart and Browne received a formal welcome by the people of Liberia, followed by a luncheon in their honor that was hosted by the widow of the former president of Liberia.[31]

Stewart and Browne had scarcely settled in Monrovia before they clashed with Blyden. "The rupture between Blyden and the two professors took place so quickly that they taught not one day in the College," wrote historian Hollis Lynch. Blyden was also a militant nationalist who harbored an irrational hatred toward mulattoes, and although Stewart's complexion was medium brown, Blyden considered both him and Browne, who had a lighter complexion, members of this class. Mulattoes, Blyden believed, had exploited Africans for their own personal gain. Blyden also disliked the autonomy that Stewart and Browne enjoyed. Since both men had been hired by the American boards of trustees in Boston and New York and were paid by the same sources, Blyden had little control over their actions. Blyden, however, had few alternatives, for he had failed to attract distinguished African scholars to Liberia College as he had hoped.[32]

Blyden was particularly suspicious of the outspoken Stewart, who appeared to have little if any respect for his authority or the mission of Liberia College. "I am very much surprised and grieved at the course the new Professors have chosen to pursue, Stewart being the leader. I hope, however, that they get their eyes opened by a larger experience," wrote Blyden to William Coppinger, the corresponding secretary of the American Colonization Society and Blyden's confidant during these personal travails.[33]

Exactly what "larger experience" Blyden had in mind is unclear, but Blyden was firmly convinced that T. McCants Stewart was the source of the problem. "You will be sorry to learn that Professor Stewart, through inexperience and hasty temper, is disposed to give trouble," Blyden continued, "and Professor Browne seems to be altogether under his influence. They pay no respect whatsoever to the College authorities here, notwithstanding the friendly advice given them by Dr. Wells as a condition of their successful work here—to obey orders." Blyden incorrectly attributed his disagreement with Stewart and Browne to their lack of racial pride. "They are not trained in America," he informed American Colonization Society official Thomas Davenport, "to respect men of their own race. They required the residence of a few years in Liberia to learn the necessary self-respect."[34]

Blyden also accused Stewart and Browne of being lazy as well as uncooperative. Since they were unaccustomed to the Liberian climate, the two Americans apparently insisted on a prolonged acclimation period before commencing their work, for fear that they would otherwise contract the African fever. Blyden noted, with a bit of sarcasm, that the female professor, Jennie E. Davis, "is quite at home [in Liberia], having apparently no apprehensions whatever, though very prudent in her movements." Blyden also complained that Stewart and Browne resisted his effort to move Liberia College into the nation's interior, where he felt it could serve the native population more effectively. "So far their influence is really with those who would keep everything on the coast, and those who look with suspicion upon every movement toward the interior," wrote Blyden.[35]

The conflict between Stewart and Blyden was part power struggle and part ideological dispute concerning the direction Liberia College should take in educating its students. Blyden, on the one hand, had hoped to stress a liberal arts education combined with industrial education. He felt that this approach to educating African students, which had already been adopted at Hampton Institute and the newly established Tuskegee Institute in the United States, would help defray students' expenses and make Liberia College more accessible economically to the native population.[36] Stewart, on the other hand, a proponent of Booker T. Washington's program of industrial education at Tuskegee Institute, clearly saw the merits and utility of combining a program of industrial education with a strong liberal arts curriculum. Nevertheless, Stewart and Browne felt that Blyden had been dishonest with them concerning not only his intentions for the college, but also his own political motives. Liberia College did not, they argued, intend to stress the liberal arts as Blyden had alleged. Furthermore, they maintained that Blyden had hoped to use their influence to further his political career by having them make speeches on his behalf. There is evidence to support Stewart and Browne's charge. Blyden wanted to become president of Liberia, and in 1885 he challenged the incumbent president, Hilary R. W. Johnson, for reelection. Despite Blyden's belief that "Divine intervention" would result in his victory at the polls, the more popular and able Johnson defeated Blyden by almost a two-to-one margin.[37]

Blyden and American Colonization Society officials were concerned that Stewart and Browne would return to the United States and circulate inaccurate and damaging reports concerning the work of Liberia College. "I shudder at the thought of the mischief their coming back [to the U.S.] dissatisfied will bring about to the interests which we have here at heart," confided William Coppinger to Blyden. "I shall begin to look forward for their return and with such representations of Liberia," Coppinger continued, "as will produce more damage to the Society and the Republic than any one thing that has taken place since their foundation." Coppinger feared, justifiably, that Stewart and Browne's criticism of the American Colonization Society's work in Liberia would cripple fund-raising efforts and destroy any realistic chance for Liberia College to succeed. Thus Coppinger and Blyden were faced with a dilemma. On the one hand, they hoped to be rid of Stewart and Browne as soon as possible, for they viewed their presence as an impediment to the progress of Liberia College. On the other hand, Stewart and Browne's departure would certainly result in criticism of Liberia College and a potential loss in funding. As Coppinger conceded, "There will be no means of refuting their statements, however false, and whites and blacks alike will believe them and quote their testimony for years to come."[38]

Stewart and Browne, both strongly opinionated and accustomed to leadership, were admittedly difficult to get along with on occasion. Blyden privately resented their inflated sense of themselves as race leaders, black nationalists, and agents of civilization. As a militant black nationalist who had lived and labored in Liberia since 1850, and a gifted intellectual, Blyden did not take kindly to anyone who challenged his authority or lectured to him concerning the direction that Liberian education should take. Blyden's inflated ego and insecurities led him to expect the worst from Stewart and Brown; as a result, they were never allowed to test their abilities. Blyden had bristled, too, at the attention Stewart and Browne received when they resigned their ministries and sailed to Liberia. Blyden was particularly critical that Stewart and Browne spent two months traveling through England, France, Germany, and Holland before coming to Liberia. Blyden felt it was a "pity that they could not have come direct from America here. Their visit to England and the treatment accorded to them there by distinguished persons for their work's sake have made them top heavy."[39] However, Blyden was unrealistic to think that Stewart and Browne's departure would not be important news in the United States, particularly in the black press, and equally naive to believe that their arrival in Monrovia would not be met with considerable excitement.

By the spring of 1884, the breach between Stewart, Browne, and Blyden was irreconcilable. Blyden, who had quickly concluded that Stewart and Browne's employment at Liberia College was a mistake, worked secretly to get rid of the two men. In a confidential letter to J. C. Braman, corresponding secretary of the trustees of donations, Blyden urged the Boston trustees to use their influence to dismiss the two professors: "I would now recommend in the interest of the institution the withdrawal of their appointment unless they change their course and work in harmony with the policy approved of by you in the new departure for the prosperity of the institution." Blyden ultimately brought a formal grievance against Stewart before the Boston board of officers. After hearing the evidence in the case, however, the board ruled in Stewart's favor.[40]

Stewart and Browne had no intention of leaving Liberia without discrediting Blyden and, if possible, getting him removed from his position as president of Liberia College. They accused Blyden before the TDEL of mismanaging the affairs of the College, an accusation supported by Hilary R. W. Johnson, the president of Liberia. Johnson also believed that Blyden's opposition to Stewart and Browne stemmed largely from their autonomy and assertiveness. "More than once," Johnson confided to the Boston TDEL, "have I had occasion to defend these men against slanderous reports put in the mouths of certain persons by Dr. Blyden, who finds in the Professors only one fault—they being men who speak for themselves—an unpardonable offense in the estimation of the President of the College, whose motto seems to be Rule or Ruin."[41]

Blyden's downfall was the combined result of his lack of tact and diplomacy, overextending himself as minister of the interior and president of Liberia College, and the serious limitations of his leadership that Stewart and Browne had exposed. Blyden was an exceedingly difficult man to work with, "mainly because he regarded himself as a 'providential agent' working on behalf of the Negro race and was always convinced about the rightness of his ideas," concluded Hollis Lynch. Thus at a meeting of the Liberian board of trustees in January 1884, Stewart and Browne "attacked Blyden with unrestrained abuse."

When Blyden realized that Liberia's president sided with the two American professors, he fled to Sierra Leone, which had become a regular sanctuary for him in recent years, leaving the presidency of Liberia College vacant. By June 1884, the Boston trustees voted to suspend Blyden as president because of his long absence from the college, proof, in their estimation, that Stewart and Browne's criticism had merit. Shortly thereafter, Edward Wilmot Blyden formally resigned as president of Liberia College. Not a single student graduated from Liberia College under Blyden's presidency, and by the spring of 1885 every senior student had left the college to seek employment.[42]

T. McCants Stewart's return to the United States in 1885 ended his work of christianizing and civilizing of the Liberian people. But his Liberian experience, albeit abbreviated, was beneficial to Stewart in several respects. Ironically, it broadened his appreciation for the importance of industrial education. Although Stewart had been fervently critical of Blyden's decision to mix a liberal arts education with industrial training, he had gradually changed his opinion on this issue. In 1884, serving as a self-appointed general agent for Liberia College, Stewart had conducted a study of Hampton Institute, where the curriculum combined industrial and liberal education, although the emphasis was on learning a trade. His favorable impression of Hampton's program probably influenced his decision during the early 1890s to send his two sons, McCants and Gilchrist, to Tuskegee Institute.[43]

Stewart's two years in Liberia had also broadened his political and intellectual horizons. In 1885, few black Americans had traveled abroad, and even fewer had lived and worked in Africa and seen the potential and the travails of the continent first hand. But Stewart had been privileged to witness the struggle of an African nation for political and economic respectability and attempted to educate its people. He synthesized his experience and knowledge of Liberia in a book, *Liberia: The Americo-African Republic,* published in 1886. He also kept an extensive diary of his work in Liberia, which has never been located.[44]

The publication of *Liberia,* which was well received in the United States and reviewed in some of the leading black newspapers and periodicals, was an important milestone for Stewart, for it heightened his reputation. "Professor Stewart is an excellent writer and his work will undoubtedly be an interesting as well as a valuable one," concluded one reviewer in the Cleveland *Gazette*. Like Paul Cuffe, who made two voyages to Africa at his own expense in 1811 and 1816 and was recognized by the U.S. government as an African authority, Stewart, too, would claim expertise in this area following the publication of *Liberia*.[45]

The book, which devotes five of its sixteen chapters to climatic conditions and five chapters to characteristics of the Liberian people, was an impressionistic account of Liberian affairs that may have done more to establish Stewart's reputation as a climatologist than as a gifted writer. *Liberia* is also significant, as historian August Meier notes, because it places Stewart among a select group of nineteenth-century African-American leaders who stressed both commercial relations and a limited migration to Africa for the purpose of Christianizing the continent. This voluntary movement of American blacks to Africa, argued Stewart, would be self-supporting and ultimately create a "new Christian Negro nationality in the Fatherland." Although Stewart denied that he was a colonizationist after his return to the United States in 1885, he did indeed advocate a "voluntary movement to the [Liberian] Republic of independent, self-reliant, and self-supporting people with capital behind them." Stewart was correct in his prophecy that a sizable infusion of capital would develop and transform the African continent but wrong in his predictions that most of this capital would come from American blacks, or that "thousands of civilized American Negroes of enterprise" would be attracted to Africa.[46]

T. McCants Stewart's two years in Liberia also irreparably strained his marriage to Lottie. But for Stewart, forging his reputation as a national leader and spokesman for the black community was more important than marital bliss and a sacrifice, he believed, that his family was expected to bear. Thus, when Stewart traveled to Liberia, he sent his wife and three young children to live in her mother's home in Columbia, South Carolina, until he could make arrangements to send for them, which he never did, establishing a pattern that he would repeat in his future travels.[47] Stewart may have felt that the African climate, particularly the possibility of catching malaria, made it inadvisable to bring his wife and three small children, including an infant, to Liberia. Furthermore, because of his feuding with Edward Blyden, Stewart never managed to establish himself firmly enough in Liberia to send for his family.

However, most evidence indicates that Stewart was less concerned about the effect of the harsh African climate on his family's health than he was about furthering his career without the distraction of a family. He seldom wrote his wife or inquired about the well-being of his children, and he provided his family with insufficient financial support during his absence. Under the terms of his contract, the New York Mission Board paid Stewart a salary of $1,800 annually, of which only $50 a month went directly to support Stewart's wife and three children. Stewart apparently believed that this amount was sufficient, despite the pleadings and protestations of his wife, and refused to increase this meager allowance. Consequently, Lottie Stewart and her three children lived on the edge of poverty for two years, and T. McCants Stewart never once appeared overly concerned with their predicament. Oddly, the glaring contradiction of Stewart's personal quest to become a national spokesman for African-Americans and his neglect of his family provoked no strong moral crisis or feeling of guilt. His career took first priority, and this fact in Stewart's mind was not a debatable issue. Within five years of his return to the United States, Stewart had divorced his wife and subsequently provided her with no financial support.[48]

In spite of the toll on his family life, T. McCants Stewart's career was progressing nicely. His three years in New York, as pastor of the Bethel AME Church, and his two years in Liberia placed him one step closer to the position of a nationally recognized black leader that he so coveted. He had already made many important inroads into New York's important black community in a relatively short time—his service in the black ministerial community alone had earmarked him as one of the most promising young ministers and "race leaders" in the city. Although emigrating to Liberia had been potentially risky for Stewart's career, his return to New York in 1885 and the publication of *Liberia* the following year brought a new status. Stewart had lived in Africa and had worked for the betterment of the African continent, a boast that only a handful of blacks of his generation could make. He had also locked horns with Edward Blyden, a highly respected black intellectual, and emerged victorious. Now that he was back in New York, Stewart would use this triumph to affirm his position as a black leader of national importance.

3

Years of Triumph and Frustration

❖ ❖ ❖ ❖ ❖ ❖ ❖ ❖ ❖ ❖ ❖ ❖ ❖ ❖ ❖ ❖ ❖

"I now face life again in the United States," wrote T. McCants Stewart, vowing that he would never return to Liberia under any circumstances. "Liberia College," he observed, "was a feeble affair, unworthy of the name," noting that there had been no real need for his services.[1] New York's bustling black community had not changed radically during Stewart's two-year absence, and Stewart was confident that he could reclaim the prominent position he had occupied before his departure for Africa in 1883. While living in Monrovia, he had kept abreast of domestic affairs in the United States and written an occasional column for the New York *Freeman*. He had also corresponded with his close friend T. Thomas Fortune, who would shortly establish himself as one of the nation's premier black journalists.[2] Once he was back in New York, Stewart realized quickly that he could not regain the pulpit at Bethel AME Church. Furthermore, it was unlikely that another influential African-American church would need the services of an experienced black minister right away. Therefore Stewart made the decision to resume his legal practice.

Since 1875, when Stewart handled his first legal case under the protective wings of Robert Brown Elliott and D. Augustus Straker in Orangeburg, South Carolina, the number of black lawyers had grown steadily. But in terms of their status, income, and clientele, black attorneys had continued to lag behind their white colleagues. Regardless of their credentials or the location of their practices, they consistently had trouble attracting white clients. The majority of African-American attorneys, therefore, established partnerships with other black lawyers or practiced alone. "Their presence and their small numbers," wrote law professor J. Clay Smith, Jr., "were not viewed as a significant threat in the legal community because they were only marginally accepted by white lawyers and white clients."[3] The legacy of slavery, the limited access of blacks to college and professional degrees, and white hostility toward black professionals in general combined to ensure an uphill battle for black lawyers such as T. McCants Stewart who planned to succeed in a predominantly white profession.

Thus, when Stewart returned to New York in 1885, he took steps to ensure that he would be taken seriously by both white and African-American attorneys. In 1886, he was admitted to practice before the New York Supreme Court. Stewart had opened an office near Wall Street and the New York Stock Exchange, in the heart of New York's prestigious financial district. He was admitted to the bar on the motion of Algermon S. Sullivan and A. M. Keily, both distinguished jurists.[4]

Only fragments of information on Stewart's legal career in New York have survived, principally as these cases were reported in the black press. These reports reveal, nevertheless, that Stewart was a highly competent attorney with a keen legal mind who proved to be an effective courtroom orator. Stewart's own assessment of his legal career, however, was more reserved. In an 1887 interview for the New York *Freeman,* Stewart described his legal triumphs but also revealed the difficulties inherent in being an African-American lawyer in New York. He stated that his practice had been progressing "slowly, and yet encouragingly," an honest admission that attracting clients of any race was more difficult than he had expected. Nonetheless, Stewart was guardedly optimistic. "New York City," he stated, "is a good field and yet it is a hard field. It is good because there is plenty of business here. It is hard because competition is so great. The struggle for existence is very intense." Stewart never cited race as a reason that his practice was moving slowly.[5]

Stewart specialized in civil law, hoping to attract a wide spectrum of clients from all races. However, he admitted that his legal calendar in 1887 was not "an extensive one." During the past year, Stewart had represented four corporations, which he chose not to identify, and appeared before the New York Supreme Court, district court, and common pleas court representing both plaintiff and defendant. His most noteworthy cases involved appearances before New York district courts, where he argued cases concerning divorce, slander, contracts, the recovery of trust funds, and damages for injury to property. Stewart affirmed that he had been "uniformly successful, losing absolutely only one motion for a bill of particulars." His success with these varied cases not only demonstrated Stewart's legal breadth, but also quickly won him the respect of the New York bar.[6]

Unlike some of his black legal colleagues in other states, who were openly referred to in court as "niggers," Stewart affirmed that he was treated with respect and dignity: "Whenever I come in contact with my brother lawyer, I find myself cordially received. Nowhere am I patronized." Stewart also pointed out that both blacks and whites sought his services, but that blacks had not utilized his services as much as he had hoped. Stewart attributed this fact to the commonly held belief that many black lawyers were less qualified than their white counterparts. "We colored people," he stated, "have little confidence in each other and little disposition to patronize one another; but such a spirit must disappear in time."[7]

Despite his success in the courtroom, Stewart had yet to establish a reputation as a successful attorney in the competitive New York market. Many black lawyers had already established solid legal reputations prior to Stewart's arrival on the scene in 1886, including Jacob H. Simms, who had been admitted to the New York bar in 1884 and handled eighty cases the following year, and John Francis Quarles, who had served in the foreign service under presidents Ulysses S. Grant and Rutherford B. Hayes before his admission to the New York bar in 1880.[8]

The young attorney's patience paid off. By 1887, Stewart was considered one of the leading black attorneys in New York and the nation. "T. McCants Stewart, Esq., beyond question the ablest colored lawyer in the country," wrote the Huntsville, Alabama, *Gazette*, "is building up a substantial practice in New York City."[9] J. Clay Smith, Jr., concluded in his detailed history of black lawyers that Stewart "later would become one of the most celebrated lawyers in the nation."[10]

Stewart's growing popularity permitted him to take on a wider range of cases as well as to increase his number of clients. In 1889, for example, Stewart represented a client in a probate case. Although he lost the case in the Surrogate's Court of New York, the judge praised Stewart's legal skill: "The masterly argument of counsel for the contestant greatly impressed me."[11] The fact that a white judge praised a black lawyer in open court was no small matter in the late nineteenth century, and it once again illustrated Stewart's solid legal training and the respect that he was accorded by the white legal community.

The following year Stewart appeared in one of his most widely publicized cases, which became known as the Trainor Hotel suit. T. Thomas Fortune, the militant editor of the New York *Freeman*, sued a saloon proprietor who had refused to serve him because of his race and then had forcibly removed him from the premises. It is plausible, as historian Emma Lou Thornbrough speculated, that Fortune deliberately provoked the incident to rally public support behind the recently formed Afro-American League. It is just as probable, however, that Fortune wished to assert his rights as an American citizen and buy a beer in a public establishment. Whatever Fortune's motivation may have been, he retained his close friend T. McCants Stewart to represent him in the case and sued the establishment.[12]

Two decades earlier, white New Yorkers, troubled by the presence of considerable racial discrimination in their state and increasingly sensitive to the pressure of African-American leaders, had passed a statewide civil rights law. This bold legislation spearheaded by New York Republicans and supported by the most prominent African-American leaders in the state, was consistent with the race policy of the national Republican party. The 1873 Civil Rights Act provided that blacks were entitled to full equality under the law and that no citizen "because of his race or color shall be excluded from the full and equal enjoyment of public facilities such as inns, common carriers, and common schools."[13] By the time the case came to trial in November 1891, Stewart was well acquainted with New York's civil rights law and had located witnesses who were willing to testify that the saloon's established policy was to refuse service to black patrons.

The Trainor Hotel suit generated tremendous excitement in New York's black community and in the black press nationally. Stewart, an adroit courtroom orator, persuaded the jury that the key issue in this case was not social equality but Fortune's right to exercise his constitutional rights. "The intelligent Afro-American," Stewart stated, "does not bother his head any more about social equality than you do about the man in the moon. What he rightly insists upon, gentlemen, is that he shall enjoy without let or hindrance every public, every civil, and every political right guaranteed him by the Constitution and the law of the land." Twelve white jurors agreed with Stewart, taking merely fifteen minutes to decide that force had been used in ejecting Fortune from the establishment, and assessed damages at $1,016.23. The defense appealed the decision, but the New York Court of Appeals upheld the verdict of the trial court.[14] The case was an important victory for Stewart personally, for it thrust his name once again into the national limelight as a racial spokesman. Booker T. Washington, for one, thought highly enough of Stewart after the Trainor case that he invited him to serve as the commencement speaker at Tuskegee Institute in 1893, a privilege that Washington reserved for the most prestigious black spokesmen in the nation, such as Frederick Douglass, Blanche K. Bruce, Francis and Archibald Grimké, and John Mercer Langston.[15]

Initially, Stewart turned down Washington's invitation, citing a busy legal calendar and his unwillingness to ride to Tuskegee, Alabama, in a segregated Pullman car. But Washington, as historian Louis R. Harlan has informed us, was not a man to be put off once he had made up his mind. In a handwritten note he chided Stewart for turning down his offer and attempted to persuade his northern friend to change his mind: "I hope you will do so [come to Tuskegee] as you will not only do us a favor, but have an opportunity of helping the race by what you will say." The "Wizard of Tuskegee" also assured Stewart that his commencement address would be "well reported in the Boston, New York, and Philadelphia papers" and that reports of segregation on Pullman coaches between New York and Tuskegee were exaggerated. "Every wide-awake, intelligent colored man like yourself who comes into the midst of the white people, and speaks to them, and looks them into the face gives them an object lesson of what the colored people are capable of doing and goes further to break down prejudice than anything else," Washington continued. "I assure you from New York to our place you will not have the slightest trouble on the Pullman car," he concluded. Apparently convinced that Washington was correct, Stewart spoke at Tuskegee's commencement in May 1893.[16]

T. McCants Stewart's legal career did not blossom dramatically, as he had hoped, following his successful defense of T. Thomas Fortune. Yet Stewart continued to attract clients on a steady basis and to argue civil, probate, and civil rights cases before the New York courts. Stewart represented Susie Frazier, a black female, who was attempting to gain a teaching position in Manhattan's white public schools. Although Frazier had graduated from New York City's Normal College (Hunter), she and other African-Americans found it virtually impossible to obtain teaching positions in the traditionally white public schools of either Brooklyn or New York City. In 1895, Frazier hired Stewart to press her case and to secure a writ compelling officials to appoint her to a permanent teaching post since she was on the eligible list. Although Stewart failed to compel New York's schools to hire Frazier immediately, she succeeded in gaining a permanent teaching position in the New York schools the following year (1896), opening the door for other African-American teachers.[17]

Arguing civil rights cases in the courts did a great deal to accelerate Stewart's quest to become a national spokesman for African-Americans. But these cases were few and far between. Most of Stewart's legal business consisted of civil cases, and though the litigants were often African-Americans, the cases did not necessarily have a racial component. In *Robinson v. Farren,* for example, Stewart represented William H. Robinson, an African-American, who sued a white defendant for false imprisonment. In this protracted case, Stewart won a judgment of $1,000 for his client. The New York *Age* reported that "the verdict showed that a man's color has nothing to do with litigation, at least in our higher courts, when the case is properly conducted.[18] In 1893, Stewart argued a criminal case, *New York v. Johnson,* where he appealed the murder conviction of a black man in the New York Court of Appeals. Even though Stewart lost the appeal, the appeals court praised his "professional ability [which was] worthy of commendation."[19]

Stewart's reputation as a capable black attorney and racial spokesman had a direct bearing on his ability to obtain a political appointment on the Brooklyn school board in 1891. He succeeded Philip A. White, an African-American wholesale druggist who had served on the school board until his unexpected death in 1891. Brooklyn's mayor Alfred C. Chapin appointed Stewart to the school board in May 1891 for a three-year term, and he was present at the roll call during the board's meeting on May 19, 1891. Stewart's appointment to the school board suggests that Chapin felt some obligation to represent the interests of African-American children in this important position. It also illustrates that black leaders such as Philip White and T. McCants Stewart had sufficient political clout to secure positions of this magnitude.[20]

The young activist and attorney took his position on the school board seriously. He never regarded his service as merely another routine committee assignment. Rather, he viewed his appointment as an extension of his service to the race as well as an opportunity to improve the educational opportunities of black children. Stewart took pride, for instance, in his appointment to the board's Free Scholarship Committee as well as his selection to the local committee for Public School 67.[21] Similarly, Stewart served as chairman of the Committee on Rules and Regulations, an appropriate assignment given his legal training and his attention to detail.[22]

Stewart worked diligently to ensure that Brooklyn's public schools were free of segregation and racial distinctions. Described by historian Carleton Mabee as the "most frequent visitor" to the black schools of Brooklyn, Stewart proposed to eliminate all use of the word "colored" in reference to Brooklyn's public schools and to merge the students and staffs of public schools number 68 and 83, forming, in effect, an integrated school. It was no small matter to create an integrated school in either Brooklyn or New York City during the nineteenth century. Not all whites agreed that the 1873 Civil Rights Act applied to schools, although African-American leaders who promoted the law believed that black students could not be denied admission to any school because of their race. Thus some cities, such as Buffalo and New York City, opened their white schools to blacks but did not close their black schools, leaving in place, in effect, a dual system of education. However, school officials in cities like Albany, Troy, and Schenectady believed that the 1873 law required them to shut down their black schools, even if the decision resulted in African-American teachers losing their jobs.[23]

Stewart's idea to consolidate two public schools was motivated by two considerations: his intense dislike of racial segregation and declining enrollments in Brooklyn's public schools. Black public school enrollment, which had peaked at 747 students in 1890, had fallen to only 443 students in 1893. Thus segregating black students, which made little sense to Stewart from an ethical standpoint, was not a fiscally sound idea either.[24]

Opposition to Stewart's plan surfaced immediately among white school board members, who argued that white parents would keep their children at home rather than permit them to attend school with black children. The school board initially decided to house the white and black schools in the same building but required them to occupy different floors. In a campaign that lasted two years, Stewart, argues historian Carleton Mabee, used the success of this joint venture to "press for the revival of the original plan for a thoroughly mixed-race school, in which the two schools, both pupils and teachers, would be merged into one school."[25]

Stewart's persistence and persuasiveness ultimately prevailed, for the Brooklyn School Board voted seventeen to eleven in 1893 to adopt the consolidation plan. The new school was organized with a white principal, a black head of department, and a mixed student body and faculty. The consolidated school was an important achievement, not only for the school board, but for Stewart personally. Like Stewart's defense of Fortune in the

Trainor Hotel segregation case, the integration of the schools added to his prestige as a national spokesman on racial issues. And in this instance, Stewart had persuaded a committee of distinguished white New Yorkers that segregated schools were fiscally impractical as well as wrong.[26]

In 1893, during his term on the board, Stewart took a break from his arduous schedule to marry Alice M. Franklin in a private ceremony at her home in Orange, New Jersey. The marriage, which was the first for Alice and Stewart's second, appears to have been unexpected. Neither the black press nor any of Stewart's personal correspondence to his children mentions the prospect of his remarrying or even the existence of a courtship. Stewart had not been involved in a serious relationship since he and his first wife, Lottie Harris, had parted shortly after his return from Liberia. He had concentrated instead on building his legal practice and on forging his career as a racial activist, displaying almost no interest in women. But he rectified this absence of female companionship shortly before his fortieth birthday.[27] (Interestingly, Stewart, who paid meticulous attention to details in both his legal practice and his personal affairs, incorrectly listed the year of his marriage to Alice as 1892 in an alumni questionnaire that he submitted to the Princeton Theological Seminary.) Unlike his first marriage to Harris, which had been fraught with chaos, dissension, and considerable ill-will on Stewart's part, Stewart's marriage to Alice Franklin was an exceedingly happy and fulfilling one. The black activist and attorney was devoted to Alice, and the two spent the remainder of their lives together.[28]

That Stewart would be drawn to Alice Franklin is not surprising. She was intelligent, outgoing, highly competent in her profession, and an attractive woman. She also interacted with the public with an ease, polish, and sophistication that his first wife did not possess. A graduate of Hunt's Dramatic College of New York and the National Conservatory in Paris, where she studied for several years, Alice M. Franklin, wrote the Cleveland *Gazette*, "is regarded as a dramatic reader of great ability." Because Franklin guarded her private life as zealously as Stewart did, little is known about her upbringing or her courtship with Stewart. According to her granddaughter, Beryl E. Kean, she was born in Middletown, Connecticut, and attended Middletown High School. A striking woman physically, with a fair complexion and long straight hair, Alice Franklin, recalled Kean, resembled an Oneida Indian.[29]

Franklin made her New York debut in the fall of 1885 at Adelphi Hall to polite critical acclaim. "The repertoire of this young lady comprised selections dramatic, humorous and pathetic. They were of a nature to give the greatest scope to her abilities, as a reciter, and was in every instance well received and generously applauded," reported the New York *Freeman*. Although the influential black newspaper found several of Franklin's dramatic interpretations to be less than praiseworthy, it concluded on an optimistic note: "There is every reason to believe that with more study and greater attention to moderation, Miss Franklin will rank here long among the foremost in her profession."[30] The editor was correct in his prediction. Over the next decade and a half, Alice Franklin Stewart emerged as one of the leading African-American dramatic readers and elocutionists in New York.[31]

By the early 1890s, T. McCants Stewart had emerged as an important political spokesman for African-Americans. This role, essentially a new one for Stewart, would be buttressed by his legal practice, his appointment to the school board, and his widely circulated appraisals of America's racial condition in newspapers, periodicals, public forums, and literary societies. Stewart's political stance also drew national attention because, unlike most black leaders in the late nineteenth century, he did not pledge his firm allegiance to the Republican party, disregarding Frederick Douglass's widely quoted refrain: "The Republican party is the deck, and all else is the sea."[32] Instead, though he had embraced the Republican party early in his career, Stewart broke ranks between 1886 and 1887 and joined the Democratic party.

What motivated this young, aspiring national leader to join a political party that represented, in the opinion of most African-American leaders, racial oppression, white supremacy, lawlessness, and racial violence? Stewart's defection to the Democratic party was part of a larger pattern of dissatisfaction and disillusionment with the Republican party that African-American leaders had been expressing openly for over a decade.[33] Following the contested presidential election of 1876, black leaders had criticized the GOP for abandoning its black constituents. T. McCants Stewart, writes August Meier, "thought it neither manly nor politic for Negroes to cling to the hem of the garments of the Republican party, to whom the Negroes owed no debt of gratitude for what was simply a war measure."[34] To be sure, Stewart represented only one of a handful of prominent African-American Democrats in New York. This small but influential group was led by James C. Matthews, a black attorney from Albany who had integrated Albany's public schools with a successful legal suit in 1874. Yet Stewart attracted considerably more attention in the black press than Matthews, even though the Albany attorney served as president of the New York State Grover Cleveland League.[35]

Stewart did not abandon the Republican party abruptly. His political metamorphosis began in the mid-1880s, a time when race relations were in a state of transition. In 1886, just one year after he had returned to the United States from Liberia, Stewart wrote President Grover Cleveland to express his respect and appreciation for the manner in which Cleveland had supported the nomination in 1886 of James C. Matthews to the office of recorder of deeds in the District of Columbia to succeed Frederick Douglass.[36]

Matthews's nomination came under fire immediately from the Republican-controlled Senate, but it was not Matthews's race the senators objected to; it was his allegiance to the Democratic party. Stewart informed Cleveland that he especially appreciated "the rebuke which you have administered to the narrow minded and prejudiced people of both parties in the reappointment of Mr. [James] Matthews to succeed Mr. [Frederick] Douglass." Although Stewart did not proclaim himself a Democrat at this juncture, he praised Cleveland's record on racial matters and appeared to be leaning toward the Democratic party: "Colored men may be slow to respond to your wise and liberal acts of friendship to the race, so long discriminated against but your administration will certainly make thousands of us less partisan and lead hundreds of us to act *with your leadership* with the Democratic party."[37]

Whether Cleveland was moved by the fact that one of New York's most prominent African-American leaders had endorsed his racial policies was not immediately clear, for Gilded Age presidents received thousands of similar letters from well-wishers and potential office seekers.[38] Perhaps knowing that this was the case and consciously seeking to distinguish himself from less prominent black leaders, Stewart enclosed a copy of the New York *Freeman,* which had printed a lengthy article concerning the resumption of his law practice and his admission to practice before the New York Supreme Court.[39]

Cleveland responded to Stewart's letter immediately. His reply marked the first occasion when a U.S. president had written to Stewart, a sign, as far as he was concerned, that he was now an African-American leader to be taken seriously. In his lengthy letter, Cleveland attempted to explain why he had named James C. Matthews again to the political appointment as recorder of deeds.[40] Stewart then replied to Cleveland informing him that he had been encouraged by his friends to publish the president's letter "so that its noble sentiments might become known to the Country, and especially to my own race."[41] However, Stewart was asking for the president's approval after the fact, for he had already decided to publish the president's letter in the New York *Herald*.[42]

T. McCants Stewart's association with Grover Cleveland and the Democratic party blossomed between 1887 and 1894. In the spring of 1887, Stewart congratulated Cleveland on the appointment of James M. Trotter to the political post of recorder of deeds in the District of Columbia, the same post that had deadlocked the Senate on two previous occasions over the nomination of James C. Matthews. Unlike Matthews, Trotter was confirmed easily by the Senate. That same year also witnessed Stewart's first public announcement that he would break with the Republican party and support Cleveland's reelection in 1888. Informing Cleveland that he would soon be addressing the Odd Fellows of Brooklyn, Stewart stated that he would "declare for President Cleveland in 1888." Attempting again to assure Cleveland that his motives were unselfish, Stewart added, "You know that I am not after office now or in 1888."[43] Although Stewart may not have been campaigning directly for a political appointment, it is unlikely that he would have refused such an offer if Cleveland had made it.

Throughout the remainder of 1887, T. McCants Stewart's support of Cleveland grew stronger and more secure. He continued to assure Cleveland both directly and indirectly, that his political endorsement was not motivated by his desire to gain a political appointment but by Cleveland's moderate racial policies. President Cleveland, argued Stewart, clearly attempting to ingratiate himself to the president, is "making it possible for self-respecting colored men to break the political shackles which have bound them fast for more than a decade." Stewart, who was apparently beginning to assume the role of an unofficial political adviser for African-American affairs, wrote Cleveland that the Democratic party was effectively dividing the "colored vote." Stewart endorsed that policy strongly, which Cleveland, no doubt, was delighted to hear. Speaking on behalf of other black Democrats, too, and echoing the famous 1857 Dred Scott decision, Stewart observed that blacks approved "seeing a democratic president insist that colored men have rights which even a republican Senate is bound to respect."[44]

Although Stewart had appeared sincere in his praise of Cleveland for the manner in which he handled the failed nomination of James C. Matthews, the black leader had engaged in political posturing and wishful thinking when he analyzed the Democratic party's position on race relations and civil rights. "The time hastens when the color line will be completely wiped out of American politics," Stewart wrote in 1887, and Cleveland's reelection "will fix, I think, a period in our history such as Washington's and Lincoln's."[45] Grover Cleveland, as historian Lawrence Grossman wrote in his analysis of the Democratic party's racial policies between 1868 and 1892, supported the Blair Aid to Education Bill, which would have provided federal money to support public education and reduce illiteracy, and reimbursement to depositors of the failed Freedmen's Savings and Trust Company, a bank granted a charter by the federal government in 1865 to encourage former slaves to save their money, that closed its doors in June 1874. Neither measure passed a Democratic House of Representatives. In light of the Democratic party's effort to restrict the civil and political rights of African-Americans, including its overwhelming opposition to the Lodge Federal Election Bill, Stewart's opinion of the Democratic party's racial policies was anomalous to say the least.[46]

Although there was no appreciable sign that race relations were improving during Cleveland's first presidential administration, Stewart continued to pledge his loyalty to the president. He encouraged Cleveland to support the rights of blacks in the Democratic party platform, arguing that his support would "paralyze any bloody shirt issue that the Republicans may make in theirs." Moreover, by supporting the rights of blacks in the 1888 Democratic party platform, Cleveland would be showing good faith, argued Stewart, to his potential black supporters. Attempting to persuade Cleveland of the importance of the black vote and presaging a modern-day political realignment, Stewart cautioned Cleveland that "we cannot expect the South to be *always* for the Democratic party, nor is it best that it should be."[47]

Grover Cleveland's defeat at the polls in 1888 must have been disconcerting for Stewart, but it was undoubtedly worse for Cleveland, only the second incumbent president at that time (after John Adams) to lose a bid for reelection. Ironically, Stewart had less faith in the ability of incoming president Benjamin Harrison to improve the status of African-Americans, even though the record of the Republican party was far superior on racial issues to that of the Democrats. Harrison's appointment of Frederick Douglass as the U.S. Minister to Haiti in 1889, and Blanche K. Bruce as recorder of deeds in Washington, D.C., should have been a sign that African-American leaders stood a far better chance of obtaining political office under Harrison than under a Democratic president.

Despite his protestations to the contrary, Stewart must have also been at least mildly annoyed that Grover Cleveland had never suggested his name for even a minor political appointment. One of these jobs, which both political parties had traditionally given to black leaders as rewards for their support, would have guaranteed Stewart a steady income and increased his visibility as a black spokesman.[48] Even so, Stewart did not waver in his support of Cleveland. He publicly supported Cleveland's reelection bid in 1892, and he continued to affirm that blacks would reap a larger share of political patronage under a Democratic administration. Others disagreed. An article in the influential New York *Age* stated that Stewart stood a good chance to be appointed to the new appellate circuit court created by the U.S. Congress in 1891. It was unlikely, however, that the Republican president Benjamin Harrison would have appointed a black Democrat, or a black Republican for that matter, to such a prestigious political post. An African-American would not be appointed to a U.S. Circuit Court until 1949, when William H. Hastie was appointed to that post by President Harry Truman.[49]

Stewart's continued support of Cleveland and the Democratic party was also puzzling in light of the defeat of the Blair Aid to Education Bill and the Lodge Federal Election Bill by northern and southern Democrats, an indication that the Democratic party would neither protect the political rights of blacks nor include civil rights in their national platform.

With Grover Cleveland's successful bid to recapture the presidency in 1892, Stewart and a small group of black Democratic supporters who had campaigned in his behalf were convinced the president would honor his promise to improve the condition of blacks throughout the nation.[50] Congratulating Cleveland on his return to the presidency in the spring of 1893, Stewart wrote Cleveland that "Afro-Americans with other patriotic Americans see in yourself and your inaugural address the assurance of national prosperity without sectional, class or racial limitations."[51] Cleveland was no doubt heartened by this vote of confidence, but it was unlikely that he could deliver the degree of sectional or racial healing that Stewart alluded to.

By 1894, however, Stewart's opinion of Cleveland had changed radically. For the first time, Stewart openly denounced the racial policies of the Democratic party and the Cleveland administration's policy of removing blacks from important political appointments. In a terse letter to Cleveland, Stewart criticized the president for the purge of African-American office-holders that had taken place under his second administration. "It cannot

be disputed, that colored men have lost ground under your present administration," he wrote angrily. "In the minor places, colored men and women
have been removed in such large numbers as to be a civil service scandal."
Stewart was particularly disturbed that the Democratic party rejected any
attempt to monitor elections by using the power of the federal government.
He also cited the removal from political office of prominent African-Americans
such as John R. Lynch, Blanche K. Bruce, and Robert H. Terrell. Yet Stewart,
perhaps naively, did not blame Cleveland personally for this turn of events.
He pointed the finger instead at white southerners within Cleveland's
administration who were opposed to both black officeholding and racial
progress. "Southern white men are opposed to Negroes holding any office
which carries honor or emolument to any extent," he informed the president.[52] That Stewart did not in this letter confront Cleveland directly with
charges of racial discrimination and racial insensitivity within his administration suggests that even though he was not ready to break with the
Democratic party in 1894, he was clearly moving in that direction. He
viewed the South as a menace and liability to the Democratic party, a
liability that he would unfortunately have to accept if he remained faithful
to the party. He urged Cleveland to push for protective tariff legislation as
well as more black political appointments.[53] In addition to the purge of
black officeholders, Stewart also criticized for the first time, the upsurge in
lynching and terrorism that had taken place in the South and the president's lax policies toward segregation in public accommodations. "Unfortunately, under your administration, we are suffering from cruel lynchings
in the South and from unjust discrimination in the public services throughout the nation," Stewart wrote.[54] "I admit that as President you cannot stop
the former, but we had hoped for much from your influence upon the
Southern white people." That Stewart ultimately reached these conclusions
is not surprising. What does come as a surprise is the fact that the militant
black leader, who had been an uncompromising proponent of racial equality from the time he arrived in New York in 1880, had waited seven years
before he brought this matter to Cleveland's attention. Stewart's self-inter-
est had apparently blinded him to the grim reality that southern race
relations were regressing rather than improving. Furthermore, by 1894, he
had also come to the realization that Cleveland would never consider him
for even a minor political post.[55]

This accusatory letter, the sharpest rebuke that Stewart would ever address to a U.S. president, essentially terminated Stewart's relationship with

the Democratic party. Although he had joined the party in 1887 as one of the most visible African-Americans in the nation and had hoped that his influence could be used to improve race relations, Stewart had grown disillusioned. He was correct in his claim that the Democrats were in part responsible for the increase in segregation, disfranchisement, racial violence, and lawlessness that swept through the South during the 1890s, culminating in the 1896 *Plessy v. Ferguson* decision, which declared the "separate-but-equal" doctrine constitutional. The Cleveland administration's policies seemed to confirm Stewart's growing apprehension that American race relations were indeed retrogressing. By 1894, Stewart would have confirmed Frederick Douglass's lament after Cleveland won the 1892 election, that the "first and natural effect of the restoration of the Democratic party to power will be to make the white people of the South still more indifferent to the claims of Justice toward their colored fellow citizens."[56]

Although T. McCants Stewart had been disappointed in the Democratic party's insensitivity toward racial issues in general, he had learned several valuable but painful lessons. Working through a political party with a strong southern base in a national climate of segregation and white supremacy was an act of profound faith, a strategy unlikely to produce even the most meager results in either black officeholding or race relations. Stewart learned that race relations under the Democrats could actually retrogress in spite of the alliance of several prominent African-American leaders such as himself and James C. Matthews with the party. Finally, Stewart learned that politics is a painfully slow and imperfect method of bringing about social change and racial progress.[57] Admittedly, a decade of affiliation with the Democratic party is not nearly enough time to erode centuries of racial hostility toward African-Americans. But by 1895 Stewart had arrived at the conclusion that it was fruitless to remain in a political party that appeared unwilling to change. Though perhaps despairing the ordeal of a ten-year relationship that had neither furthered his personal career nor improved the plight of African-Americans, Stewart had grown considerably wiser. He continued to work toward the betterment of African-Americans, but this time he chose to work within the Republican party.[58]

4

The Talented Tenth

❖ ❖ ❖ ❖ ❖ ❖ ❖ ❖ ❖ ❖ ❖ ❖ ❖ ❖ ❖

T. McCants Stewart was fundamentally a man of ideas. That fact allowed him to wear many hats during his long public career—minister, professor, writer, racial activist, attorney, and black nationalist—and to become an important African-American intellectual. The quality and breadth of Stewart's mind earned him the respect of some of the foremost black thinkers of his generation. His ideas, disseminated through some of the leading black newspapers and periodicals, allowed him to challenge the ideas of competing African-American leaders. His association with prominent black leaders such as Booker T. Washington, Frederick Douglass, Bishop Alexander Payne, T. Thomas Fortune, Blanche K. Bruce, Edward Blyden, Alexander Crummell, and Francis and Archibald Grimké significantly enhanced his prestige as a major African-American spokesman. Yet Stewart's respect as a man of ideas notwithstanding, his intellectual thought lacked originality. He was most effective as a sounding board of the dominant racial thought of his generation.

Juggling a career as an attorney and racial activist with the roles of husband and father was never an easy task for Stewart, so he established priorities. Like numerous nineteenth-century leaders, irrespective of race or nationality, Stewart consciously placed his career ahead of his family, believing that the two were closely intertwined and that his wife and children should be willing to make whatever sacrifices were required to advance his career. T. McCants Stewart was by nature a great joiner. He believed that it was in his interest as a black spokesman to affiliate with as many racial organizations as was humanly possible, even if his membership was merely a token one. Such was the case with Stewart's affiliation with the American Negro Academy (ANA), the first major African-American learned society in the United States. Founded in 1897 in Washington, D.C., the ANA attempted to organize a forum where black intellectuals and writers could express their ideas in a scholarly public institution. Alexander Crummell, an Episcopal clergyman educated at Queen's College and Cambridge University, was the guiding force behind this organization and served as the ANA's first president.[1]

Crummell, himself a man of wide intellectual breadth, shaped the aims and the focus of this black literary society, which was designed as a forum for the "Talented Tenth," that small circle of college-educated African-American leaders who W. E. B. Du Bois believed would lead the race and serve as "missionaries of thought among their people."[2] The ANA's constitution defined its purpose and objectives succinctly as "an organization of authors, scholars, artists, and those distinguished in other walks of life, men of African descent, for the promotion of Letters, Science, and Art."[3] During its thirty-one year history, the organization attracted hundreds of distinguished African-American leaders to its annual meetings, exhibits, and presentations of occasional papers, twenty-two of which were published.[4]

T. McCants Stewart was invited to join the ANA in March 1897. Stewart attended the ANA's inaugural meeting along with thirty-one distinguished black leaders, four of whom were also attorneys. Citing a busy schedule, Stewart declined the ANA's invitation to become an active member and refused to make any financial commitment to the organization. Predictably, Stewart attended few of the ANA's meetings and never presented an "occasional paper" before the organization, even though it would have been in his interest as a black leader of rising stature to do so.[5]

Although he did not participate actively in the ANA, Stewart did express his ideas on numerous subjects in a variety of forums. He was among a small group of black intellectuals who were influenced by the single-tax philosophy of Henry George. It was probably T. Thomas Fortune, Stewart's close friend and editor of the militant New York *Age*, who introduced him to George's ideas. Fortune, as historian August Meier has written, was the leading African-American student of George's philosophy in the late nineteenth century. Power, Fortune asserted, "resided with the group that owned the land," clearly a reference to George's idea that those who owned the land received an unearned increment in wealth. George asserted, moreover, that no one had a right to the value that accrued from the land, for that value was created not by its owner, but by the community. Consequently, Fortune urged blacks to acquire homesteads first, before embarking on politics, a view that Booker T. Washington would also express forcefully in his philosophy of racial accommodation.[6]

Although not nearly as eloquent as T. Thomas Fortune on this issue, Stewart, too, expressed his views on the single-tax in the AME *Church Review*, one of the leading forums of African-American intellectual expression in the nation. Like Fortune, Stewart criticized unrestricted or unregulated capital, although his criticism never went as far as Fortune's. These ideas surfaced publicly for the first time during the 1880s, when Stewart supported a tariff reduction. High protective tariffs, he argued, were detrimental to the interest of the American working class, for they depressed wages. In 1888 Stewart wrote "that under our high protective tariff system capital is importing, free of duty, the pauper labor of Europe, to the injury of American workmen both as to employment and wages," and, he continued, the overstocked market caused many industries to languish, "furnishing irregular and unremunerative employment to those that are dependent upon them."[7] These views explain why Stewart encouraged President Grover Cleveland in 1892 to reduce the protective tariff.[8]

In 1898, when he wrote an article critical of wealth for the AME *Church Review*, Stewart took an even firmer position on this issue: "Institutional capital is seldom benevolent; it is never philanthropic; it is not always for the public good."[9] Stewart conveniently ignored the fact that American corporations and industrialists such as John D. Rockefeller, Andrew Carnegie, and C. P. Huntington possessed the capacity to be benevolent as well as ruthless, and that these industrial giants contributed liberally to black colleges and universities, including Hampton Institute, Spelman College, and Tuskegee Institute, where two of Stewart's sons matriculated during the early 1890s.[10]

Nevertheless, Stewart, by 1898, had moved closer to the critique of monopoly capital that T. Thomas Fortune had made in the 1880s. He affirmed that "great power in any form is always dangerous, whether it flashes out in the face of lightening, the ocean, or the whirlwind. Institutional power wields great power in lobby and legislatures, in store and factory, in bank and trust room.[11] Stewart was correct. The great corporations of the late nineteenth century, as historians Harold Livesay and Allan Nevins have written, wielded enormous power in virtually every area of society, including education, politics, and the arts—all the more reason for shrewd African-American leaders such as Booker T. Washington to cultivate longstanding relationships with industrialists and entrepreneurs.[12]

In addition to his fame as a critic of capitalism, Stewart also gradually became one of the leading African-American proponents of industrial education. In an article that first appeared in the New York *Globe* in 1884, a segment of which was reprinted in T. Thomas Fortune's book *Black and White*, Stewart analyzed the importance of industrial education for African-Americans and explained how learning trades would prepare them to compete in the modern world.[13] Citing the contributions of General Samuel Chapman Armstrong at Hampton Institute in assisting African-Americans economically and morally, Stewart praised the value of an industrial education. He was especially impressed with the wide variety of trades that Hampton offered its students (Native Americans as well as blacks) and confident that the practical application of these skills would advance the economic and social position of Hampton students in the larger society. Describing a segment of a visit and fact-finding tour that he made to Hampton in 1884 to ascertain whether industrial education should be incorporated into the curriculum of Liberia College, Stewart applauded the school's industrial education program. "Standing in the carpenter and paint shops, and in the saw mill, and seeing Negro youths engaged in the most delicate kind of work, learning valuable and useful trades," he wrote, "I could not help from feeling that this is an excellent institution, and that I would like to have my boys spend three years here, from fourteen to seventeen, grow strong in the love for work, and educated to feel the dignity of labor, and get a trade."[14]

In addition to the multifaceted industrial curriculum that Hampton offered its students and the school's well-maintained physical plant, Stewart believed that Hampton's location, on a peninsula between the James and York rivers at the mouth of Chesapeake Bay, provided an idyllic educational setting for African-American college students. Yet he was even more impressed with the quality of Hampton's programs and summed up his analysis in metaphorical language: "There is no question about the fact that this is a 'beehive' into which a bee can enter, if accepted, with nothing but his soul and his muscle, and get a good education."[15]

Stewart's sudden enthusiasm for industrial education can be explained in several interrelated ways. Following his disappointing two years in Liberia, Africa, from 1883 to 1885, when he feuded with Edward Blyden, president of Liberia College, Stewart had come to the conclusion that in their struggle for economic and political equality, African-Americans must develop a secure economic base before they entered politics. In Stewart's mind, the most direct path to this economic base was encouraging African-Americans to learn skilled trades and purchase their own farms and businesses and promoting racial solidarity. These ideas, as historian Louis R. Harlan has written, would find their fullest expression under Booker T. Washington at the Tuskegee Institute. Nevertheless, Stewart and numerous African-American leaders, including David A. Straker and T. Thomas Fortune, were also influential proponents of industrial education.[16]

In many respects, Stewart and Booker T. Washington shared similar views regarding the importance of industrial education and the plight of the freedmen in the wake of slavery. In an 1891 lecture delivered in Boston in honor of the noted abolitionist Wendell Phillips, Stewart traced examples of political discontent throughout history, including the travails of blacks in the South following slavery. Stewart painted a grim picture of conditions he had seen first-hand in Charleston, South Carolina. It was not dissimilar to the portrait that Washington would paint before thousands of northern and southern audiences when he raised money for Tuskegee and preached the gospel of industrial education. "The masses of the colored people are poor and ignorant," wrote Stewart, "but they are aspiring." However, it would take time to erase the "trammels of slavery."[17] Although Stewart echoed both Booker T. Washington and Samuel Chapman Armstrong in these views, he never went as far as Washington, who argued that slavery had been beneficial to African-Americans because it taught them useful skills and how to work—the myth of the plantation as a school of civilization, a fiction maintained by southern planters and popularized by historian U. B. Phillips. As the product of an antebellum free black family from Charleston, Stewart had learned from experience that African-Americans were quite capable of learning discipline and work skills apart from bondage.[18]

Stewart's views on industrial education remained remarkably consistent over time, and he believed that they were as applicable to Africans as to African-Americans. In 1912, when he served as an associate justice of the Liberian Supreme Court, Stewart delivered the commencement address at the College of West Africa (formerly Liberia College) and embraced the importance of industrial education as firmly as he had done two decades earlier. Stewart informed the graduating class that "we have been neglecting the education of the masses, and have been attempting to put finishing touches at the top without laying a firm foundation. Young men, you have not caught the spirit of manual labor. You think it degrading; you do not understand that it dignifies." Stewart, therefore, encouraged Liberian students to stress farming and the skilled trades and to cease exporting their labor for the benefit of other nations. "We must lay the foundation for farms by immediately placing our education on an agricultural and industrial basis," he declared.[19]

Ironically, Stewart, in his 1912 speech, ridiculed the significance of a liberal arts education, like he had received at Howard University and the University of South Carolina, and on which his rise to national leadership was in part based. Heretofore, Stewart had believed that industrial education and the liberal arts complimented each other and prepared blacks for not only employment but also, as W. E. B. Du Bois was fond of saying, to face the vicissitudes of life. Stewart now saw little utility in a liberal arts education as an instrument for elevating the socioeconomic status of either Africans or Africans-Americans. His conclusion may have been predicated on the vast untapped economic potential of the Republic of Liberia as well as the brutal economic and political reality that many African-Americans faced during an era that historian Rayford Logan has appropriately called the "nadir." These were not the best of times for African-Americans, and Stewart's views reflected this growing despair.[20]

Stewart's decision to embrace industrial education was his attempt to answer in part, two larger questions that he grappled with throughout much of his career: What role should blacks play in the labor issue? And what is the most expedient course for blacks to follow if they hope to advance economically as a race? Like many black intellectuals of his day, Stewart examined his answers to questions in public forums and literary societies, modifying his views when he discovered new information or received incisive critiques from his contemporaries. In a paper read in 1889 before the literary society of the St. Augustine's Protestant Episcopal Church in Brooklyn, Stewart asserted that the "history of mankind, from nomadic tribes to civilized states, is the history of labor."[21] In Stewart's opinion, again reflecting the influence of Samuel Chapman Armstrong and Booker T. Washington, as well as his first-hand experience as a young boy of modest means growing up in antebellum Charleston, all labor was dignified, no matter how menial. He also preached consistently to his three children that they should always endeavor to be frugal and industrious and to make their own way rather than depend upon their father for financial support.[22]

Stewart's lecture before the St. Augustine literary society was only one of many that Stewart presented before numerous secular and religious organizations. An accomplished orator, Stewart was in constant demand as a speaker. In a paper delivered before the Young Men's Guild of St. Philip's Protestant Episcopal Church in New York entitled "Heredity in Character," Stewart shared his interest in genetics and biological determinism, but maintained that character, unlike most other human traits, "is often shaped and formed by environment in spite of the forces of heredity."[23] Environment alone, however, could not account for an individual's character and behavior, for some human character traits were independent of environment. Stewart affirmed that an individual "who has inherited evil forces of character has a mighty hard struggle to get into the kingdom of truth and righteousness."[24]

This paper, which addressed a topic far afield from Stewart's academic training at either the University of South Carolina or the Princeton Theological Seminary, illustrated his intellectual breadth. However, the ability to speak cogently on a variety of subjects was not uncommon among nineteenth-century African-American leaders, many of whom, such as Frederick Douglass, believed that their college education or multifaceted experiences had prepared them to address a broad range of subjects. Thus Stewart did not hesitate to deliver a eulogy in honor of the renowned poet John Greenleaf Whittier at St. Mark's Lyceum in New York, or to attend the centennial commemoration of President George Washington's inauguration in 1889. Stewart never earned the same degree of respect that the venerable black leader Frederick Douglass received for the quality of his mind, for Douglass was widely regarded as one of the leading nineteenth-century abolitionists and as one of the greatest African-American leaders and thinkers who ever lived. Stewart, nevertheless, was highly regarded for his intellectual rigor and praised for the power of his discourse.[25]

Despite Stewart's intellectual eclecticism, he was primarily a racial spokesman, and the majority of his public debates, lectures, and writings dealt with racial matters. Often searching for a broader framework in which to place his ideas concerning African-American progress, Stewart frequently sounded like the young college professor that he had once been at the South Carolina State College in Orangeburg. His description of "The Life and Character of Frederick Douglass," presented at a symposium in honor of the great abolitionist following his death in 1895, illustrated his professorial erudition: "Like Aristides, Frederick Douglass was just; like

Lincoln, he was generous; like Pericles, he was cultured; like Webster, he was eloquent. In himself, he combined the elements which characterized such heroes of human history."[26]

The final two decades of the nineteenth century marked a renewed interest in emigration to Africa, and T. McCants Stewart was part of this broad intellectual and spiritual identification with the African continent.[27] Yet Stewart did more than simply write about a glorious African past in newspapers and literary journals; he also lived and worked on the African continent during two distinct intervals of his life and could speak with confidence and authority about Africa's vast potential for development as well as its travails. Thus Stewart, along with Alexander Crummell, Edward Blyden, Presbyterian minister Henry Highland Garnet, Episcopal bishop James Holly, and Henry McNeal Turner, was a forerunner of Pan-Africanism, a sense of identification with Africans. Pan-Africanists also believed that the peoples of the African diaspora composed a common community, shared a common destiny and history of oppression, and that their past as well as their future were linked. These black leaders, wrote David L. Lewis, "formed an articulate chorus calling for the cream of Afro-America to be resettled in Haiti or South America or West Africa."[28]

Stewart also shared with his black ministerial colleagues an abiding belief that Africans were socially and religiously primitive, and that African religion in particular should be discarded in favor of Christianity, a position that one might expect an ordained Methodist minister to assume. Yet despite the fact that he harbored many of his society's prejudices toward Africa, Stewart never adopted the white majority's view that Africans were intellectually or racially inferior. Nor did he support the view of black nationalists such as Edward Blyden that the European partition of Africa was justified because it would "teach the natives to make the best use of their own country."[29]

Using African-American literary organizations as his forum, Stewart lectured widely on his impressions of the African continent and occasionally wrote articles on African history or the historical relationship between African-Americans and black Africans. He wrote, for example, the introduction to Rufus L. Perry's book, *The Cushite or the Descendants of Ham*. Perry, a respected New York minister, theorized that the ancient Ethiopians and Egyptians were Cushites or "Negroes descended from the race of Ham" and supported his controversial thesis by tracing the evolution of the Cushites from the time of Noah to the present.[30]

Stewart's four-page introduction to Perry's book reveals his keen interest in biblical history, his familiarity with African ethnology, which he had probably studied as a graduate student at the Princeton Theological Seminary, and his wide reading in African history, a subject in which he had no formal training. Citing an article that had appeared in the *Princeton Review* in 1878, Stewart maintained that "the Ethiopian race, from whom the modern Negro of African stock are undoubtedly descended, can claim as early a history as any living people on the face of the earth. History as well as the monumental discoveries, gives them a place in ancient history as far back as Egypt herself; if not further."[31] Moreover, Stewart observed, some scholars believe that Africans "led the way, and acted as the pioneers of mankind in the various untrodden fields of civilization."[32]

This discussion intrigued Stewart, who conceded that experts disagreed on whether modern blacks were direct descendants of ancient Ethiopians and Egyptians. But in Stewart's mind, there was no doubt that Egyptians and Ethiopians were the "direct ancestors of the slaves who for centuries were exported from the West Coast of Africa," and that Africans were descendants of Noah. In making these arguments, T. McCants Stewart and Rufus Perry were attempting to disabuse their readers of the prevalent belief that Africa was a backwards continent and that civilization sprang entirely from whites. "The fruitful imagination of the modern Egyptologist who can see nothing great in the black man, but finds unlimited wisdom in the white man," wrote Perry, "delights to robe all ancient Egypt in white," a conclusion that Stewart shared.[33]

Stewart's insistence that Africans could boast a glorious past and that African-Americans should therefore be proud of their racial heritage were ideas he shared in many public forums. Speaking before the Hampton Institute Alumni Association in 1884, at the invitation of Booker T. Washington, its president, Stewart told his predominantly African-American audience that they were "descendants of a great people whose ancient civilization was the wonder and glory of the world."[34] This public address, Stewart's first formal speech on the topic of African history, emphasized two beliefs that Stewart espoused throughout his career: Africans had produced some of the most advanced civilizations in the history of the world and black Americans were the descendants of these African peoples whose cultures were once the envy of the world. Drawing upon the writings of the respected black historian George Washington Williams and the works of Martin Delany and Edward W. Blyden, Stewart maintained that "these writers show conclusively that the early inhabitants of the Nilotic and Nigrition regions of Africa, where the earliest civilizations flourished were Negroes."[35] Stewart probably hoped that his speech would instill a stronger sense of racial pride in black students at Hampton, and that his words would also inspire future generations of blacks to believe that significant accomplishments were also within their grasp.

Stewart's quest to obtain recognition for Africa's contribution to world civilization would eventually lead him to challenge former president Theodore Roosevelt's use of the word "savage" in reference to Africans as well as Roosevelt's unwillingness to capitalize the word "Negro" in his formal writing. Although Stewart conceded that Roosevelt applied the term savage uniformly to all unclothed people that he had met in his extensive travels, he argued, nonetheless, that the term was insensitive and inappropriate.[36]

Though Roosevelt could have dismissed Stewart's letter as a nuisance, he responded to Stewart's letter promptly. Roosevelt wrote that he appreciated "very deeply" receiving Stewart's letter and that he had not intended to offend either Africans in general or Stewart personally. He informed Stewart that he customarily wrote the words *Negro* and *white* in lowercase, but that he was willing to capitalize the word *Negro* if Stewart preferred. Roosevelt also attempted to explain his use of the word *savage:* "I think you are right in your criticism of my use of the word savage, but I don't in the least regard gentlemen with manners and hospitality as inconsistent with being a savage. I should have made my meaning clear, for there are very different stages of culture which I group under that term."[37] Roosevelt's response was open, direct, and revealed that he did not wish to appear racially insensitive. Nor did Roosevelt, who seldom shirked a challenge, political or otherwise, seem offended by either the content or tone of Stewart's letter, the purpose of which was simply to request that a former United States president acknowledge the dignity and humanity of African peoples.

T. McCants Stewart's letter to Theodore Roosevelt revealed his strong sense of pride in his African heritage and his determination that blacks should be accorded respect. Indeed, Stewart, like his close friend T. Thomas Fortune, who later became the leading advocate of the term "Afro-American," urged blacks to refer to themselves as Afro-Americans rather than as Negroes or Colored. Stewart believed that the word *Negro* in particular was an inaccurate description of black Americans as well as a term of contempt. Stewart challenged the views of W. E. B. Du Bois, who refused to use the word *Afro-American* and criticized its use as an "ark of refuge from the term Negro." Stewart replied that he preferred Afro-American "because it rids us of the word 'nigger,' and it has within itself an element of dignity and solidarity which helps to promote aspiration in ourselves and to command respectful mention from others." Even though he admitted that the term *Afro-American* "lacked scientific precision" because most black Americans were in fact of mixed blood, Stewart defended it as a dignified though imprecise description of black Americans. This debate with Du Bois is also important because it is in this context that Stewart suggested that blacks could construct their own racial identity in a society that viewed them with contempt and branded them as racially inferior, a conclusion with which Du Bois would readily agree.[38]

After African-American newspapers and periodicals, literary societies were perhaps the most important public forums for Stewart to express his ideas. His presidency of the Brooklyn Literary Union was particularly important because of the group's interracial makeup. The New York *Age* reported that the organization served "as a forum for the discussion of public questions, which brought to its platform eminent speakers of both races."[39] Indeed, Stewart, in spite of his busy schedule, took his tenure as president of the Brooklyn Literary Union very seriously (in marked contrast to his association with the American Negro Academy).

The group generally met on a bimonthly basis in one of Brooklyn's African-American churches. Stewart and the society's officers, which included Charles A. Dorsey, principal of a Brooklyn primary and grammar school for black children, and Reverend W. H. Dickerson, encouraged African-Americans and whites to attend these free public programs, and they responded enthusiastically. Stewart was pleased when a large audience gathered to hear a paper by Dr. Philip A. White, a Brooklyn pharmacist and the first African-American appointed to serve on the Brooklyn school board. He also took great pride in the fact that in the fall of 1886, after he was reelected president of the organization, thirty individuals were granted membership.[40]

A gifted public speaker, Stewart occasionally exercised his presidential prerogative to present the literary society's keynote lecture. These talks not only provide a window into Stewart's intellectual thought, but they also reveal that he, like numerous nineteenth-century white reformers and African-American leaders, used literary societies to present papers as trial balloons before submitting them to national magazines for publication.

Thus Stewart's lectures entitled "Heredity in Character" and "Tariff Reduction, the Problem of the Hour" were warmly received by the Brooklyn Literary Union prior to their publication in the AME *Church Review*. Similarly, because Stewart was among only a handful of African-Americans in New York to have lived in Africa, he spoke before the Brooklyn Literary Union on his African travels and presented a well-received lecture on Stanley, the renowned African explorer.[41] The interracial thrust of the Brooklyn Literary Union, which paralleled the mission of the more prestigious Cosmopolitan Society in New York, was also consistent with Stewart's abiding belief in interracial cooperation and the obligation of both races to make an effort to improve race relations and to discuss issues of mutual interest.[42]

Although T. McCants Stewart often lacked originality as a racial thinker, he was especially adept in articulating the dominant racial themes of his era. Yet Stewart was one of the earliest African-American leaders to suggest that racial segregation had not worsened during the post-Reconstruction years, noting that in some southern states the practice of segregating blacks on public conveyances was not practiced widely until the 1890s. As a victim of discrimination on public transportation in both the North and South, Stewart was well versed on this issue. In April of 1885, as an editorial correspondent for the New York *Freeman*, Stewart journeyed from New York to his native state of South Carolina after a ten-year absence. In a series of columns for the paper Stewart shared his impressions of southern race relations and the unique problems that blacks encountered when they traveled throughout the South. Stewart's observations are interesting in two respects. First, he had expected to find considerable racial tension and animosity between blacks and whites but, to his surprise, found none. "I put a chip on my shoulder," wrote Stewart after he left Washington, D.C., "and inwardly dared any man to knock it off." The black activist and attorney reported that he sat next to white passengers consistently without the least bit of fanfare, and heard not so much as a single racial slur. Stewart wrote that he took a seat in a dining room in a train station just south of Petersburg, Virginia, and was seated at a table with other whites. "The whites at the table appeared not to note my presence," he wrote. On only one occasion did Stewart report that he was treated even with the slightest bit of discourtesy, and his detractor, ironically, proved an African-American waiter aboard a North Carolina steamboat who seated him at a separate table, though in an integrated dining room.[43]

Stewart's 1885 columns reflected his personal experience and his optimism that southern race relations were remarkably benign, at least on
southern trains and steamboats and in railway stations. The black-New
Yorker-turned-investigative-journalist seemed generally surprised that white
passengers not only took seats beside him in first-class compartments, but
that they never raised even the slightest objection to his presence. "I think
the whites of the South," he wrote, "are really less afraid [to have] contact
with colored people than the whites of the North." He also reported that
thus far he "had found travelling more pleasant [in the South] than in some
parts of New England."[44] Stewart's observation that blacks traveled more
freely on southern public transportation would soon be proven accurate:
he was denied first-class accommodations on a New York steamboat in
1886 because of his race, approximately one year after he had completed
this column.[45]

Stewart's description and analysis of southern race relations remained
cheerful after he arrived in South Carolina. Regarding Columbia, the Palmetto state's capital, Stewart noted that "I can ride in first-class cars on the
railroads and in the streets. I can go into saloons and get refreshments even
as in New York. I can stop in and drink a glass of soda and be more politely
waited upon than in some parts of New England."[46] These observations are
instructive for several reasons. As a native South Carolinian, he had seen
first-hand the condition of slaves and freedmen in Charleston, Columbia, and
Orangeburg during the Civil War and Reconstruction. He had witnessed both
segregation and intermittent racial violence. His 1885 eyewitness account,
however, revealed that conditions had improved considerably. Stewart noted,
for example, a peaceful review of hundreds of African-American troops,
blacks and whites dining in the same establishments, and a black policeman
arresting a white man "under circumstances requiring coolness, prompt decision, and courage." Stewart concluded sentimentally that South Carolina
was among the most progressive states in the South, a conclusion that Vir-
ginians and North Carolinians certainly would have contested and one that
no modern historian shares.[47]

The historian C. Vann Woodward in particular was persuaded of the
accuracy of Stewart's description of southern race relations in 1885. Woodward, citing lengthy passages from Stewart's columns in the New York
Freeman, used the young writer's observations to support his argument that
southern race relations were indeed more benign and less tightly con-
stricted in the 1880s than when Jim Crow laws and formal segregation

became the rule in the South during the 1890s and early 1900s. "More than a decade was to pass after Redemption before the first Jim Crow law was to appear upon the law books of a Southern state, and more than two decades before the older states of the seaboard were to adopt such laws," Woodward wrote in his influential study, *The Strange Career of Jim Crow*.[48] Woodward stated clearly, however, that both extra-legal segregation and racial discrimination existed before the passage of Jim Crow laws, and that segregation and discrimination differed in intensity across space and time. Nevertheless, he was convinced, on the basis of experiences reported by Stewart and other African-Americans, that the 1880s represented an enlightened period in the South when race relations were relatively fluid and the prospect of solving the nation's racial problem was a realistic one.[49]

Although Woodward was correct in noting that African-Americans like Stewart were permitted to ride first-class railroad coaches and to dine at the same table with whites in the mid-1880s, he erred in concluding that this arrangement represented the norm for blacks in the southern states. Indeed, Stewart's lengthy journey from New York to Charleston was remarkable precisely because Stewart failed to report even a single racial incident—and even more remarkable when one considers that African-Americans were denied access to these same facilities in some northern and western cities during the late nineteenth century.[50]

Stewart's experiences were not typical. As historian Charles A. Lofgren writes, "It would be perfectly possible to cite contemporary experiences and testimony of a contrasting character."[51] Yet those blacks who were properly dressed and properly behaved "evidently came to be accepted into first-class accommodations" during the 1870s and 1880s. T. McCants Stewart's experience, then, including his observation that African-Americans were permitted to ride in first-class coaches in Georgia, suggests that southern race relations, while not free of racial discrimination, were indeed less rigid in isolated instances than they would become by the 1890s, when Jim Crow laws were enforced widely throughout the South.[52]

Stewart's observations on southern race relations were also important for a reason that historians have overlooked. Grover Cleveland, a Democrat, was elected president in 1884, the first Democrat to occupy the White House in twenty-four years. As C. Vann Woodward noted, the New York *Freeman* "had opposed Cleveland, and propaganda had been spread among Negro voters that the return of the Democrats would mean the end of freedmen's rights, if not their liberties."[53] Yet Woodward failed to acknowledge a critical point concerning Stewart's political leanings. Even though the New York *Freeman* and its editor, T. Thomas Fortune, opposed the Democratic challenger, Stewart did not. He later became one of the leading black Democrats in the nation. It is therefore possible that Stewart exaggerated the degree of race liberalism in the South in order to cast the Democratic party in a more favorable light, although to what degree we cannot be certain. It is just as plausible to conclude, however, that Stewart's description of southern race relations in 1885 is accurate, but that his experience could not necessarily be replicated by every African-American, irrespective of class, who traveled throughout the southern states. Rather than dismissing Stewart's rich and extensive observations out of hand, or accepting them blindly, one should read them carefully and critically with these factors in mind.

Stewart's racial thought, while occasionally fraught with inconsistencies, placed him squarely among the leading African-American thinkers of his generation. Although he was not a prolific writer in the mold of W. E. B. Du Bois, Frederick Douglass, or Alexander Crummell, T. McCants Stewart produced an important body of writings. Stewart's articles in black newspapers and periodicals, his well-received book on Liberia, his published speeches, and his presidency of the Brooklyn Literary Union circulated his ideas among a broad spectrum of the white and black communities.[54] Occasionally, his speeches and articles were heard and read by Africans, such as his commencement address at the College of West Africa in 1912. But Stewart always considered himself first and foremost an activist rather than a man of ideas, although unlike his close friend Booker T. Washington, Stewart felt comfortable in both camps.

Stewart's writings and public speeches also reveal his evolving nationalism, which was evident as early as 1883 when he emigrated to Liberia. Although he was only one in a long line of nineteenth-century black nationalists, Stewart's contribution is seldom acknowledged. Stewart's ideas also reveal the "Talented Tenth's" commitment to finding solutions to the problems of inferior and underfunded schools, disfranchisement, and the marginal economic status of African-American workers. Finally, Stewart's writings and speeches reveal a genuine pride in African history and African civilization, as well as his belief that he and other black intellectuals had an obligation to help shape Africa's future.

5

New Challenges, New Frustrations

Hawaii, Liberia, and St. Thomas, 1898–1923

❖ ❖ ❖ ❖ ❖ ❖ ❖ ❖ ❖ ❖ ❖ ❖ ❖ ❖ ❖

After residing in New York for almost two decades, where he had established a reputation as an important and respected national leader and an advocate of civil rights, T. McCants Stewart migrated to Hawaii in 1898. The black leader never revealed publicly his reasons for leaving New York or, for that matter, why he chose to move to such a distant location. However, he had been restless in New York for several years. He had become increasingly pessimistic over blacks' chances to advance politically or economically in the continental United States. Furthermore, despite his support of both Democratic and Republican administrations during the late nineteenth century and his close friendship with Booker T. Washington, Stewart had failed to obtain an important political appointment. His legal practice, while generating a modest income and a steady stream of clients, provided neither the lifestyle nor the security that Stewart had hoped for. Thus Stewart was in search of new opportunities when he and his family sailed to Hawaii in 1898, shortly after the islands had been annexed by the United States. There he hoped to enter politics, practice law, and to invest in local businesses, notably the sugar industry. The Honolulu *Pacific Commercial Advertiser,* the largest daily paper in Honolulu, reported Stewart's arrival, noting that he was accompanied by his wife Alice, "whose education was finished with three years in Paris and a daughter, an accomplished young lady."[1]

Few blacks had migrated to Hawaii before the Stewarts. Anthony Allen, who arrived in the islands in 1810, was apparently the first. Allen, a fugitive slave from Schenectady, New York, had migrated to Hawaii to escape bondage and the deplorable condition of free blacks, and to improve his social and economic status. Opportunities, indeed, were considerably better for Allen in Hawaii. He became a respected merchant, married a Hawaiian woman, and served as one of the "trusted advisers" of Kamehameha the Great.[2]

But Allen's success did not stimulate an exodus of blacks to Hawaii during the nineteenth century. Although several dozen black missionaries, laborers, and seamen came to Hawaii for various reasons, only a handful remained more than a few years. The vast majority of black Americans resided in the southern states, and with the exception of an "exodus" to Kansas during the 1870s, there was no significant movement of blacks outside of the South during the nineteenth century.[3]

The distance and expense involved in migrating to Hawaii made it impossible for most blacks to even contemplate such a move. Unlike many ethnic and racial groups, such as the Japanese, Chinese, Portuguese, or Puerto Ricans, who were recruited to Hawaii as laborers and contract workers in sizable numbers, black agricultural workers from the South were seldom recruited. At least one U.S. official, however, Secretary of State James G. Blaine, urged the importation of blacks as early as 1881 in order to lessen Hawaii's dependence on Asian labor. Blaine, admittedly no advocate of racial equality or the economic betterment of black workers, simply argued that Hawaii was "a part of the productive and commercial system of the American states" and that blacks would be a suitable substitute for Asians in the cultivation of such staples as sugar and rice. The Hawaiian legislature, however, was opposed to large-scale black migration, and Blaine's recommendation was never adopted. However, a few industrialists disagreed with the legislature. The Hawaiian Sugar Planters' Association recruited at least 200 blacks from Tennessee in 1901 to work on sugar plantations. Six years later about thirty black families were recruited by the association from several southern states. Even so, the number of black laborers imported remained modest, and black workers never became an important segment of Hawaii's labor force.[4]

Several other factors discouraged large-scale black migration to Hawaii during the nineteenth century. Hawaii was accessible only by ship, and the cost of passage was beyond the means of most blacks who worked as sharecroppers, tenant farmers, domestic workers, and unskilled laborers. Without systematic recruitment by either American or Hawaiian industries, Hawaii's black population was unlikely ever to increase in proportion to other racial groups that had migrated to the islands. Finally, Hawaii was not a geographical area that most blacks, including members of the middle class, were familiar with. Unlike Mexico, Africa, the Caribbean, Canada, and South America, which received small black in-migrations and periodic coverage in black newspapers or periodicals, Hawaii was rarely mentioned as a potential oasis for black workers. Only 233 blacks lived in Hawaii in 1900, two years after T. McCants Stewart arrived, and they represented but 0.2 percent of the total population.[5]

Despite the minute black population, T. McCants Stewart believed that Hawaii offered an ambitious man like himself the opportunity to prosper. The Honolulu *Advertiser* wrote that Stewart came to Honolulu "highly commended," with letters of commendation from former president Grover Cleveland, the United States minister to Spain, and the financier and industrialist C. P. Huntington. In many respects, Stewart's relocation to Hawaii was consistent with the pattern he had established early in his career. He had shown a pioneering determination to better his condition when he moved from South Carolina to New Jersey, then to New York, then to Liberia, and now to Hawaii. Stewart perceived Hawaii as a frontier community, and he wanted to take advantage of the economic and political opportunities in the islands during the early stages of American settlement. Yet Stewart stated that he was also attempting to escape racial discrimination in the United States, which had grown more intense and virulent as the century drew to a close. "I am a victim of the white man's unholy color line," he wrote in a letter to his eldest son. "In 1878 I left South Carolina to escape it. In 1883 I left New York for Africa to escape it. And now, ah, whither shall I flee?"[6]

Stewart wasted little time in making his presence felt in Hawaii. He established a law practice in Honolulu, enrolled his daughter Carlotta in Oahu College (the Punahou School), and became active in Republican party politics. Stewart was easily the most prominent black leader in Hawaii, since he was the *only* black leader in Hawaii in the early 1900s. He also received an occasional distinguished visitor from the mainland such as his son Gilchrist, who worked briefly as a census taker in Honolulu before returning to New York to practice law, and his close friend T. Thomas Fortune, the militant editor of the New York *Age*, who stopped off in Hawaii to visit Stewart en route to the Philippines. The prominent black military chaplain Theophilus Gould Steward also visited Stewart shortly after his arrival, who reported: "I went ashore [in Honolulu] and passed the night with T. McCants Stewart, baptizing his infant child. While in his residence on the evening of November 3rd I there met a fine Hawaiian family, Mr. Fernandez and his two daughters. The young ladies were clad in Hawaiian style, pure white dresses with no girdles or bands. They sang a number of the Queen's songs and also sang 'Sweet Alice, Ben Bolt' for me, very sweetly."[7]

T. McCants Stewart also immediately distinguished himself as an attorney in Hawaii, at least among his colleagues. He was admitted to the Hawaiian bar in 1898, and during his seven years in Hawaii, Stewart made sixteen appearances before the Hawaii Supreme Court and argued five cases before the U.S. District Court of Hawaii. Moreover, T. McCants Stewart "became the first lawyer in Hawaii to litigate a case in the newly established federal court."[8]

Stewart's first appearance before the Hawaii Supreme Court in 1899, in a case involving police powers of the state, marked the first occasion when an African-American appeared before Hawaii's highest court.[9] Just one year later, Stewart eulogized Albert Francis Judd, chief justice of the supreme court, an illustration of the esteem that Stewart had earned in Hawaii's legal community in less than two years.[10]

The majority of Stewart's Hawaiian jurisprudence involved civil cases, which had also composed the bulk of his cases in New York.[11] He worked occasionally with white lawyers as cocounsels but apparently decided not to establish a joint practice, handling the majority of his legal cases alone.[12] In 1901, for example, Stewart argued three cases before the newly established federal court in Hawaii. In one instance, Stewart prosecuted a negligence case involving a wrongful death on board a schooner and won a judgment of $1,577. That same year, Stewart represented Chinese laborers in two separate deportation cases, both of which he lost. Two years later, however, Stewart successfully defended a seaman of undetermined race and nationality who sued after receiving injuries on board the ship *James Turf*. He also won a case in admiralty for injuries to a seaman on board the ship *Erskine M. Phelps,* resulting in a judgment in the amount of $1,800 for his client.[13]

However, these cases, even viewed collectively, are unimpressive. They reflect the same sort of marginalization of black lawyers that Stewart had experienced in New York. But they also demonstrate Stewart's lifelong commitment to defending the rights of ordinary people against the state or large corporate entities. Although Stewart never shared his thoughts on the complex labor situation in Hawaii, it is reasonable to assume, given his own working-class background and his earlier writings on the labor question, that he identified with the plight of Chinese laborers and equated their struggle to advance economically with the struggle of African-Americans in the South. After all, was it not, by extension, the mission of the "Talented Tenth" to improve the lot of the dispossessed and downtrodden of all races and nationalities, including the Hawaiians and the Chinese?[14]

Within two years after his arrival in Hawaii, Stewart had assumed a prominent role in Republican party politics. By the spring of 1900, the *Advertiser* reported that Stewart had managed a Republican party meeting in Honolulu, and that he and a group of political leaders were attempting to organize the GOP on the island of Oahu. In that same year, Stewart was appointed by the Republican Territorial Central Committee to draft an act granting the Hawaiian people local government.[15] At another GOP meeting, Stewart was described as the "most prominent man in it." The conservative *Advertiser* also reported that Stewart favored including a broader sector of the Hawaiian electorate in the Republican party than the party bosses did: "We reckon that if [T.] McCants Stewart had managed the Republican meeting the Portuguese would not have been overlooked."[16]

That Stewart rose so quickly in Republican party circles was remarkable given his lack of familiarity with Hawaiian history, culture, and language, not to mention the intricacies of Hawaiian politics. On the one hand, Stewart identified with the plight of the Hawaiian people and their quest for greater political autonomy. On the other hand, he was a political opportunist. His support of a greater political role for the Hawaiian people was consistent with his own political ambition, which rested in large measure on cracking the island's centralized government.

The ambitious black leader's political fortunes, however, never measured up to his expectations. For a variety of reasons, he never became a dominant figure in Hawaiian politics. Nor did Stewart's investment in Hawaiian sugar produce the returns that he anticipated, for these industries were dominated by American industrialists before his arrival. Similarly, Stewart never received a major political appointment, though in 1905 the governor of Hawaii appointed him to a County Act Commission, a relatively minor political post. Stewart wrote his son McCants in 1905 complaining of his predicament: "We have a centralized government, the Governor appointing every official, even a policeman."[17] Though he did not deny that progress had taken place on the island, Stewart was dissatisfied with his own status. "I am a Boss here as compared to New York," he informed McCants. "But I don't relish heartily being 'a King' among dogs." This harsh comment was atypical of Stewart, for he had been sympathetic to the plight of the Hawaiian people. But it did illustrate his thwarted ambition and growing frustration. Stewart also acknowledged that his wife's health "is not vigorous here," a problem that he would confront almost every time he relocated.[18]

Stewart's inability to either make a comfortabe living or advance his stagnant political career was his biggest disappointment. So in July 1905, Stewart and his family returned to the United States on the *S. Sonoma.* Stewart informed his son McCants that "I left Honolulu because it was busted and there was no field for individual or community growth." Thus in Stewart's mind, it was time to move on to another challenge. Yet his eldest daughter Carlotta perceived the opportunities in Hawaii for African-Americans quite differently than her father. Carlotta chose to remain in Hawaii, where she taught at the Sacred Heart Convent, a private Catholic school for girls, after which she established a respected career as a teacher and principal in the Hawaiian schools that lasted for over four decades.[19]

Stewart's reference to Hawaii being "busted" is inaccurate, for the territory enjoyed decades of economic growth after his departure. In reality, it was Stewart who was busted. He had taken out a sizable mortgage on his Honolulu home that he could not repay, and his legal practice there, although promising, never thrived. After more than a year following his departure, Carlotta informed her brother McCants that their father's home "is not sold yet. Papa took out a large mortgage on it before he left, but the mortgage is greater than the present value of the property."[20]

Stewart also cited racial discrimination as a factor in his decision to leave Hawaii. He was correct on the one hand: racism had become more pronounced in Hawaii in the early years of the twentieth century. The *Advertiser* regularly published articles, editorials, and cartoons that maligned not only blacks but Asians and Puerto Ricans as well.[21] Stewart wrote his son that he had also been libeled in the press on at least one occasion and noted just two months before his departure, "I must confess that I am not happy, and I have been for the past two or three years under a cloud of race prejudice."[22] Stewart had never before used racial discrimination as a reason to leave a community or to shirk a challenge, either publicly or privately. He had also discouraged his children from doing so. This admission, then, indicated that Stewart had grown tired of fighting racial prejudice and was searching for a community where race would not be a significant factor in his career advancement or an impediment in the lives of his three daughters from his second marriage.

In the space of seven years, Stewart had come full circle in his opinion of Hawaii's race relations and the territory's economic potential. In 1898 he had praised Hawaii's racial tolerance and believed that the islands were an excellent location to raise a family. "I see in Hawaii a better outlook for old age than here [New York]," Stewart had exclaimed on the eve of his migration to Hawaii. "I see a better social life for my children and grandchildren, a social life in which color won't be the dead line." He was clearly impressed with the extent of racial intermixture in Hawaii, an important sign of racial progress in his opinion, and he wrote to his son that miscegenation would also improve the status of blacks on the mainland. "In my opinion Mac [McCants], the Negro's only hope of *equality* of *opportunity* lies in amalgamation," he asserted boldly.[23] This was indeed an unusual position for a black leader and particularly for a black nationalist to take. It was certainly not a position that Stewart could state publicly. It reflected less the reality of the racial situation in Hawaii, which he had analyzed only superficially, than his own dissatisfaction with the nature of race relations in the United States and his failure to find a solution.

After leaving Hawaii in 1905, Stewart had planned to return to New York and resume his legal practice and political career, but a group of British investors persuaded him to settle in London instead. Why did Stewart at the age of fifty-two choose to settle in England, a nation he knew little about? Apparently the entrepreneurs convinced him that Africa offered the potential for unlimited opportunity. He hoped to use London as a base to pursue trading and investment opportunities with Africa as an earlier black nationalist, Paul Cuffe, had done in the early nineteenth century. Stewart and his business associates believed that investing in Liberian trade, in particular, would bring lucrative returns. Stewart was willing to take the risk, and still smarting from his failed financial ventures in Hawaii, he moved to London in 1905.

Stewart continued to express contempt at the idea of ever residing permanently in the United States. In the strongest language he ever wrote privately, Stewart explained to his son, "Indeed Mac, I could *never* live in the United States happily." London, he felt, was a more tolerant society racially than the United States, and he enjoyed higher social status there: "Miss Alice [Stewart] and I are wined and dined; clubs are open to me— houses too; and in one instance a private carriage at my disposal."[24] Stewart also noted the presence of a black Charlestonian, Edmund Thornton Jenkins, "who had covered himself and our race with glory in his career as a student and sub-professor in the London Royal Academy of Music."[25] Several years later, Stewart again expressed disdain for his country and shared the happiness he had found in London. "We are contented and happy—I would not live in America for a *gold mine,* if the conditions was [*sic*] *that I must reside there,*" he wrote his two sons from London.[26] Although Stewart had attacked racial discrimination consistently throughout his career, he had always been an optimist. Now, however, Stewart expressed grave doubts about the ability of blacks and whites to improve the racial situation in the United States sufficiently for blacks to achieve full equality.

Stewart exaggerated the degree of racial harmony in London, for the city was not the racial melting pot that he alleged it to be. London's small black community, composed largely of African and West Indian immigrants, not only faced racial discrimination in employment and housing but intermittent racial violence as well. England's black community in the early decades of the twentieth century, according to historian James Walvin, consisted of "depressed people, eking out a living on the poverty-stricken fringes of society." The black population in some years constituted one massive relief roll, with needs so acute that they were beyond the means of charitable organizations and government programs. The black unemployed, many of whom were former sailors, maritime workers, or unskilled laborers, were "confronted with blatant discrimination," concluded Walvin. Many found it difficult to obtain work because white employers were reluctant to integrate their labor force or because white workers would threaten to strike if they were forced to work with blacks.[27]

Stewart's favorable treatment in London, due in large measure to his class standing and his association with influential white Englishmen, therefore, had little relationship to the lives of most black Britons, who lived on the margins of English society. White Englishmen discriminated against people of African descent on the basis of class as well as color, though Stewart seemed oblivious to this fact when he arrived in London in 1905. As he had done when he reported on southern race relations for the New York *Freeman* in 1885, concluding that they had improved considerably,

Stewart misinterpreted his own acceptance in London society as a sign that conditions for all blacks had progressed.[28]

Stewart was attracted to London for several other reasons. It was a cosmopolitan city, and he had missed the pace, energy, and culture of large urban centers. He had been born and raised in Charleston, the cultural and intellectual capital of South Carolina, and he had spent the majority of his adult years in New York, the cultural capital of the United States. He also wanted to raise his three young daughters from his second marriage in a more benign world racially than the one in which he raised McCants, Gilchrist, and Carlotta. And, to a large extent, he had been successful. Two of Stewart's daughters, Gladys and Kapulani, had been born in Hawaii, and they had experienced none of the racial restrictions that blacks faced on the Mainland at the turn of the twentieth century. But Stewart was not naive. The restriction-free haven that he sought for his family existed neither in England nor in the United States. As W. E. B. Du Bois had written in 1903, "The problem of the twentieth century is the problem of the color line, the relation of the darker to the lighter races of men in Asia and Africa, in America and the islands of the sea." As a keen student of both history and politics, Stewart knew that people of African descent were subjugated by whites throughout the world. But this fact did not deter him in his search for a more hospitable environment.[29]

Stewart's years in London were happy ones. He had grown very fond of his three daughters, Anna, who he named after his mother, Gladys, and Kapulani. With them, he attempted to be the warm, affectionate father that he had failed so miserably to be with his earlier children. He informed McCants that his daughters were receiving a well-rounded education and that raising them had proven to be a joy. Anna, he boasted, "can talk a bit of history, mythology, botany, French, and plays piano." Stewart's daughters would later attend the University of Notre Dame in Belgium before returning to London to attend the Academy of Music and the Polytechnic School of Art. "They are not brilliant girls," Stewart confided later to his childhood friend, Francis J. Grimké, "although our art student passed her last month's exams at the head of her class; but they are good and splendid girls." He also wrote McCants, to whom he had grown closer as he aged, that he was enjoying the winter in England and had spent "not a dollar for doctors." The itinerant black patriarch also admonished his son to settle down and establish roots: "Dear Mac [McCants], I wish you were *settled*. Don't follow me in restlessness."[30]

But almost as abruptly as he had left Hawaii in 1905 to sail to London, Stewart, as rootless in his middle age as he had been in his youth, moved to Liberia in 1906. He wrote his son McCants shortly before his departure to the African nation that he had renounced two decades earlier: "I am again in touch with African interests—large interests; and you know I move quickly."[31] Although Stewart never revealed the names of his African interests, he promptly established a legal practice in Monrovia and was asked by the Liberian government to use his legal expertise to revise Liberia's statutes, a project he completed in 1906 and again in 1911.[32] Stewart also wrote the legal code for Liberian justices of the peace in 1907 and was the pivotal figure in establishing the Liberian National Bar Association. How Stewart gained the favor of the Liberian government so quickly is uncertain. It is reasonable to assume that his London contacts paved the way, in part. Stewart's prior residence in Liberia, however, and his reputation as a skilled and careful attorney were probably also important factors and whatever the source of his success, his move to Liberia appeared to be paying immediate political dividends: Stewart's star was rising.[33]

T. McCants Stewart moved much more cautiously within Liberian political circles as a mature man in his fifties than he had as a volatile young black leader in his early thirties. He was careful initially in his public statements to offend neither Liberia's president nor any high-ranking government official, and his perceived loyalty was rewarded in several ways. He was included in the Liberian government's inner circle of leadership and had the ear of the president, Arthur Barclay. Stewart was also invited to organize the Liberian National Bar Association, and he presented the formal address at the second annual meeting of the organization, held in the executive mansion in 1908.[34]

Stewart's Liberian affairs were well publicized in both American and African newspapers. *Liberia*, a quarterly bulletin that succeeded the *African Repository*, reprinted Stewart's letters from the republic and described his political progress. It reported that Stewart and his family had arrived in Monrovia in November 1906 and that the black leader had accomplished a great deal in the space of a year. "We are pleased to know that he is a full-fledged Liberian citizen."[35] *Alexander's Magazine*, a black American periodical, also reported on Stewart's work in Liberia and published his appeal to black farmers—provided they were industrious—to migrate to Liberia.[36]

Since Stewart had gained the confidence of President Barclay, a West Indian–born politician who led one of the most progressive administrations in Liberia's history,[37] he was offered the cabinet position of secretary of education or the opportunity to serve as an associate justice on the Liberian Supreme Court. Presumably, these were the types of political appointments that Stewart had been desiring all of his career. (Neither he nor any other black American would receive such appointments in the United States until the 1960s.) A cabinet position and a judicial post offered not only prestige but also a stable income. Surprisingly, Stewart declined both positions. His reasoning was straightforward. "I want to go *home established* as soon as possible," he wrote McCants.[38] It is not clear what Stewart meant by "home," for he had pledged never to live in the United States again. In fact, he reiterated that pledge. Perhaps he had planned to return to London, his latest of many homes. But to his son McCants, who had become his closest confidant, he wrote, "We are contented and happy."[39]

Stewart's decision to decline a political appointment proved only temporary, for in 1911 he accepted a position as an associate justice of the Liberian Supreme Court. This appointment represented a significant political victory for Stewart personally and for black Americans in general. No African-American had been successful in obtaining a judicial post at this level in the United States or abroad by 1911. Thurgood Marshall's confirmation on the United States Supreme Court would not occur until 1965, more than five decades after Stewart sat on the Liberian Supreme Court. The appointment also revealed Stewart's emerging influence in Liberian politics and the esteem he had gained in the eyes of President Barclay.[40]

Stewart apparently had several reasons for changing his mind and accepting this prestigious political appointment. His African investments had been less lucrative than he had anticipated, and it is unlikely that Stewart earned more than a modest living as an attorney in Monrovia. He had hoped in 1910 to start a produce company in Liberia and to allow McCants to represent the company as its attorney. But Stewart had insufficient start-up capital to launch this venture, and he could not attract American or European investors.[41] Stewart had purchased an unspecified amount of land in Liberia, but it failed to appreciate in value as he had hoped. Thus Stewart's decision to accept a judicial post was based in part on his need to generate a steady income to support himself and his family, who would accompany him to Liberia this time. Accepting a judicial appointment also meant that Stewart had changed his mind about staying in Liberia. He was fifty-eight years old in 1911, and although his health had always been robust, he probably sensed that his career was winding down.[42]

Little is known about Stewart's years on the Liberian Supreme Court. His legal training at the University of South Carolina and his thirty-six years of experience as an attorney probably made him as qualified to serve on the court as any jurist in Liberia. And although Stewart had not lived in Liberia for three decades, his work in revising the statutes of Liberia and establishing the Liberian National Bar Association illustrated his familiarity with the laws and legal apparatus of the nation.

Stewart's role and responsibilities as a Supreme Court justice, however, were considerably broader than merely issuing opinions from the bench. President Barclay also utilized the black jurist occasionally as an envoy to negotiate sensitive diplomatic matters and to secure small loans for Liberia. Clearly the Liberian president wanted to take advantage of Stewart's American and European connections. Shortly after Stewart was appointed to the Supreme Court, for example, he sailed to the United States to meet P. G. Knox, the American secretary of state, to request a loan from the United States government. William D. Crum, who had gained an important political appointment under Theodore Roosevelt as customs collector of the port at Charleston, South Carolina, described Stewart as "a friend of my youth" and stated that he should be useful "in throwing light on many matters which may aid your Department in dealing with Liberian affairs." Crum described Stewart's character as exemplary, and he urged Knox to assist him in any way that he could.[43]

The purpose of Stewart's 1911 visit was two fold: he was attempting to keep communication open between the Liberian government and the United States and to secure a loan for Liberia. The U.S. State Department was advised, however, to withhold the loan until the revised 1911 statutes of Liberia were securely in place. This may also explain why Stewart personally supervised the completion of the revised statutes of Liberia in 1911.[44]

Despite the confidence that Stewart had established with the Liberian government, his tenure on the Supreme Court was short-lived. By a joint resolution of the two houses of the Liberian legislature, Stewart was removed from the Supreme Court in October 1914. The reasons for Stewart's removal from the court may never be revealed in their entirety. Stewart charged that he was a political pawn who refused to support the policies of a corrupt president and legislature. The Liberian government, however, denied that his removal was politically motivated. It was based instead on Stewart's violations of Liberian law; Stewart's criticism of the Liberian judiciary and the Supreme Court justices, whom he charged in 1909 with "ignorance," accepting bribes, "excessive use of intoxicants," and "shocking immorality"; and Stewart's accepting retainers from private parties, which probably damaged his image in the eyes of the legislature. The decision was made in secret caucuses of the Liberian legislature, and Stewart had no opportunity to present witnesses on his behalf or to answer the charges that were brought against him. The resolution, adopted at the September 1914 session of the Liberian legislature, directed the president to "remove T. McCants Stewart, one of the justices of the court and to appoint another in his stead." The resolution passed by a two-thirds vote of both houses of the legislature and was approved on October 28, 1914. Thus, in the short space of three years, Stewart's star, which had risen so rapidly, fell just as quickly.[45]

It is likely that Stewart's removal from the court was, at least in part, politically motivated. Stewart alleged that his unwillingness to engage in corruption was a pivotal factor in his removal. After returning to London, he informed McCants of his plight: "The fact is that I am unpopular with the corrupt political bosses from the President down because I am clean and they are steeped in sexual and other mud."[46] Stewart also alleged that his removal from the court was unconstitutional, for the Liberian constitution specified that a Supreme Court justice must be removed by an "Address" and not by a joint resolution. Although Stewart stood little chance of regaining his political post, he vowed to fight. "I am a bad man to tackle, you know," he boasted to his younger son, Gilchrist. Stewart also noted that he was "in perfect health and fighting form" and that he would press this issue until he reached a satisfactory resolution. "We will bite the rascals to the bone (a Liberian expression) before we get thro [sic] with them." He urged both of his sons to write the U.S. State Department to inform them of this episode: "If you can stir up the [State] Department at Washington to call a halt [,] these chaps who fear nothing but the whip will yell for mercy. They are arrant cowards afraid of me like the devil."[47] This correspondence is revealing because it illustrates the influence that T. McCants Stewart believed he had established with the United States government during his tenure on the Liberian Supreme Court.

Gilchrist Stewart followed his father's advice and wrote the U.S. State Department to protest his father's removal from the court, though there is no indication that McCants did likewise. To his older brother Gilchrist wrote that "we must try and save dad now." He also suggested to McCants that the U.S. government "establish a quasi Protectorate that would bring about law and order [in Liberia], seeing how American investors are protected in their court."[48] Gilchrist Stewart acknowledged frankly, however, that his father had handled this delicate situation poorly. "I think he could have been quite a little bit more diplomatic," he observed, understating a well-known fact about his father's obstreperous temperament. In their correspondence neither Gilchrist nor McCants mentioned the nature of the dispute between their father and the Liberian president. But as Gilchrist observed, "His recall was due to the fact that he was considered persona non grata."[49]

Stewart had been quite satisfied with the direction that his career had taken in Liberia and had expressed no intention to leave Africa. Now, suddenly, he was perceived as a disruptive element in the Liberian government. For the second time in his career, T. McCants Stewart left Africa following a bitter dispute. The stakes were considerably higher in 1914, however, than they had been in 1885 when Stewart left after feuding with Edward Blyden. In the earlier instance he had left Africa on his own accord; in 1914 he had been removed from office in disgrace. Stewart's removal from the Supreme Court was also problematic for immediate, practical reasons: he had no income. Worse, he could not use his former judicial post as a springboard to another political appointment in Africa as he had planned. But Stewart had faced adversity before, and he was confident that he would weather this storm.

Without a job or a country of his own, Stewart returned to London in 1914, where he remained for the next seven years. In letters to his children he continued to assail President Barclay for political corruption and moral turpitude, and he took some satisfaction in learning that the Liberian government was in considerable debt as a consequence of the disruption of its wartime trade with Germany.[50] London's black community had swelled considerably during Stewart's absence, with the large influx of Africans and West Indians who flocked to the city during World War I. Many of these immigrants were former British colonial subjects trying to improve their standard of living during the war, while a handful served in the British military.[51] Stewart seemed oblivious to these changes. He spent most of his time searching for new economic opportunities and raising his three daughters. Yet Stewart had not tired of politics or racial activism altogether. Still a committed black nationalist, though a discouraged one, Stewart continued to follow African affairs and was invited by W. E. B. Du Bois to attend the Second Pan-African Conference in Paris. Though it is not clear whether Stewart attended the international meeting, the invitation revealed that Stewart was still regarded as an important civil rights leader and activist.[52]

Soon Stewart left London in search of new challenges and opportunities, citing the damp London weather as an impediment to his wife's health. Stewart and his family moved to the Virgin Islands in 1921. The Stewarts arrived in February of that year aboard the *S.S. Prins Der Nederlanden* from London via Amsterdam, and they settled in the town of Charlotte Amalie on Frenchmen's Hill overlooking St. Thomas's majestic harbor. Stewart's decision to move to the Virgin Islands was similar in several respects to his earlier move to Hawaii. Both were recently acquired U.S. possessions, and Stewart believed in each case that a sparsely settled community would provide greater political and economic opportunities. He informed his oldest daughter, Carlotta, in 1922, in what had become an all too familiar refrain: "Well, you should not be surprised to find me here [in St. Thomas]." Carlotta, now a respected principal in the Hawaiian public schools, was not surprised. She had expected him to continue his restless pursuit of peace, respect, and economic opportunity.[53]

During this period Stewart was attempting to reestablish the rapport he and Carlotta had enjoyed when they lived together in New York and Hawaii. That father and daughter had drifted apart emotionally had less to do with Carlotta's attitude toward her father than Stewart's lax correspondence and his frequent moves. Carlotta also resented her stepmother, Alice Franklin Stewart, a resentment that grew stronger as the years passed. Carlotta saw her father's second wife as an interloper and apparently never completely forgave her father for his terrible treatment of her mother. She had no desire to comply with her father's wishes to promote family unity.[54]

Stewart was one of only several black attorneys in the Virgin Islands, and he established himself quickly. He formed a joint legal practice with Christopher H. Payne, a noted black attorney who had lived in the Virgin Islands since 1903. Like Stewart, Payne came to the Virgin Islands to further his political and legal career. An ordained Baptist minister and attorney, the West Virginia native had served as U.S. deputy collector of internal revenue for Charleston between 1889 and 1893. In 1896 he had become the first black elected to the West Virginia State legislature. In 1903, Payne was appointed U.S. consul to the Virgin Islands by President Theodore Roosevelt. He remained in St. Thomas, where he became a prosecuting attorney and a police judge for the district of Frederiksted, St. Croix. Together, Payne and Stewart established one of the most successful legal practices in the Virgin Islands.[55]

Although he was no longer the vigorous and outspoken leader he had been earlier in his career, Stewart was still an active and respected member of the community. His former civil rights campaigns and his brief tenure as a supreme court justice in Liberia had made him one of the most experienced racial leaders in the Virgin Islands. Age, admittedly, had taken its toll, and Stewart informed Carlotta that "it has not been an easy task of late to bear the burden and heat of the day."[56] Yet Stewart continued to represent clients, write articles in the local newspaper, attend literary and social gatherings, and speak at political functions.

Within four months of his arrival, the St. Thomas *Mail Notes* described Stewart as one "of the ablest minds among us."[57] The local press reported regularly on Stewart's legal affairs and noted that he was one of the most astute attorneys in the Virgin Islands. In the case of *Levi v. the Director of Police*, the *Mail Notes* wrote that "Judge McCants Stewart Makes Brilliant Defense" and concluded that his counsel was instrumental in persuading the district court to reverse an earlier ruling against his client, Lyall Levi, whose dog roamed the streets without a leash.[58] In a more pressing legal matter, Stewart defended a man who was charged with manslaughter when his boat collided with another and killed two women who were aboard. The jury was swayed by Stewart's defense of his client and returned a verdict of not guilty. Although Stewart had a steady flow of business, most of his cases concerned relatively routine legal matters such as estates, divorces, and wives who sued their husbands for nonsupport.[59]

Stewart's reputation as an attorney soon attracted the attention of Governor Sumner E. Kittelle, who appointed him to the Board of Law Examiners, an appointment that met the widespread approval of the local community. "The action of the Governor in appointing this eminent lawyer to the position shows much foresight," wrote the *Mail Notes*.[60] The appointment, though largely symbolic, placed Stewart among the political elite in St. Thomas. In the space of six months, he had emerged as an important black leader in St. Thomas, no small achievement in a country that distrusted outsiders. However, neither the political appointment nor his status in the community discouraged Stewart from criticizing the inefficiency of some aspects of the judicial system in the Virgin Islands. He recommended, for example, that the district court's jurisdiction be expanded to include police cases, in effect, merging the police court into the district court. He also suggested that the annual salaries of judges be raised to $4,000 from their current level in order to attract more qualified jurists. Stewart stated that he had no interest personally in another judicial post and that his only motivation in making these recommendations was to improve the judicial system.[61]

Stewart's image and visibility in the Virgin Islands were also enhanced by periodic articles in local newspapers and speeches at political functions. Not only did he express his opinion regarding the Virgin Islands' legal apparatus, but he also wrote human interest stories about his experiences or eulogized important people he had known. A well-read and well-traveled man, Stewart expressed his opinion in the local press about a variety of subjects, including African history. Stewart considered himself well versed in African history, for he had written and lectured on the subject widely and had lived in Africa on two occasions. He also contributed an obituary, for example, on Prince Jonah Kuhio Kalanianaole of Hawaii, whom he had known during his residence in Honolulu. "In all the years of my residence in his native home," wrote Stewart, "he was my friend and my associate in the public and political affairs of Hawaii." It is doubtful that Prince Kuhio was actually an associate of Stewart's, given the black attorney's tenuous economic status when he lived on the islands. Yet namedropping had been a characteristic of Stewart throughout his career, since he believed that his association with important political figures would elevate his status among his colleagues.[62]

Stewart also spoke at churches, literary events, and political functions, rarely passing up an opportunity to express his opinion on a subject or to play the role of elder statesman. After reporting on the content of a sermon at the Anglican Church in St. Thomas for the *Mail Notes,* Stewart also noted that public works programs "would at once furnish employment for our working men and women." Yet Stewart did not wish to superimpose the entire American economic model on the Virgin Islanders. He feared that the people would lose their identity in the process. Nevertheless, Stewart believed that the Virgin Islanders should emphasize economic development first and foremost. This Washingtonian doctrine, which Stewart had embraced throughout his career and instilled in his children, was still a cornerstone of his racial philosophy.[63]

Time and age did not change Stewart's opinion on most subjects. He continued to advocate thrift, morality, and diligence as blacks' best route to economic success. In a speech before a group of middle school students, Stewart urged them to pursue any honest labor or toil in their quest to excel. The dignity of labor was a theme that he had raised repeatedly throughout his long life. It was also an illustration of the impact that the

Washingtonian influence still had on Stewart's views, despite the many twists and turns his career had taken.[64]

Stewart's reputation as an attorney and his appointment by Governor Kittelle to the Board of Law Examiners meant he was a member of the political elite, it did not automatically place him in the same social circle with St. Thomas's black elite, some of whom had resided in the islands for many generations. Although highly regarded, Stewart was still viewed in many respects as an outsider. Stewart did not attend many of the most important social functions in St. Thomas. He was not included, for example, among the distinguished guests who attended a large party at the governor's home to celebrate his silver wedding anniversary.[65] On the other hand, Stewart may simply have decided to shun most social affairs at this point in his career. He traveled sparingly and devoted most of his time to his legal practice and family matters. He also minimized his organizational affiliations, choosing not to join the Virgin Islands chapter of the Universal Negro Improvement Association (UNIA) or any other political or protest organization, a major departure from the habits of his earlier years.

Surprisingly, Stewart did not speak out publicly against the deplorable conditions of black workers in some industries or protest racial slurs as readily as he had done in his youth. He was silent following the performance of a minstrel show in St. Thomas and offered no protest after the publication of derogatory cartoons about blacks in the local press. Clearly, some of the fire had been extinguished from Stewart's soul. Though there were still battles to be fought, Stewart was considerably more selective in choosing his confrontations.[66]

As Stewart approached his sixty-ninth birthday, he resolved to wage one final battle. He joined the Virgin Islanders in their campaign to wrest greater political and constitutional guarantees from the United States government. In the quest to secure these rights, the Virgin Islanders had organized a committee in 1922 that planned to bring their plight before President Warren G. Harding and the United States Congress. Stewart supported the campaign, so his absence from the official delegation to Washington, D.C., was a conspicuous omission. He was one of the most experienced attorneys in the Virgin Islands and had gained the respect of the U.S. State Department while serving as an envoy of the Liberian government. If Stewart was disappointed in this oversight, he did not express his dejection publicly. Rather, he was content to work behind the scenes.[67] He urged local leaders to close ranks behind the delegation as a demonstration of unity. "Now that the local legislature has decided upon the delegation we should all do whatever we can to make their mission a success. Unless we deal with public matters broadly, calmly, unselfishly and without personal feelings, we shall go up against the rocks."[68]

The official delegation was headed by Conrad Corneiro, a successful black merchant, member of the Harbor Board, and legislator. It also included George A. Moorehead and Adolph Sixto, both important leaders in the Virgin Islands. Moorehead, too, was a member of the legislature, and Sixto, who was elected delegate-at-large to the committee, established the first repertory theater in the Virgin Islands and wrote an early history of the islands. Stewart had been one of the first political leaders to recommend that Corneiro head the delegation to Washington and to explain to the Virgin Islands people the purpose of their mission. Although at least one militant faction of the Virgin Islands' political leadership, headed by Casper Holstein, criticized this delegation as too conservative, Stewart defended the choice as essentially sound and urged the people to rally around these leaders.[69]

The delegation arrived in Washington in July 1922, and the St. Thomas *Bulletin* noted that the delegates, having "started their work, find it up hill work as it is rather difficult to reach the different men they have to interview." While the delegation called attention to the political plight of the Virgin Islanders, they failed to persuade President Harding and the U.S. Congress that their grievances were just and that they deserved a civil government and broader constitutional liberties. This failure, however, did not discourage the more militant faction of the Virgin Islands' political leadership. Casper Holstein, who was elected president of the New York-based Virgin Islands' Congressional Council in 1923, continued to lobby the U.S. government. The council demanded that the people of the islands receive the same rights as any United States citizen as stipulated in the U.S. Constitution. It also attempted to win the support of the American people but initially succeeded only in gaining the backing of the New York branch of the UNIA. Thus neither the official delegation nor the Virgin Islands' Congressional Council had any immediate impact on the attitudes of the American government.[70]

Although he was not part of the official delegation to Washington, Stewart visited the Mainland in early November 1922 as a private citizen. The St.Thomas *Mail Notes* wrote that Stewart "will sail this week on the [S.S.] Surinam for a visit to the mainland, [and] while on private business, the

Judge says that he will deliver a course of lectures before his return and that he will lose no opportunity to endeavor to help the islands."[71] Similarly, the St. Croix *Avis* reported that Stewart would be visiting the Mainland "to give lectures on the Virgin Islands with the hope that they may create more interest in them." The *Avis* also noted that Stewart had been away from the United States for more than two decades, and "we daresay he will find many changes."[72]

It is not surprising that neither T. McCants Stewart nor the official delegation succeeded in convincing Congress of the merit or urgency of the Virgin Islanders' political demands. The U.S. Supreme Court had ruled in an earlier opinion that the Constitution did not "require the granting of full citizenship rights to the people of unincorporated territories, and that Congress enjoyed complete command over them."[73] Unrestricted citizenship would not be granted to all Virgin Islanders and to persons residing in any American insular possession or territory until 1932, and full political rights would not be granted until June 1936.[74]

Stewart's return to the United States, however, was personally if not politically rewarding. He spent two months there visiting friends and fulfilling several speaking engagements that he had arranged before his departure. Stewart's precise itinerary is not known, but he had planned to visit New York as well as Washington, D.C., and to see his son Gilchrist, who was practicing law. While visiting the nation's capital, Stewart worshipped at the Fifteenth Street Presbyterian Church where his childhood friend, Francis J. Grimké, served as pastor. In addition to attending the Sunday service, Stewart, wrote Grimké, "took supper with us and spent the evening and a most delightful evening it was."[75]

Despite the time and distance that separated them, the two men had maintained a sporadic correspondence for five decades, and these letters served as a source of comfort to each. Grimké held his friend in high regard and maintained a great deal of affection for him. "We were like brothers, and felt for each other a brothers love," he wrote.[76] In 1920, while living in London, Stewart had confided to Grimké that "as I grow older my memory turns to and lingers around Charleston and the days of our early boyhood there." Stewart also assured Grimké that despite his ouster from Liberia in 1914, the young republic was still very much on his mind. "Having taken and re-taken hold (1883 & 1905) of the Problems of Liberia, I do not give up, but am trying to help solve it." Yet by the 1920s Stewart was more realistic in his appraisal that developing the resources of Liberia, while possible, would be more difficult than he had realized early in his career. "No denying the fact," he wrote Grimké, "that it [the problem of Liberia] is a tough one involving ignorance, self-sufficiency, and other factors known and unknown. But roads and railways and better education which I am helping to bring about will let in the light."[77]

Several months before seeing Grimké in Washington, D.C., in 1922, Stewart had written him a nostalgic letter partly critical of his own restlessness and drifting: "It is a long way, Frank, from old Charleston 1865 and 1922—I here and you—where you anchored 44 years ago. I wish mine had been a steadier life. But alast [*sic*], I have tried to do some good in every port where I have let down my anchor, and I do not feel that my life has been exactly in vain. But I sometimes feel like the Prodigal Son."[78] For the first time, Stewart revealed misgivings regarding the course that his life and work had taken. Had he "anchored" in one location like his close friend Francis Grimké, his contribution to the economic and political progress of African-Americans might well have been even more significant. His life, however, would have certainly been far less adventurous.

In late December 1922, Stewart prepared to sail from New York to his adopted home in St. Thomas. For a man of sixty-nine he was in reasonably good health, though inconvenienced by a cold. The cold, however, grew worse. After Stewart got caught in a blizzard as he attempted to board his ship for departure, it quickly developed into pneumonia. The return voyage exacerbated the illness and, according to the St. Thomas *Bulletin*, "the Judge landed [in St. Thomas] in pretty bad shape, and at once placed himself under medical care."

The respected African-American leader, who had won so many battles as an attorney, minister, politician, and racial activist throughout his long life, could not conquer this illness. He died at midnight at his home on Frenchmen's Hill on January 7, 1923.[79] Stewart had probably never grasped the seriousness of his illness. His final words, which he spoke to his wife and three daughters, were, "The doctor did not say that I was going to die did he? for I do not want to die. You folks need me."

T. McCants Stewart's sudden death took everyone, including his family, by surprise, for he had been robust and in excellent health since his arrival in the Virgin Islands. Indeed, one of the many remarkable aspects of Stewart's life had been his ability to avoid serious illness. Stewart was laid to rest on the island of St. Thomas. A large gathering of Virgin Islanders turned out at the Moravian Church, and hundreds of people lined the streets to pay their final respects to a man who had dedicated his life to the cause of racial and political equality. In a simple, dignified ceremony, Stewart was buried with the Liberian flag wrapped around his body, a request that he had made to his family some years earlier, and a sign that he remained devoted to Liberia despite his conflicts with the Liberian government. The *Mail Notes* wrote that "the Judge was one of the best Americans who made St. Thomas their home" and called Stewart "a true American" who "loved his country and his race." Thus the black leader who had promised never to return to the United States permanently died not on foreign soil, but on a possession of the United States government.[80]

Stewart's death would be mourned in the United States and abroad. In a moving tribute to his memory, William Shepperley, who served as president of the Little Society of John Keats and vice-president of the William Blake Society of Arts and Letters in London, submitted a poem to the St. Thomas *Times* in honor of Stewart's life. Shepperley noted that Stewart's "London friends" were also grieved at his passing and that they, too, held the black leader in high esteem. "Such men as he it is who make our poor world rich," Shepperley wrote.[81] Many black newspapers and periodicals also noted Stewart's passing and praised his multifaceted career as well as his contribution to the civil rights struggle. The New York *Negro World,* the official paper of the UNIA, led by Marcus Garvey, wrote that Stewart "helped dig the foundation of everything the race has in New York City and Brooklyn." The influential journal *Crisis* also paid a moving tribute to Stewart: "Most men are satisfied with success in one land. T. McCants Stewart sought and obtained it in many."[82]

T. McCants Stewart had served his race and his country well during his long career. Not only had he been a consistent champion of equal rights for African-Americans, but he also labored to secure broader freedoms for Africans, Hawaiians, and Virgin Islanders. However, like many leaders of his generation, Stewart had a tendency to be pompous and arrogant, and his faults as both a husband and provider to his first wife, and as a father to his three children from that marriage, were apparent. In fact, he seemed to delight in being perceived as a stern patriarch.

But despite his faults as a husband and father and his waning energy in his later years, Stewart never compromised his ideas in the struggle to improve the social, political, and economic status of African-Americans. Like his close friend Booker T. Washington, Stewart never renounced his position that all labor was dignified, no matter how lowly or menial, and he, like Washington, encouraged blacks to work with whites in order to improve their condition. But here Stewart apparently drew the line in being compliant and cooperative. Stewart did not work behind the scenes, as Washington did, but fought openly for racial equality in the courts, in newspapers and periodicals, and in public and political forums. In this respect, Stewart was much closer to Frederick Douglass and T. Thomas Fortune than to Booker T. Washington.[83] The *Negro World* and the *Crisis* were correct in their assessment that Stewart had made a major contribution to the struggle of blacks to achieve racial equality in New York and throughout the nation. Stewart would have been proud, although not surprised, to hear these compliments, for he believed that his contributions to improving the status of African-Americans was part of his mission and obligation as a black leader.

T. McCants Stewart

T. McCants Stewart

Gilchrist Stewart

McCants Stewart

Robert Flippin

Verina Morton-Jones

Anahola School, Hawaii, Class of 1928

Carlotta Stewart

Carlotta Stewart Lai (on right). Grade officers and
principal, Hanamaulu School, 1933.

Mary Delia Weir

Katherine Stewart Flippin

Charlotte Harris Stewart Stephens

Katherine Stewart Flippin

Mary Stewart and family

Part Two

❖ ❖ ❖ ❖ ❖ ❖ ❖ ❖ ❖ ❖ ❖ ❖ ❖ ❖ ❖

Race, Obligation, and

the New Generation

6

McCants Stewart

The Struggle of the African-American Professional

in the Far West

❖ ❖ ❖ ❖ ❖ ❖ ❖ ❖ ❖ ❖ ❖ ❖ ❖ ❖ ❖

T. McCants Stewart's children shared his sense of duty. His two sons, McCants and Gilchrist, and his daughter, Carlotta, were reared and educated not only to succeed, but also to assume leadership positions in their respective communities and work to uplift the race. Thus all three attended college and embarked on professional careers, the expected course of action for the black elite and their descendants. Although none achieved the national renown that their father had earned in his lifetime, McCants and Gilchrist, in particular, played important roles as African-American leaders in their communities, and Carlotta became a respected educator in the territory of Hawaii.[1] As a father, T. McCants Stewart led largely by example. Yet he also imparted to his children both verbally and through his letters his sense of duty, mission, and racial obligation. He expected his children not only to earn his respect, but also to work unselfishly to improve the condition of those less fortunate than they. No matter how far removed from his presence, they never forgot their father's advice.

It surprised virtually no one in either his extended family or his immediate circle when Stewart named his first son, whom he hoped to mold into an important leader, McCants. Born in Orangeburg, South Carolina, on July

11, 1877, McCants spent his formative years in this small rural southern community, where his parents taught at Claflin University, an historically black college. Charlotte Stewart taught piano and organ at Claflin. Stewart, who taught mathematics, had been admitted to the South Carolina bar in 1875 and supplemented his income by practicing law.[2] Because of the heavy demands on his schedule, his frequent travels, and the two years that he spent in Liberia, Stewart often attempted to exercise parental discipline and to shape the upbringing and values of his children through written correspondence. Stewart's letters to his children, therefore, which first appear in 1885, are rich, poignant, and revealing. They not only illustrated the type of upbringing that this absentee father expected for his children, but also allowed McCants, Gilchrist, and Carlotta a window into their father's complex world of politics, African affairs, and race leadership.

As an ordained Methodist minister, Stewart expected his children, above all, to be devout. It is essential, he informed them, "that the Bible be made your rule of conduct and Christ your example. To be *good* should be the chief aim of your life every day; and the best time to begin is *now*." Stewart encouraged his children to read the Bible regularly, and he was certain that if they followed his advice that they would find tranquility and good fortune. "If you grow up *good* depending daily upon God for strength and guidance," he continued, "then you will not *lie*, nor steal, nor do injury out of malice or retaliation to your fellow men. People will love you, and God will bless you."[3]

Stewart also instilled in his children the importance of education, accumulating capital, and helping those less fortunate than they. As a self-made man, he hoped to impress upon McCants and Gilchrist that success, both financial and spiritual, required commitment and hard work. "To be greatly useful, you must have education and money. Honestly and honorably get all you can of these two powerful agencies which move the world. Get your farms; buy houses and lands, but at all times use your money so as to make poor people happy."[4]

Reared in the "Age of Booker T. Washington," McCants and Gilchrist embraced the principles of thrift, self-help, and moral reform, and their parents instilled these ideals into their children at an early age. "It will delight your papa to see you grow up and to be a good and great man," Stewart informed McCants, seven months before his tenth birthday in 1887. Stewart urged McCants, who he had hoped would follow in his footsteps as a racial activist, to lay "the foundation now in your boyhood" and assured him that "you will be a Man of Mark, if you strive hard to be always busy and economical." As he had done two years earlier, Stewart encouraged his son never to neglect his biblical studies, for "if you make this Book the rule of your life while a boy, it will be easy for you to follow it in later life when the storms come and the winds blow." Stewart also encouraged McCants to start thinking about his career,—a tall order for a boy of nine—but this advice was probably motivated by his own propensity to shift from one profession to another, a pattern he did not want his son to emulate. He advised, "But having decided upon your course, you must stick. Papa has changed from the law to the ministry, and from the ministry back to the law. He does not want history to repeat itself in the case of either of his boys." This moral-laden advice characterized the correspondence between Stewart and his two sons throughout their lives.[5]

McCants and Gilchrist attended Claflin University between 1889 and 1891, where they had hoped to learn a trade and make themselves "useful" and productive as their father had done at an early age. Like numerous black colleges during the latter years of the nineteenth century, Claflin was initially a college in name only. As historian Joel Williamson writes, "The level of instruction at Claflin during Reconstruction hardly deserved the appellation higher education."[6] By the early 1890s, however, Claflin's enrollment had grown to more than 500 students, and the school offered a wide array of courses and programs, including art, music, agricultural and mechanical training, domestic science, religion, a normal department, and a college preparatory program.[7] Claflin was also reasonably close to Columbia, the state's capital and the home of Charlotte Stewart's parents, in whose care Stewart had left his children at regular intervals.

McCants and Gilchrist loved their years at Claflin. Both, according to the 1890-1891 school catalogue, were enrolled in the fifth grade, and each, as their father had instructed, was earnestly learning a trade. McCants was learning carpentry and the blacksmith's trade, while Gilchrist pursued carpentry and printing.[8] Although both McCants and Gilchrist had hoped to attend Claflin for their secondary education and college training, their father had other ideas. Without consulting his two sons and contrary to their wishes, he enrolled McCants, at the age of sixteen, and Gilchrist, at age thirteen, in Tuskegee Institute. The protests and shrill complaints of McCants and Gilchrist apparently fell on deaf ears. "At present boys, the problems of your life lie at Tuskegee [and] there will be no change," wrote Stewart to his sons. The boys even attempted to get their grandmother,

Anna Morris Stewart, to intercede on their behalf but to no avail. "She [grandmother] understands my views concerning your training, and when you get older, you will appreciate more than you do now my effort to make you self-reliant," the patriarch exhorted.[9] Stewart had established a close friendship with Booker T. Washington prior to the latter's "Atlanta Compromise" speech in 1895, which catapulted him into the national limelight, and the two men remained lifelong friends. Thus, on the eve of their departure to Tuskegee, Stewart assured his sons that Booker T. Washington was "a warm personal friend of mine," and he "will be a father to you."[10]

Stewart's reasons for enrolling his sons in Tuskegee, however, were more complex than the assurance that Booker T. Washington would serve as their surrogate father. Tuskegee, though a relatively young black industrial college, had considerably more prestige than Claflin and, according to Stewart, a more impressive physical plant. "It is larger than Claflin, having 18 buildings on the grounds and several trade shops. Frederick Douglass delivered the annual oration there last year and says that it is one of the finest educational institutions in the South," Stewart wrote, clearly attempting to mollify his sons' disappointment.[11] Stewart believed that the black race's future was tied to the South. "There is something in Northern surroundings that takes manhood out of our young men," he informed McCants, and "I would rather see you a blacksmith like your grandfather, than a good for nothing northern tramp." He also believed that the matriculation of his sons at Tuskegee Institute, which within the space of a decade had gained a national reputation for its work, would accelerate their development as leaders. This belief may explain why Stewart informed McCants and Gilchrist that "I am not quite satisfied with your career at Claflin; but I have great hopes of your future." Moreover, the development of his sons as leaders of the race, Stewart argued, must be cultivated in the South. Stewart confided to Booker T. Washington that he hoped that his sons grew up in the South because, "I see very little hope for the Negro out of it."[12] Ironically, none of his three children remained in the South after completing their formal education, and none became blacksmiths.

Tuskegee Institute was eleven years old when McCants and Gilchrist Stewart entered the Middle B class in 1892. With Booker T. Washington serving as principal, the school already commanded respect throughout the nation and drew attention from around the world. Tuskegee's mission was personified in Washington himself, a former slave who believed zealously in hard work, frugality, sound character, and learning a trade. Stressing industrial education and the principles of modern farming, Tuskegee sought to mold its students into a class of independent black artisans and farmers who would become landowners, skilled tradesmen, and respected citizens. In the process of working their way up the economic ladder, these African-Americans, Washington believed, would gain the requisite tools for citizenship and, ultimately, the acceptance and esteem of whites.[13]

McCants Stewart rebelled against Tuskegee's rigid structure and adjusted slowly to the school's discipline. "I see no reason why you should be treated different from the other students," wrote Booker T. Washington after learning that Stewart was eating his meals at improper times. Two months later, Washington firmly rebuked Stewart: "I had hoped that after your promise to me that you would do so and try to make a man of yourself, but I am sorely disappointed." After denouncing Stewart's obstinate behavior, Washington threatened to notify the young student's father adding, "The trouble with you McCants is that you are determined to have your way in regard to everything that does not go to suit you." McCants's behavior finally resulted in his suspension for one semester. The heretofore rebellious student then reentered Tuskegee the following semester, modified his behavior, and graduated in 1896.[14]

Immediately after graduation, McCants moved to New York and enrolled in New York University for one year. He earned a law certificate in 1896 and worked as a legal assistant in his father's law practice. Yet McCants discovered that his father was as hard a taskmaster as Booker T. Washington. When Stewart invited McCants to join the family business, for example, he required a signed contract which specified in detail the terms of his son's employment and compensation: "Well, my intention is to pay you $3 per week to cover your fare, lunches; allow you 5% of all my fees; at 21, I shall make you Notary Public and put your name on the door." His son accepted the invitation. This arrangement revealed, among other things, that T. McCants Stewart had changed very little since his sons were children, continuing to rule his children with an iron fist. It also illustrated that McCants initially felt it necessary to remain under his father's protective wing, even after his graduation from Tuskegee.[15]

However, McCants quickly grew tired of his father's supervision. After one year, he left New York to enroll in the University of Minnesota Law School. He never revealed his reasons for choosing a northern school or a state with a small black population, but the presence of a former Tuskegee classmate and associate, Jay Moses Griffin, may have persuaded Stewart to enroll. McCants' attitude during his brief interlude in Minneapolis was characterized by maturity and a sense of purpose. He was a serious graduate student who excelled academically, wrote for the school newspaper, participated in moot court, and was an active member of the Kent Literary Society. McCants was also "acquainted with the printers trade" and an experienced player of the flute."[16]

In only one instance did local whites remind McCants of his race and the inferior status that African-Americans were accorded. A Minneapolis restaurant refused to serve him because of his race, the white proprietor charging that black customers had driven away his white patrons. The young law student filed a formal complaint with the assistant city attorney, who sued the establishment on the grounds that an 1897 state civil rights law prohibited racial discrimination in public accommodations. A jury of twelve white Minneapolis citizens agreed and convicted the proprietor of violating McCants Stewart's civil rights. However, this lone episode of racial bigotry, though deplorable, did not seem to taint McCants's law school experience or his residence in Minneapolis. When he completed his law degree in 1899, he was the second African-American at the University of Minnesota to have achieved that distinction. Two years later, he also earned an L.L.M. degree (master's degree of law) from the University of Minnesota Law School.[17]

When McCants arrived in Minneapolis in 1897, the Twin Cities could boast a small black professional and leadership class with attorneys, editors, ministers, businessmen, and railroad workers at its center. African-American political leaders such as J. Q. Adams and F. L. McGhee, who served on the executive committee of the Minnesota chapter of the National Afro-American Council, were respected community leaders. As business manager of the *Twin-City American* and, later, the *Afro-American Advance,* McCants was also a visible figure in the black community. In his first "public appearance" following his graduation from the University of Minnesota Law School, Stewart was invited to present an oration at a testimonial concert in honor of J. M. Griffin, editor of the *Afro-American Advance.* "As a speaker Mr. Stewart's future seems bright. His oration was excellent," noted the *Advance.* McCants worked to secure his bright future by taking every opportunity to participate in the city's African-American community. He spoke often at local black churches and occasionally debated topics of local and national interest with other African-American leaders.[18]

Despite his interest in establishing a legal practice in the Twin Cities, his admission to the state bar in 1899, and his community activism, McCants Stewart never successfully challenged the established professional and leadership class. William R. Morris, a black attorney who had migrated to Minneapolis in 1889 and organized the Minnesota Afro-American League in 1892 and the American Law Enforcement League in Minnesota in 1898, remained the preeminent black lawyer in the Twin Cities. Thus when the *Advance* published the names and photographs of the Twin Cities' most prominent black leaders in 1899, McCants Stewart was not included. Perhaps sensing that the competition was too keen in Minneapolis and St. Paul, Stewart moved to Portland, Oregon, in 1902, where he prepared to practice law.[19]

McCants never revealed his reason for selecting Portland over a city with a more substantial black population. However, by 1902, he had already demonstrated independence as well as a degree of impatience. He had also shown himself not only willing to take risks, but willing to disregard his father's advice. His decision to migrate to the Pacific Northwest was consistent with the rebelliousness, independence, and the stubborn determination he had exhibited since his Tuskegee years.[20]

T. McCants Stewart objected vehemently to his son's relocation to the Pacific Northwest and, three years later, was still urging McCants to reconsider: "But for the life of me, I can't see why you are 'using up' your life where you are." The elder Stewart felt that his son's professional career could be better served if he left the United States altogether. "Why not strike out for [the] Philippines," he suggested, "grow up with your new country and at 60 have your 'nest egg.'" McCants rejected his father's advice and remained in Portland, a luxury his financial independence allowed him. Admitted to the Oregon Bar Association in 1903, apparently without difficulty stemming from his race, he worked to build a successful legal practice and to earn the respect of the white legal community and black leadership. He practiced law in Portland for the next fourteen years.[21]

In August 1905, he returned to Minneapolis and married Mary Delia Weir, his college sweetheart. After a brief honeymoon, McCants returned to Portland, where he and Mary started a family. Although McCants's meddling father had hoped that his son and Mary would have a boy as their first child to carry on the family tradition of racial activism and service, and had even selected a suitable name, he was apparently only mildly disappointed with the arrival of his granddaughter, Katherine, in 1906.

In Oregon, as in Minnesota, the black population was small during the early twentieth century. However, two-thirds of black Oregonians resided in Portland. These blacks worked primarily as unskilled, menial laborers and service workers, although a smattering of black businesses had been established throughout the city.[22] Portland's black leadership also embraced the Washingtonian emphasis on industrial education, business enterprise, and self-help as the best means of racial advancement. "The [Portland] *New Age* had held all along that the solution to the race problem would come when the industrial and financial development of the Negro made him an integral part of the great commercial life of this nation," wrote the paper's editor, A. D. Griffin. A personal friend of Booker T. Washington, Griffin had established a chapter of the Washington-dominated Afro-American Council in Portland.[23]

As McCants settled into Portland's black community, he found it difficult to earn a decent living. Indeed, the odds of any black attorney succeeding in Oregon were formidable, given a black population that never reached 1 percent of the state's total before World War II. Custom dictated that whites rarely hired black attorneys, and the prevalence of unskilled laborers and service workers in Oregon's black population guaranteed a modest black trade. Thus McCants and other black attorneys in the West struggled. Stewart never purchased property in Portland, and most of his legal cases resulted in small fees.[24] Nor did Stewart's wife work outside of the home to help supplement his meager income, even though she was a graduate of the University of Minnesota and the Manning College of Music, Oratory, and Language and had earned a teaching certificate in the Minneapolis public schools.[25]

Despite the financial difficulties he faced, the young black attorney did not confine his Portland activities to advancing his legal career. McCants was active in promoting black journalism and in 1903 was one of the ten cofounders of the Portland *Advocate*, which lasted at least until 1933 and became the city's second oldest black newspaper. Stewart also lobbied the Oregon legislature in 1916 to repeal anachronistic and unenforced sections of the Oregon constitution that both prohibited the franchise and denied basic property rights to blacks. But the Portland *Oregonian* argued in an editorial that "both [laws] are relics of another age. Neither has the slightest force nor effect." Nonetheless, Stewart felt that the presence of these laws on the state's statute books was an affront to black Oregonians. His efforts to repeal them, however, proved unsuccessful.[26]

Although only fragments of information have survived concerning McCants's skill as an attorney, he was well respected, both among his legal colleagues and in the judicial community. Henry L. Benson, an associate justice of the Oregon Supreme Court, wrote that McCants "has established an exceptional record for industry and ability as a lawyer and his work before the Supreme Court has been commendable." Similarly, Oregon Circuit Judge John P. Kavanaugh praised McCants's work before the court: "His professional standing is excellent, and he enjoys the respect and confidence of the Bench and Bar." John H. Jones, judge of the District Court of Portland, was also laudatory. Stewart "has not only been a leader of his people but has proved himself in every way to be a man of worth, and a credit to this community," stated Jones. Finally, two of McCants's legal colleagues, of the Portland firm of Bernstein and Cohen, called the black attorney "a perfect gentleman, a good lawyer, and a fair opponent."[27]

However, McCants's early legal cases were unimpressive. Acting as a court appointed lawyer in 1903, he represented Charles Shanley in a larceny case. He argued that his client, whose guilt was beyond question, had perpetrated his crime as a result of unemployment and asked for the court's mercy. The court, however, convicted Shanley and sentenced him to serve "nine months work on the rockpile." Larceny cases appeared to be one of Stewart's specialties, for that same year he defended a Japanese client also charged with that crime. Despite a spirited defense, McCants's client was convicted. The following year Stewart represented a female client charged with assault with a dangerous weapon. The alleged victim, another woman, claimed that McCants's client had "tried to cut her heart out with a pocket-knife because she cussed her for making free with a man and a bucket of beer." The young attorney was more successful in this instance, for he convinced the jury that the victim, though shaken, had suffered no injury. His client was acquitted.[28]

The highlight of McCants's rather uneventful legal career involved a civil rights case, *Taylor v. Cohn*, which he argued successfully in 1906. The case involved a black Pullman porter, Oliver Taylor, who was denied box seating at Portland's Star Theater. When informed that the theater prohibited the seating of blacks in that section, Taylor refused to exchange his tickets and sued the establishment for $5,000. In his brief, McCants Stewart maintained that protecting the rights of blacks against discrimination was accepted as a matter of public policy, even though Oregon had not passed a civil rights bill. "We have always regarded our rights in every respect to have been secure," he argued. "So well founded has been our belief until we regard that legislation, known as civil rights law, which has been enacted in other states, to be unnecessary." Indeed, in some respects, Oregon was more racially progressive than many western states. Oregon state law did not segregate schools, housing, or public accommodations. Blacks served, however, in segregated military units throughout the state, and intermarriage between blacks and whites was prohibited. Nonetheless, the Portland *New Age* applauded Oregon's race relations when it editorialized, "In no other state are the colored people given more privileges and accorded more respect than in Oregon."[29]

The influential *Oregonian* sided with the theater's right to exclude blacks or any other race from its premises: "It is obvious that any place of public amusement would speedily lose patronage if it were not understood that certain discriminations might be made with reference to certain classes of people." Although the paper attempted to cloak its opinion in nonracial language, it showed contempt for blacks such as Oliver Taylor who crossed over the accepted social boundary in Oregon: "Colored people are wise who accept conditions that they cannot change or control, and go their way cheerfully, realizing that after all, their condition in this country is much improved over that of their ancestors of a century or two ago." Moreover, the editor asserted that "it is simply a well known fact" that whites object to sitting next to blacks. Hence, the Star Theater "must govern itself accordingly."[30]

The Oregon Supreme Court disagreed with the *Oregonian* and awarded McCants's client a favorable judgment. But McCants's victory in *Taylor v. Cohn* did not turn out to be the hoped-for boon to his legal career. "How is business now? Brisk?" his mother inquired. It was not. Business was as slow as ever and not likely to change in the foreseeable future. Searching for options, McCants attempted to supplement his income by purchasing stock in numerous companies, including the American Telephone Company, the Bonanza Queen Mining Company, and the Portland Coal and Development Company. Unfortunately, each company dissolved shortly after incorporation.[31]

McCants Stewart's early professional career and his collective civil rights activities reveal that he was strongly influenced by both the Washingtonians and the more militant positions of such northern black leaders as William Monroe Trotter and W. E. B. Du Bois. Stewart even lectured his former principal, Booker T. Washington, on the importance of business training and business education, especially the study of contracts and commercial law. Washington must have felt pleased that his former rebellious student had come to embrace the importance of business training as a prerequisite to business enterprise. Moreover, for two decades following his graduation from Tuskegee McCants continued to correspond with both Booker T. Washington and his wife, Margaret Murray Washington. On one occasion she wrote, "I certainly hope that you and those of you who have gone out from Tuskegee will not let the old flag trail in the dirt, but will remember that it is to you that we look for continued influence." McCants believed in Tuskegee's mission, and on occasion he lectured on behalf of his former school, presumably to raise funds. He was also appointed in 1908 by Oregon's Democratic governor, George Earle Chamberlain, as the state's representative to the National Negro Fair Association meeting in Mobile, Alabama, where he delivered a keynote address.[32]

While a Washingtonian, on the one hand, Stewart pressed for the abolition of Jim Crow laws in both the city of Portland and throughout the state of Oregon, and occasionally criticized segregation laws in southern states. Unlike many northern black leaders who espoused a more militant approach to solving racial problems, however, Stewart never broke with Booker T. Washington. He also avoided the inflammatory rhetoric of northern black leaders, perhaps partly to protect his professional career, and he never criticized Washington, publicly or privately. Taking the middle ground, Stewart believed that in order to achieve racial progress, industrial education and business enterprise must be combined with an assault upon white supremacy and segregation laws, an idea that his father had also embraced throughout his long public career.[33]

Yet McCants, on occasion, abandoned his cautious stance. In 1914 he publicly attacked President Woodrow Wilson for his failure to stop the widespread mob violence and lynching of African-Americans in the South. Following the lead of his father, who had condemned the Cleveland administration in the mid-1890s for its failure to halt the rising tide of segregation and racial violence against black southerners, McCants Stewart also attacked a Democratic president for his inept racial policies. McCants was particularly disturbed about a report that five African-Americans had been lynched in Shreveport, Louisiana, within a span of ten days, and he assailed Wilson for not taking a more aggressive approach to safeguarding the lives and civil liberties of blacks.[34]

McCants Stewart eventually attempted to take advantage of his numerous contacts in Oregon's political and legal community to gain a political appointment. His associates represented a cross section of Portland's legal, political, and ecclesiastical community. For example, he secured letters of recommendation from Henry L. Benson and Lawrence T. Harris, associate justices of the Oregon Supreme Court; Samuel White, president of the Oregon Bar Association; John P. Kavanaugh, Oregon Circuit Court judge; and the archbishop of Portland. An undisguised Republican, McCants found that his political support was also solicited by Oregon Circuit Court Judge John B. Cleland, and by C. B. Moore and Edward D. Baldwin of the Republican State Central Committee.[35]

Although McCants was respected among his white peers, he was not in a position to demand political favors of any magnitude. Furthermore, few blacks obtained significant political appointments. With the exception of A. D. Griffin, who was appointed sergeant-at-arms at a special session of the Oregon legislature, blacks were customarily appointed only to menial posts as janitors and porters in return for their loyalty to the GOP. The moderate *New Age*, a staunchly Republican paper, lamented the neglect of black Republican leaders and requested "something besides manipulating the brooms and cleaning spittoons" when the party doled out political patronage. Although McCants did receive a commission as a notary public, he never obtained a major political appointment. Similarly, his aspiration to become Portland's public defender in 1914 was naive, given the city's small black voting-age population and the reluctance of whites to vote for black candidates.[36]

In addition to the burden of supporting a wife and a child, several physical problems exacerbated Stewart's financial difficulties. In a freak accident he slipped while running to board a streetcar. One leg was severely mangled and required amputation. Shortly thereafter, Stewart began to have difficulty with his vision and feared he would ultimately lose his sight. While neither of these ailments halted Stewart's legal career, they did hurt his confidence and thereby hindered his struggling practice. Consequently, the black attorney was forced to rely on charity for a brief time; but he resumed his practice about a year after the accident, attempting once again to support himself, his wife, and his daughter.[37]

His inability to establish a successful legal career in Portland finally prompted McCants Stewart to relocate to San Francisco in 1917 leaving his family in Portland. He confessed that leaving Portland was not a difficult decision: "The business was not there [in Portland]—I stuck to it—lived in debt—starved and worried but it was not there." Surprisingly, though, he blamed not overt racial discrimination but rather Oregon's declining economy for his faltering legal practice. "We are suffering here in this section of the country. The slump seemingly has come to stay," McCants wrote to an old friend. Undoubtedly, though, racial discrimination in Portland's legal community had been a significant factor in his inability to earn a decent living. The fact that he was Portland's first black lawyer and that he was only able to attract a few white clients illustrated white racial attitudes. His reluctance to cite racial prejudice in explaining his difficulties may have been a holdover from the Washingtonian attitude that working hard, demonstrating impeccable character, and seeking the goodwill of whites would ultimately transcend racial prejudice. This reluctance may also have been in prideful recognition of how far he had come despite racial obstacles.[38]

In San Francisco, McCants formed a partnership with Oscar Hudson, a respected black attorney who was the first African-American admitted to membership in the San Francisco and California bar associations. Hudson had been admitted to the California bar in 1911 and also served with the Office of Adjutant, Colored California Volunteer Regiment.[39] Although he was broke when he arrived in San Francisco, he was optimistic that he could "ruff [*sic*] it and dig my way." He proclaimed the move "the beginning of a new chapter." Yet McCants's optimism was guarded. His rich and moving correspondence with his young daughter, Katherine, reveals a black professional who was experiencing considerable anxiety over his future and his ability to support his family in the new locale. He confided to Katherine, shortly after his arrival in San Francisco, that "everything is very quiet here at this time and no one seems to be making any money." McCants mentioned that he had only five dollars in his savings account, noting that, much like in Oregon, "the war is having its effect upon business conditions."[40] Even Katherine's innocent request for a watch was not only difficult for McCants to fulfill, but also stressful. Yet he assured Katherine, "I will do all in my power to get the watch for you. He [Papa] is not making much money here nor doing so very well."[41]

McCants's relocation to San Francisco in 1917 was the first time he had been separated from his family for a prolonged period, a situation that had been all too common with his own father but was nevertheless agonizing for him. He attempted to fill this void by writing to his wife and daughter on a regular basis. On one occasion, for example, he informed his daughter that "you must not feel slighted when you do not get a letter from me. I think of you all of the time and mean to write but just do not get the time—you know how I am always doing something even if there is no pay in it."[42] He also informed Katherine on that occasion that he had experienced "a howling nightmare last night," clearly a sign of the mounting anxiety, and that he had been busy seeking new clients. Although preoccupied with his work and the challenges that a new city offered, McCants promised to answer her letters promptly in the future and concluded his letter warmly: "My dear child, I must beg to remain and to be remembered as your loving and affectionate old pal and Pa."[43]

McCants kept his promise. The following month he informed Katherine that he had established an office in San Francisco's financial district and business had improved. He had taken on a divorce case since his last letter, he wrote, and represented another client who was incarcerated. Moreover, he had joined Oscar Hudson's family for Thanksgiving dinner, the first indication of a social engagement since his arrival in San Francisco.[44]

By the following spring, the Stewarts were still separated. McCants was dismayed that the family had remained apart for so long. Perhaps the long separation was evidence, to McCants, of his own inadequacy as a provider; perhaps it was also a painful reminder of the lengthy separations from his own father that he had endured as a child. But despite the painful separation, he took great pleasure in his daughter's progress in school: "I am so glad you made such good marks in school. Try and beat them this term." He thanked her for a box of food he had received recently and urged her to continue writing him regularly, for he had become homesick once again. "I hope you are sending me a letter today so that I may know what you have done today," McCants told his daughter.[45]

Like the earlier correspondence between T. McCants Stewart and his two sons when they attended Claflin University and Tuskegee Institute, the correspondence between McCants and Katherine transcended routine family matters and examined the spectrum of McCants Stewart's business affairs. Thus McCants, while never denying that Katherine was only a child, occasionally addressed her as an equal. One of his letters, for example, described a routine day to his daughter: "I did not get up until 10 o'clock this morning—shaved and hung about the room until noon and came here [to my office]. I'll stay here until 9 o'clock tonight—go to the room and get some sleep and be out early in the morning to Oakland and back by noon."[46] McCants seemed to feel compelled to share with Katherine some of the travails that he had experienced as a black professional, as his father had done with him. He also may have believed that a frank appraisal of his situation would contribute to Katherine's broader education and increase her racial awareness. Whatever his motivation, he did not shield Katherine entirely from the vicissitudes of his profession.

Even letters from Katherine, however, could not remove the pain of McCants's separation from his family. Nor did San Francisco offer the immediate financial success that he had hoped for. Despite his law practice, McCants had no steady source of income, and he instructed his wife and daughter to sell some of the household items from their Portland home in order to raise money. "As soon as the weather is good you and mother can sell our heating stove," he informed Katherine. He also begged Katherine to write soon. "Its all I can do to make myself stay here without you and mother—I feel just like coming right home." The following week he informed his daughter that "this is the first Easter Sunday I was ever away from you in your life and I hope it is the last." He continued to rebuke his daughter mildly for not writing promptly or keeping him apprised of family matters.[47]

The news that Katherine and Mary would be joining him in San Francisco in June 1918, after a separation of nearly eight months, did a great deal to lift McCants's sagging spirits. Illustrating a jovial side of his personality that was seldom evident in his formal correspondence, McCants asked Katherine playfully, "How would you like to walk down? Camp along the streams and rivers—the bears might get you!!!"[48] Kidding aside, McCants was still extremely anxious about his ability to support his family in San Francisco. At forty-one years of age, McCants had yet to distinguish himself as an attorney. He had received neither a political appointment nor an opportunity to work in an established law firm, either of which would have eased the financial pressure he faced daily. In 1918, for example, Stewart had applied at the assessor's office in Oakland, California, to be commissioned as a notary public, a position he had held in Portland and one in which he could occasionally expect to earn small fees. His application, however, was rejected. Even these minor political posts were exceedingly difficult for African-Americans to obtain in the San Francisco Bay area.[49]

In fact, the plight of the black professional in the San Francisco Bay area was little better than that in Portland. True, the Bay communities contained a larger black population and professional class than existed in Portland, but few African-Americans had succeeded in establishing lucrative careers. Not a single black teacher, policeman, or fire fighter was employed by either San

Francisco or Oakland in 1917, and civil service discrimination eliminated blacks from many white-collar jobs. Bay area hospitals did not permit black physicians to use their facilities, and black nurses were segregated in some nurse training programs and prohibited from entering others.[50] Similarly, black attorneys were barred from jobs as legal assistants, clerks, or partners in most white law firms throughout the Bay area. As Charles Houston, Howard University's dean of law, noted about black attorneys in general, "White offices are reluctant to take in young Negro law graduates and the Negro lawyers cannot afford to."[51]

Consequently, McCants's legal partnership was ill fated from the start. His partner, Oscar Hudson, lamented: "I had to make these extra trips on each pay day to collect what little we had coming, for I find, that if you do not collect what little we had coming on pay day you will not likely collect until the next pay day." Yet Hudson encouraged Stewart to be optimistic: "The field is here [in San Francisco] and you and I will work it out."[52]

Despite Hudson's assurances that conditions would improve, McCants grew more pessimistic each day that his legal practice would succeed. Moreover, his vision deteriorated further, and he feared that blindness was imminent. In resignation and despair, the forty-one year old attorney committed suicide on April 14, 1919, leaving behind a family and numerous debts. His suicide note, addressed not to his wife and daughter but rather to his legal partner, was brief: "I am going blind. I am going to cash in. I cannot stand it any longer."[53]

McCants Stewart's struggles demonstrate poignantly that opportunities were restricted for black attorneys in western cities because of exclusion, racial discrimination, and the small black population. During the early decades of the century, neither Portland nor San Francisco had African-American communities sizable enough to support a class of black attorneys; and nor did Oakland, Los Angeles, or Seattle.[54] "I note what you say about prejudice in your professional life," T. McCants Stewart wrote in 1908, attempting to console his son, but "you can't escape it—not anywhere."[55] Barred from most white law firms, black attorneys were forced to form partnerships with other African-Americans and generally to rely on black clients, who compensated them poorly if at all. Although a few gained political appointments, the majority, like McCants Stewart, were fortunate to scratch out even a modest living. Economic opportunity for blacks may have existed in the West in unskilled jobs, personal service, and menial labor, despite competition from the Chinese and other immigrants.

But the success of black professionals demanded a more egalitarian racial climate and larger and more economically stable black communities similar to those in Cleveland, Chicago, or Milwaukee. Thus historian W. Sherman Savage's conclusion that "the West has given blacks an opportunity to make a better life for themselves" is not substantiated by the experiences of black professionals in western cities such as Portland and San Francisco during the early decades of the twentieth century.[56]

McCants Stewart's life and ordeal suggest that racial lines had hardened in Portland, San Francisco, Seattle, and Los Angeles by the early twentieth century. This was particularly true in employment, though racial lines were also drawn more firmly in housing and public accommodations in some western cities. As organized labor and trade unions gained strength in some western urban centers, black workers began to lose ground. Thus the economic fluidity that nineteenth-century black pioneers experienced and benefited from during the early histories of Seattle, Portland, and San Francisco had waned by the time of McCants Stewart's death in 1919. Racial discrimination, increasing economic competition between black and white workers, and the growth of the black western urban population resulted in racial patterns and attitudes similar to those found in northern and eastern cities. Collectively, these factors, as McCants Stewart and other African-American professionals discovered, made the challenge of being an effective "race leader" a particularly difficult one in the Far West.[57]

7

Gilchrist Stewart

Forgotten Black Leader in the Age of

Booker T. Washington

❖ ❖ ❖ ❖ ❖ ❖ ❖ ❖ ❖ ❖ ❖ ❖ ❖ ❖ ❖

Gilchrist Stewart was one of the most promising young black leaders in the nation in 1911. An attorney, politician, and civil rights activist, Stewart had distinguished himself for his work in behalf of the Constitution League, an interracial civil rights organization, and by conducting an investigation of the 1906 Brownsville riot. He was also one of the most active members of the New York branch of the National Association for the Advancement of Colored People (NAACP) during its formative years. By the time of his death in 1926, however, he had been largely forgotten. Gilchrist Stewart's life and professional career illuminate many of the national civil rights issues that local black leaders embraced between 1900 and 1915 as well as the relationship between local leaders and prominent national leaders. His life also illustrates how T. McCants Stewart's youngest son, despite financial difficulties and personal adversity, attempted to fulfill the Stewart family tradition of service and racial obligation. Finally, his life serves as a painful reminder of the hardships that African-American professionals faced daily in American society as they attempted to establish careers, support their families, and contribute to their communities.[1]

Born in 1879 in Orangeburg, South Carolina, Gilchrist Stewart, the second child of T. McCants and Charlotte Stewart, was reared, along with his brother McCants, in this quaint southern rural community.[2] Little is known about his formative years; however, Gilchrist, together with his older brother McCants, was educated to lead and to uplift the race. This had been the expectation for both of T. McCants Stewart's sons, and this demand was nonnegotiable. Yet most of Gilchrist's early parenting came not from his father's firm hand, but rather from his mother. Charlotte Harris Stewart raised her three children during her husband's frequent absences from home, although she relied heavily upon the support of her parents in nearby Columbia.[3]

In 1892, at the age of thirteen, two years shy of the mandatory fifteen years of age that the school required, Gilchrist entered the Middle B class, a preparatory program, at Tuskegee Institute. An allowance was no doubt made in Gilchrist's case because of the close personal friendship that his father, T. McCants Stewart, had established with Booker T. Washington, and because his older brother, McCants, was enrolling at the same time.[4] Gilchrist's tenure at Tuskegee was probably typical for male students at the college during the 1890s. Despite his initial objections to attending Tuskegee, he proved to be a very competent student. He did, however, have trouble adjusting to the rigorous discipline of Booker T. Washington, admittedly no easy task. Washington's strict code of conduct governed the behavior of students and faculty alike. Students, for example, could not drink, smoke, dance, possess firearms, gamble, play cards, or leave the school grounds without permission. Courtship rules were so restrictive that boys could not escort girls home from chapel on Sunday evenings. And though they were not always followed to the letter, Tuskegee's rules, noted Louis Harlan, were "particularly oppressive because the discipline there was so rigorous that it allowed few safety valves in its restraint of natural impulses." Yet Gilchrist, who was known affectionately on Tuskegee's campus as the "little corporal," overstepped these boundaries on at least two occasions. In one instance, he was taken before the faculty on unspecified charges and, in another, he was "read out in chapel" for violating school rules.[5]

Gilchrist's behavior at Tuskegee was neither unusual for college students nor for a boy of thirteen. Compared to his older brother McCants, who was expelled from Tuskegee for one semester for repeatedly violating school regulations, his behavior was exemplary. "Chris [Gilchrist] is in line with our plans," his father informed Booker T. Washington after receiving a disturbing report concerning the behavior of McCants, "but Mac [McCants] kicks." Although the boys' adolescent rebellion both embarrassed and angered T. McCants Stewart, he still had great expectations for his sons, and reminded them that their "li[ves] will honor and ornament the family and the race. So never forget that."[6]

The Middle B class curriculum, taught over three terms during the course of a nine-month semester, consisted of courses in alegebra, U.S. history, composition, literature, physical geography, physiology, and botany. In addition, students were required to take drawing and vocal music, regardless of whether they had an aptitude in either. Tuskegee also expected students to participate in rhetorical discussions on a weekly basis and to attend informal talks on current events. No student was excused from manual labor, for Booker T. Washington insisted that academic learning and manual labor must go hand in hand in order to produce a well-rounded student. "Some manual labor is required of all, for the purpose of discipline and instruction, and of teaching the dignity of labor," noted the 1893 school catalogue.[7]

Unlike his older brother McCants, who followed Tuskegee's most rigorous academic program, Gilchrist hoped to become a dairy farmer. The dairying major at Tuskegee consisted of a structured two-year program and combined practical knowledge of a growing industry with solid academic courses. The first year of study, for example, included classes in the scientific work of the dairy industry, cleaning and ventilating dairy barns, grooming, bedding, and milking cows, the care of cows and calves, and the extermination of ticks and lice. The program's second year offered more of the same but also covered different breeds of dairy cattle, the treatment of sick cattle, the specialized study of both raw and cooked dairy products, and an exploration of the future of Alabama's dairy industry.[8]

After graduating from Tuskegee with a degree in dairy science in 1895, one year before his brother McCants, Gilchrist, at the age of sixteen, was expected to support himself and to make his own way. Indeed, the young Tuskegee graduate worked briefly at several jobs in the dairy industry and, wishing to expand his knowledge of the industry and enhance his future employment prospects, attended the University of Wisconsin for graduate study in dairy science. This decision paid almost immediate dividends, for Gilchrist's academic training and personal contacts at Tuskegee and the University of Wisconsin helped him obtain employment at Hoard's dairy at Fort Atkinson, Wisconsin. There he reportedly managed one of the largest creameries in the United States. For reasons that are unclear, Gilchrist left his position in the Wisconsin dairy industry and moved to Brookins, South Dakota. He taught there for one year in the dairy department at the South Dakota Agricultural College and later at Ontario Agricultural College at Guelph, Ontario. Finding little satisfaction in a career as either a dairyman or professor, Gilchrist moved to Honolulu, Hawaii, where his father had relocated to practice law and enter politics in 1898. Gilchrist remained in Hawaii until 1903, where he worked briefly as a census enumerator. Restless, immature, still uncertain about his future, and perhaps sensing that he had no future if he remained in Hawaii, Gilchrist moved to New York in 1903. As his brother McCants had done before him, Gilchrist attended New York University Law School. Although he did not graduate from the prestigious school, he opened a law office in New York City.[9]

Stewart divided his time in New York between law, politics, and a variety of odd jobs that he did for small fees. Like numerous black attorneys throughout the nation, Stewart had difficulty supporting himself and maintaining a legal practice, so he formed a partnership with Clark Smith, another African-American attorney.[10] Gilchrist still managed to amass a large debt, by living beyond his means and investing in several unprofitable business ventures, a habit he had unfortunately inherited from his father. As early as 1900, for example, Gilchrist informed Booker T. Washington from Sioux Falls, South Dakota, shortly before he sailed to Hawaii, that he was "almost penniless" due to a recent bank failure. He assured Washington, nonetheless, that he would mail his financial pledge to Tuskegee as soon as his business affairs were in order.[11] He never fulfilled that obligation. Similarly, Gilchrist wrote Washington's personal secretary, Emmett Scott, to seek advice about the African Union Company, which invested in gold mines. Gilchrist informed Scott, however, that he was unlikely to invest in this company, although he had been advised to do so, because of the numerous poor investments he had made in recent years. "I don't go strong on these stock propositions," he wrote to Scott. "I have one little drawer that I am looking at now that is full of worthless stock."[12]

Blaming his predicament on bad timing rather than poor management or his own ineptitude, Gilchrist Stewart believed that he was only one step away from making a lucrative financial deal or arguing an important legal case that would transform his career. In reality, however, Gilchrist was not a brilliant attorney. He supplemented his sporadic legal income by working as a real estate broker and managing a small business that cleaned local restaurants and office buildings. He continued to mismanage his personal finances throughout his life. "I could weep over him if it were worthwhile," wrote his aunt Verina Morton-Jones, a respected Brooklyn physician and racial activist.[13] T. McCants Stewart also believed that Gilchrist deserved the blame for the majority of his problems because he lacked focus, drifting aimlessly from one job to another. "I wish Chris would settle down," he wrote his eldest son McCants.[14]

T. McCants Stewart also disapproved of his son's pursuit of a political career, which he felt was a waste of time and talent. Gilchrist, he argued, should have remained in the dairy business, drawing upon his education and practical training at Tuskegee and the University of Wisconsin. He believed, moreover, that Gilchrist was unwilling to make the sacrifices and commitment required to establish a career. "He is not frank, and I cannot connect with him," lamented T. McCants Stewart. "But I am trying to get him down to business."[15] Two years later, T. McCants remained agitated that Gilchrist had made few inroads into a stable career and offered his frank assessment: "As to Chris, he is no good. Not unlucky. He lacks character."[16] Although these were strong words for a father to use in describing his son, T. McCants Stewart never wavered in his low opinion of Gilchrist. No matter how much prominence his son attained later, he was always a failure in the eyes of his father. "Boy, I am proud of you," the stern patriarch wrote to McCants with warmth and compassion. But he never exchanged words of this sort with Gilchrist, and the bond between them remained strained throughout their lives.[17]

Gilchrist Stewart was far more successful as a politician and civil rights activist than as an attorney or businessman. He was considerably more active in protest campaigns than either his brother McCants or his sister Carlotta, joining the Constitution League, Niagara Movement, and the NAACP. Stewart played an important role in the activities of these organizations during their formative years and gained the respect of some of the most prominent civil rights leaders in the nation, including Joel Spingarn, W. E. B. Du Bois, T. Thomas Fortune, William Monroe Trotter, John E. Milholland, and Mary Church Terrell.[18]

The Constitution League, an interracial civil rights organization established in 1906 by John E. Milholland, had a strong affiliation with the Republican party and the Niagara Movement and also aligned briefly with the NAACP. Both organizations rejected the racial accommodation of Booker T. Washington and pushed militantly to achieve full equality for African-Americans. Gilchrist Stewart's decision to join an organization opposed to

Booker T. Washington was probably an error in judgment, for Washington had served as a surrogate father, and Gilchrist had continued to write Washington following his graduation from Tuskegee requesting advice, counsel, and an occasional political favor.[19] Aware that Gilchrist was an accomplished speaker and political organizer, and that the New York Republican Campaign Committee had sent him in 1904 on a speaking tour in the West to discuss the "Philippine question" in the wake of the Spanish-American War, Milholland asked Stewart to investigate the 1906 Brownsville riot on behalf of the Constitution League.[20]

The Brownsville affair was a particularly important case for the Constitution League because it drew national attention and served in many respects as a test case for this embryonic civil rights organization.[21] It involved the dismissal of three companies of black infantrymen who were discharged without honor after an alleged raid and shooting spree in Brownsville, Texas. The soldiers were dismissed by President Theodore Roosevelt without the benefit of a trial or public hearing.[22]

Despite a lackluster career prior to this time, Gilchrist Stewart took his charge from Milholland seriously. Indeed, the enormity and significance of this task seemed to awaken dormant qualities he had not shown heretofore. Like Ulysses S. Grant, a former quartermaster in the United States army who had compiled an undistinguished military record prior to 1861 but discovered that Civil War combat stimulated unacknowledged qualities of leadership and decisiveness, Gilchrist Stewart also exceeded all expectations of his ability.[23] He conducted a thorough investigation and interviewed local residents and black soldiers in Brownsville, Texas, and Fort Reno, Oklahoma, where the soldiers were sent following the alleged riot. Gilchrist's detailed investigation concluded that much of the evidence against the soldiers was "flimsy" and that President Roosevelt should not have discharged them without honor.[24] Emboldened, the Constitution League circulated Gilchrist's findings. The report was eventually read by Ohio senator Joseph B. Foraker, who was also convinced that black soldiers at Brownsville had neither plotted a conspiracy nor rioted against the townspeople. Foraker laid the Constitution League's findings before the Military Affairs Committee of the U.S. Senate and scheduled hearings before that same body in February 1907.[25]

The Foraker committee hearings were followed widely by black leaders throughout the nation. The Reverend Francis J. Grimké, perhaps the most distinguished black minister in the nation, wrote: "Again you have placed the whole colored race under an additional debt to you for your masterly defense of the colored soldiers in your great speech before the Senate yesterday. As a race we can never forget you." Despite Foraker's resolve to correct this miscarriage of justice, the Senate hearings had no impact on Theodore Roosevelt's decision to dismiss the black soldiers. Instead of exonerating these men as Foraker had hoped, they actually strengthened Roosevelt's resolve that they were guilty and that his decision to dismiss the black troops had been the proper one.

Despite its unfavorable outcome, Gilchrist's investigation into the Brownsville episode was significant. Gilchrist Stewart, wrote historian Louis R. Harlan, "was one of the earliest persons to reach what is now the generally accepted conclusion, that the two black regiments dismissed from the Army for alleged rioting were innocent."[26] Thus, despite the contention of Roosevelt and his secretary of war, William Howard Taft, that both black regiments were guilty, and despite the opinion of such prominent black leaders as Booker T. Washington and W. E. B. Du Bois that some of the soldiers were probably guilty as charged, Stewart never deviated from his findings that the black soldiers at Brownsville were innocent of all charges and that the punishment meted out to them was arbitrary and unfair.[27]

Stewart's investigation for the Constitution League enhanced his visibility nationally and his status within the Republican party as a political organizer. He was chosen to serve, for example, on several Republican party councils and caucuses and informed Booker T. Washington that he was "often times the only colored man [present]."[28] Stewart's political activities were also praised by William Monroe Trotter and T. Thomas Fortune, two of the leading African-American editors in the nation. Fortune, the editor of the New York *Age*, supported Stewart and the anti–Theodore Roosevelt faction in the Republican party in the 1906 primary election in New York.[29]

While Gilchrist Stewart's work was applauded in some circles within black leadership and the Republican party, he was roundly criticized in others as an opportunist. Charles W. Anderson, a prominent black politician in New York and Booker T. Washington's closest northern confidant, charged that Gilchrist had attempted to replace him as the major black political organizer for the Republican party in his state.[30] There was more than a grain of truth to Anderson's accusation, for Gilchrist's political savvy had earned him a position on the advisory committee of the Colored Republican Club in New York, and he had gained a wide political following as a result of his work in the Constitution League. Yet as early as 1904, he had been named as a delegate to the Republican state convention at Saratoga to line up the black vote. He had also been selected by the Republican party as "captain at large" of one of the largest black districts in New York, and some of his political associates had encouraged him to run for alderman.[31] Gilchrist Stewart's political career looked especially bright in 1904.

Yet his participation in the Constitution League and, later, in the Niagara Movement placed him in an awkward position. The Constitution League had become much more militant in the defense of civil rights and racial equality, openly criticizing Booker T. Washington's accommodationist philosophy.[32] So Gilchrist faced a dilemma. Loyal to Washington, he was torn by the direction in which the Constitution League, in particular, had drifted. As a demonstration of his loyalty to Washington, he informed him and Emmett Scott periodically of the Constitution League's activities. Although Stewart acknowledged that the league opposed Washington's ideas by 1906, he urged Washington that he should, nonetheless, remain an active member of the organization. If he remained a member, Gilchrist wrote, "I think that I can be of more valuable assistance in turning the rudder the other way."[33] Gilchrist also informed Washington that certain leaders in New York were pressuring him to denounce the Tuskegee president, a "position I have never taken or will I ever take." Stewart pledged he "never has joined or intend[ed] to join" any organization opposed to Washington."[34] For the moment, then, Stewart worked both sides of the fence, playing an active role in the Constitution League and serving as an informant to Washington regarding the league's activities.

Gilchrist's assurance to Washington that he had not and would not join an organization opposed to his ideas was disingenuous, for he had already embraced the radical Niagara Movement, a militant civil rights movement organized by W. E. B. Du Bois and a precursor to the NAACP. He also joined the New York branch of the NAACP during its formative years and played an important role in several campaigns to secure racial justice for black New Yorkers. Gilchrist and Joel E. Spingarn, for example, were featured jointly as the NAACP's "Men of the Month" in August 1911, and W. E. B. Du Bois praised Gilchrist's leadership and civil rights activities in *Crisis* magazine. "He has been identified with a good many movements for the betterment of the condition of the colored people on the west side," reported the *Crisis,* and the magazine praised Gilchrist's effective work as executive chairman of the NAACP's vigilance committee, which made sure that the city's laws concerning racial justice and equality were enforced. Gilchrist expected, perhaps naively, that his leadership and service would lead to his selection as the NAACP's national secretary. He wrote privately that he was better qualified for the position than anyone within the association, including W. E. B. Du Bois. His inflated ego notwithstanding, Gilchrist Stewart did play an active and important role in the NAACP's early history.[35]

Gilchrist's association with the Niagara Movement, Constitution League, and the NAACP made Washington understandably suspicious. Washington followed Gilchrist's activities in these organizations largely through Charles W. Anderson, who urged him to not be deceived by Stewart's professed loyalty. Anderson, who disliked Gilchrist personally, informed Washington in 1906 that Gilchrist, "who has been on the road for the Constitution League, is now at work in this city [New York], trying to get some of the local Colored Republican Clubs to go over to the League. He is their organizer."[36] Similarly, Anderson wrote Washington that Gilchrist Stewart had attended a speech by W. E. B. Du Bois promoting the Niagara Movement, a clear indication, as far as Anderson was concerned, that Stewart had broken with Washington. If these events did not convince Washington that Gilchrist no longer believed in his accommodationist philosophy, Anderson, clearly intending to fuel the fire, mentioned some disparaging personal remarks that Gilchrist had made about Washington. "I think he [Washington] is now altogether convinced of the true character of this fellow," Anderson confided to Emmett Scott. Although Washington never broke with Stewart publicly over these events, much to Anderson's regret, he probably considered Stewart both friend and foe, and certainly someone who was moving in a more militant direction.[37] In the meantime, he kept a close eye on his former student.

Washington had another reason to be distrustful of Gilchrist. He had raised money on at least one occasion in Tuskegee's name for his own personal use. While not the first Tuskegee graduate to commit this type of fraud, the news was particularly troubling to Washington because of his close relationship with Gilchrist's father. This incident explains, in part, why Gilchrist wrote Emmett Scott in 1914 about his relationship with Washington: "Ever since I was at Tuskegee the last time there has been a growing coldness between us—until I cease to hear from him at all."[38] Although Washington never used his vast influence to hurt Gilchrist's political or civil rights career as he did with many of his rivals, he was known as a man who held grudges. It is unlikely that he ever forgot the incident.

Gilchrist's personal life was as unstable as his political career and contributed to his declining health and, ultimately, his premature death. By his own admission, he was grossly overweight and in poor physical condition by the time he had reached his early thirties. When his close friend Joel Spingarn suggested, for example, that he would be a good candidate for the segregated officers' training school established in 1917 in Des Moines, Iowa, and supported by the NAACP, he demurred: "I don't think I could stand the training. For ten years I have done no [physical] work or exercised any. I have a pouch that weighs fifty of my one hundred and ninety-six pounds. My muscles are flabby and soft. In other words, I have been almost a creature of luxury." At 5 feet 8 inches tall and nearly 200 pounds, Gilchrist had little chance to qualify for any branch of the armed forces, and his poor physical condition stood in stark contrast to that of his father, who reported excellent health throughout his long life. He also expressed some reservations about the segregated training camp and informed Spingarn that the white leader's endorsement of the segregated facility was being "widely misunderstood and criticized" in numerous cities Stewart had visited.[39]

Unlike his brother McCants, who married his college sweetheart, Gilchrist never married. The instability of his legal and political career and his early drifting from one job to another mitigated against starting a family. But the instability of Stewart's employment alone does not explain his desire to remain single, for the majority of African-Americans worked in unskilled and menial jobs at this time, and their lowly wages, though an impediment, did not prevent most from marrying. Rather, Gilchrist Stewart, a handsome man, though a bit rotund, and a smart dresser, with charm, wit, and the gift of gab, chose to remain single for a more complex and vexing reason: he had fallen in love with Cecilia Cianci, a woman of Italian descent employed as a secretary in his New York law office. "To have married the girl he loved," wrote Katherine Stewart Flippin, Stewart's niece, "would have been to disgrace his family and ruin his career."[40] Alice Franklin Stewart concurred, writing succinctly to Carlotta Stewart that "it would be social suicide" if Gilchrist and Cecilia Cianci married.[41] Indeed, interracial marriages, although legal in New York and in many northeastern and New England states, were not advisable for an African-American professional who had his career, family, and social circle to consider. And even though Gilchrist's sister Carlotta married interracially, her husband was a man of Chinese ancestry rather than of European descent, and they lived in the territory of Hawaii, a more racially tolerant society than the mainland.[42]

Gilchrist Stewart's sudden and unexpected death from what the newspapers called "acute indigestion" in August 1926, while attending a national convention of the Elks lodge in Cleveland, Ohio, rendered the potential storm regarding his relationship with Cianci moot. Although in poor health, Gilchrist attended the convention against the advice of his personal physician. He had hoped to demonstrate to his fraternal brothers that if elected by the national membership he could manage a prominent position. He also hoped that an important position within a national lodge would help his struggling legal practice and his stagnant political career by showcasing his talents before a broader constituency. Disregarding the advice of his doctor, however, proved to be fatal. Gilchrist Stewart dropped dead in the street during a welcoming parade.[43]

Gilchrist's life, tragic in some respects, reveals much about black leadership and racial strategies in the early 1900s. He demonstrated tremendous promise early in his career, yet never fulfilled his potential due to the difficult circumstances he faced. In that regard, his life was probably typical of black leadership on the local and state level during the late nineteenth and early twentieth centuries. Thus his career illuminates an important strata of leadership that has received only marginal consideration by historians.[44]

Gilchrist Stewart's political and civil rights activities also reveal a wide range of contacts with prominent black and white leaders as well as his role in such prominent organizations as the Constitution League, Niagara Movement, and the NAACP. Through these associations, Stewart played an important role as a political organizer for the Republican party in the state of New York, as a spokesman for his local constituency in the New York branch of the NAACP, and as a radical voice for African-Americans across the nation. His successful tenure as chair of the NAACP's vigilance committee was a component in shaping the organization's aggressive legal strategy, a strategy that characterized the civil rights organization throughout much of its history. Yet Gilchrist Stewart's most enduring contribution remains the important investigation he conducted for the Constitution League in the wake of the 1906 Brownsville riot. His findings revealed that every African-American soldier dismissed at Brownsville by President Roosevelt was innocent of all charges. Moreover, the U.S. War Department, he concluded, had conducted its investigation hastily and lacked the evidence to prove its case. More than six decades after Stewart conducted his investigation, the United States government acknowledged officially that it had erred in this case and granted each of the soldiers an honorable discharge and an apology.[45]

Yet Gilchrist's political and civil rights career stagnated after 1912, and he never measured up to this early promise. Overshadowed by a domineering father whose respect and admiration he could never obtain, he sought friendship and counsel with his former Tuskegee principal, Booker T. Washington, and his close associate, Emmett Scott. But neither Washington nor Scott could provide the friendship and support that Gilchrist demanded of them, particularly in light of his evolving radicalism. In fact, his active affiliation with the Constitution League, Niagara Movement, and the NAACP placed him in direct opposition to the accommodationist philosophy of Washington. Thus Gilchrist's life and public career illuminate several interrelated themes: the plight of black leadership on the local and state level; the dynamics of interracial organizations during the early twentieth century; the pressure exerted by a demanding father who expected his son to become a great leader but found it virtually impossible to express his love; and the interaction and infighting among black leadership on the local and national levels. Finally, Gilchrist's life, despite its travails, reveals the sense of duty, obligation, and mission that T. McCants Stewart had instilled in his son. Regardless of his difficult personal circumstances, Gilchrist Stewart never shirked his responsibility to serve the race, to improve the African-American community, and to assist those less fortunate than himself.

8

Carlotta Stewart Lai

An African-American Teacher in the Territory of Hawaii

❖ ❖ ❖ ❖ ❖ ❖ ❖ ❖ ❖ ❖ ❖ ❖ ❖ ❖ ❖

When T. McCants Stewart left Hawaii in 1905, his daughter Carlotta decided not to follow her peripatetic father. She remained in Hawaii for the rest of her life, defying the odds and overcoming racial prejudice against black professional women by becoming an accomplished teacher and principal, by living in integrated communities, by marrying interracially, and by building a multiracial network of friends and associates on the islands of Oahu and Kauai. Though she was occasionally troubled with misgivings, Carlotta Stewart was convinced that she had made the correct decision. She believed that the impediments to a professional career for black females were far fewer in Hawaii than on the mainland.[1] Carlotta's lengthy residence in Hawaii, from 1898 to 1952, reveals that some African-American women were willing to sacrifice the familiarity of large black communities and the companionship of their families for economic autonomy and the opportunity to earn respect in their chosen profession. It also provides a rich mosaic by which to examine the African-American female experience in perhaps the most multiracial location in the Pacific and to test the conclusions of many early writers and scholars that Hawaii was a melting pot with virtually no racial problem.[2]

Carlotta Stewart was eighteen when she accompanied her father to Hawaii in 1898, probably at his urging, to continue her education and to begin planning her future. The third child of T. McCants Stewart and Charlotte

Pearl Harris, Carlotta was born September 16, 1881, in Brooklyn, New York, where she attended public schools and spent her formative years.[3] Even though there is no record of her initial impressions upon landing in Hawaii, she could hardly avoid being struck by the contrast between Hawaii and her native Brooklyn. Few black women had come to the islands during the nineteenth century. Although Betsey Stockton, the first reported black female, had arrived in Hawaii in 1823 to work with Christian missionaries, the majority of black settlers had been males. Yet Stewart's experience in Hawaii was different from black female immigrants in another significant respect. Although she made periodic trips to the mainland to visit her family and relatives, Carlotta remained in the islands to complete her education, pursue a professional career as a teacher and principal, and to settle permanently.[4]

Hawaii had been in the throes of profound change in virtually every area of its society between 1874 and 1898. The monarchy had been toppled during the reign of Queen Lilioukalani, and on January 17, 1893, the Hawaiian Kingdom officially came to an end. Shortly thereafter, a provisional government headed by Judge Sanford B. Dole was established. Dole used his influence to push through a new constitution, and on July 4, 1894, the Republic of Hawaii was created. The new Hawaiian constitution, to no one's surprise, named Dole as president, a position he held for six years. In 1898, Hawaii was formally annexed by the United States, and in 1900 President William McKinley appointed Dole Hawaii's first governor.[5]

During the same period, the population of the islands almost doubled, increasing from 57,000 in 1872 to 109,000 in 1896. Honolulu's population alone rose 100 percent during these years, creating congestion and the need for additional services. As a result, Hawaii began to modernize, establishing a new water supply system and street railway system to serve the growing population. Waikiki had only recently become a popular resort for tourists, and the district's first hotel, which was short-lived, was constructed in 1884. Aware that the islands' natural beauty was a potentially powerful magnet for throngs of visitors from around the world, the islanders organized a tourist bureau in 1892. But even the most carefully charted Hawaiian vacation presented formidable challenges, since roads into exotic areas, if they existed at all, were rugged. Prior to the 1880s, a trip to the volcano of Kilauea, one of Hawaii's greatest attractions, wrote historian Ralph Kuykendall, "required fortitude." The journey began by sailing to Hilo, "and from there on horseback over a rugged trail which struggled up thirty miles through the forest and lava to a very primitive hotel near the edge of the crater." Not until the mid-1880s did local steamship companies provide more efficient service to Hawaii's largest island to permit the growing tourist trade to witness this spectacular sight.[6]

The Hawaiian economy had also undergone a profound transformation. The whaling industry, dominant for many decades, was in sharp decline and being supplanted by sugar. Indeed, much of Hawaii's economic future appeared tied to sugar production. Between 1855 and 1857, when whaling was still the dominant industry, the islands' annual sugar production averaged only 500,000 pounds. By the early 1870s, Hawaii exported more than 19 million pounds of sugar annually, a thirty-seven-fold increase from the export levels of the 1850s, and the demand for this agricultural commodity appeared inexhaustible. Between 1874 and 1898, the area of land in Hawaii devoted exclusively to sugar cane production increased tenfold, from 12,225 acres to 125,000 acres. More importantly, sugar cane production had become more efficient, for an acre of sugar cane in 1898 produced twice as much sugar as an acre had produced in 1874. Thus, the islands' economic future looked especially bright.[7]

Despite its beauty and bustling economy, Hawaii was a peculiar setting for a young black woman from Brooklyn. Although her father had spent several years in Liberia, Carlotta had never traveled outside of the continental United States before coming to Hawaii. And while her brothers, McCants and Gilchrist, had attended Tuskegee Institute, Carlotta had lived with her father following a bitter divorce from his first wife.[8]

The first record of Carlotta's activities in Hawaii stems from 1902. In that year, she graduated from Oahu College (Punahou School). The *Oahuan*, the school annual, noted that Carlotta, one of eight members in the senior class, had completed one year at the school, had been a member of the literary society, and had played on the girl's basketball team. Apparently she had been assimilated into the school and accepted by her peers. Moreover, the excellent education she received at the college prepared her for a white-collar career. The course of study at Oahu College included classes in philosophy, religion, English, Latin, Greek, French or German, history, economics, mathematics, and science. After graduation, Carlotta completed the requirements for a Normal School certificate, which she received in 1902. In July of that year she accepted a teaching position in the Practice Department of the Normal School. Carlotta remained at the school for several years, where she taught English, her major at Oahu College. Her name appears in the biennial *Report of the Superintendent of Public Instruction to the Governor of the Territory of Hawaii* between 1902 and 1924.[9]

Though surviving records do not provide a detailed account of Carlotta's professional career, they do offer insight into the opportunities and challenges that a black professional woman faced in Hawaii during the early twentieth century. For example, Carlotta's annual salary in 1902 of $660 placed her comfortably in the black middle class in both Hawaii and on the mainland.[10] Within four years, her salary had increased to $900, which she supplemented by typing during her spare time.[11] By 1908, her salary had reached $100 per month, providing not only a comfortable standard of living, but also the means to travel throughout the islands and occasionally to the mainland by ocean steamer to visit relatives. Thus Carlotta enjoyed a degree of security and independence that few black or white working women had achieved by the early twentieth century. And since her salary exceeded the annual salary of some other black professionals, including nurses, she was able to provide limited financial assistance to her mother and two brothers.[12]

The young African-American teacher had also established a network of close friendships and created an active social life. "Sometimes I get quite blue not having a single relative in the Islands," she wrote her oldest brother, McCants, in 1906. "I soon get over it, for I have such good friends. I want for nothing."[13] She informed McCants during the 1906 school year that in addition to teaching, she was busy with classes, vacations, camping, surfing, and frequent parties. "We took in two dances a week at the Seaside Hotel [in Honolulu] and played cards at home the other evenings or made up moonlight bathing parties," she boasted. Carlotta also attended Sunday baseball games on the islands and served as coach of the junior and senior female teams in her local community.[14] Carlotta's career advancement, her acceptance in the larger Hawaiian community, and her strong friendships were pivotal factors in her decision to remain in Hawaii following her father's departure in 1905. The frequency with which she reported attending social functions also reveals that she was accepted into the social circles of her middle-class peers. Carlotta's exuberant descriptions of these events also reveal an outgoing, jovial side of her personality that contrasts with the staid, formal teacher and principal described in the public record.

Similarly, the ease with which Carlotta obtained housing in Hawaii revealed that even though racial hostility and tensions were evident during the early 1900s, a black woman could live openly in an integrated community. Carlotta had resided initially with her father, who had purchased a large house in Honolulu. In time, however, she became more independent and shared a residence on Beretania Avenue in an attractive neighborhood with a young female friend and, later, with a widow. "We have a pretty place here being on the main thoroughfare to the beach and cars running out here and to town pass here," she wrote McCants.[15] These living arrangements allowed Carlotta not only independence, but also the opportunity to save money, to interact with a variety of people, and, ultimately, to purchase property.

While conditions may have been neither difficult nor racially oppressive for a black professional woman in Hawaii, there was no substantial black community before World War II, and Carlotta saw few blacks, either in her classrooms or in the local community. Although Hawaii's black population had tripled between 1900 and 1910, and more black professionals had come to the islands to pursue their careers, a handful of black professionals did not constitute a community.[16] But if the absence of a black community presented particular problems in respect to dating or having a peer group of black professionals to interact with, Carlotta rarely complained. Most of her social activities, such as travel and parties, occurred in groups, relieving her of the pressure to find a companion whose racial and social background were comparable to her own.[17]

Occasionally, however, the absence of a black community proved an inconvenience, such as the time when Carlotta wrote the Madam C. J. Walker Manufacturing Company, a black business that made cosmetics and hair products for African-American women, seeking products that were not available locally. She requested advice and hair preparations to counteract the effect on her hair of swimming in saltwater. "These treatments," wrote the company's export manager in reply to Carlotta's inquiry, "will produce the straightened effect upon the hair and will last [a] considerable time."[18]

Despite her assimilation into the social circle of the middle class, Carlotta remained isolated from her family. Following the death of her mother Charlotte Harris Stewart in 1906, Carlotta felt distraught and guilty. Although her mother was an 1872 graduate from Wilberforce University, she had struggled financially throughout much of her life because of the limited employment opportunities available to college-educated African-American women. Carlotta had promised to help her mother financially following her divorce from T. McCants Stewart, an obligation she had neglected, partly as a result of pressure from her father. When T. McCants Stewart remarried in 1893, he had prohibited his children from contacting their natural mother while they were under his care. "I should have done more for her," Carlotta lamented to her brother McCants. "You see when Papa was here [in Hawaii], I was not allowed to write her."[19] Furthermore, she reminded McCants, "Papa made it understood that his former wife was dead when we children were small." This situation also resulted in strained relations between Carlotta and her stepmother, Alice Franklin Stewart, and may explain in part why she did not follow her father and stepmother to London in 1905. Carlotta resented this interloper, and throughout the remainder of her life she had little to do with either her stepmother or her three stepsisters.[20]

As Carlotta had done in the past when she desired advice and reassurance, she confided in McCants. Admittedly depressed, she lamented, "O Mac, it is terrible. I am so far away and not a soul here to comfort me, as I can not tell any one."[21] Indeed, McCants, who was four years older than Carlotta, had often served as a surrogate father for his younger sister, providing advice and solace, and his encouragement proved particularly important to Carlotta during this difficult period.[22] Carlotta also complained of her rootlessness and the need for a family in 1906. "T'is terrible to think how we have been without home, mother or father, since we were babes, practically. It is hard enough for boys. But a girl certainly does need a home with mother and father until she gets one of her own."[23] This statement was the first in her correspondence to indicate that Carlotta resented her father's frequent absences from home and the dislocation and disunity that his ambitious and peripatetic career had brought to her life. Moreover, it reflected the emotional bond that had developed between the Stewart children, particularly Carlotta and McCants, in light of T. McCants Stewart's absence and the death of Carlotta's mother.

In 1907, for the first time since her arrival in Hawaii, Carlotta responded favorably to a suggestion by McCants to return to the mainland, citing both personal and financial reasons. "Yes Mac, let us go East. I do not want to stay here any longer. I am too far away from loved ones."[24] She also revealed that she was dissatisfied with her financial situation: "The Islands are not what they used to be financially any way. Have thought of settling here [but] will not now." Carlotta assured McCants that she would relocate to the mainland no later than September.[25]

Carlotta's dissatisfaction stemmed, in part, from the impact of the Panic of 1907 on her personal finances and on the Hawaiian economy in general. Her salary had been cut 3 percent, and teachers were prohibited from working part-time jobs to supplement their salaries. Food prices, she noted, had also risen sharply and, for the first time, her debts had become a financial burden. "I have never met such a streak of ill luck," she complained. "Will simply *have* to let everything go and start all over again."[26] These financial travails caused Carlotta's weight to drop to 109 pounds, but she believed that she could weather the storm. In her characteristically optimistic tone, she wrote, "[I] will not let these difficulties conquer me."[27]

After careful reflection, however, Carlotta decided that it was not in her best interest to return to the mainland. Despite her intermittent loneliness, the depression following the death of her mother, and her financial problems, she was an established professional in the Hawaiian schools. Because of the racial descrimination in the early twentieth century, it is unlikely that she could have achieved the same status in any Pacific Coast community. Although still somewhat ambivalent about her decision to remain in Hawaii, Carlotta wrote McCants, "The thought of staying out here three or four years longer wears on me at times. But I am perfectly sensible about it now as I see the situation East. I would not leave now for anything."[28]

The young black teacher's decision to remain in Hawaii proved to be an advantageous one. Within two years she had been promoted to principal of the Koolau elementary school and received an increase in salary.[29] Carlotta's upward mobility in the space of seven years was impressive. Though many black women had established careers as teachers and a handful as administrators by 1909, it was unusual for a black female at the age of twenty-eight to serve as principal of a multiracial school. Carlotta's achievement was particularly striking for a black woman in a society with a small black community where blacks had no political influence to press for jobs of this importance. Carlotta's advancement illustrates the fact that blacks were more likely to obtain professional jobs in Hawaii than in many West Coast cities, including San Francisco, Oakland, Los Angeles, Portland, and Seattle.[30] In fact, teaching and administrative positions would not be open to African-Americans in most western cities until the 1940s.

It is impossible to reconstruct Carlotta Stewart's professional career in its entirety, yet fragments of information taken from official reports to the Superintendent of Public Instruction, school and island newspapers, and Carlotta's personal correspondence provide some insight into the Hawaiian schools and Carlotta's administrative career. Hawaii's school-aged population, which grew rapidly between 1900 and 1940, reflected the racial and ethnic diversity of the islands, and the backgrounds of Stewart's students were no different. In 1933, for example, her pupils included Hawaiians, Japanese, Filipinos, Koreans, Chinese, and Portuguese. Sixteen Americans (Caucasians) were listed among the student population, but no blacks were included. In fact, it is unlikely that Stewart had contact with more than a handful of school-aged blacks prior to World War II, and most of those were the children of U.S. military personnel. Moreover, most black Hawaiians lived on the island of Oahu; between 1916 and 1950, Carlotta resided and worked on the island of Kauai, where she was likely to encounter few African-Americans.[31]

The number of pupils who attended Carlotta's schools when she served as principal ranged between 200 and 300. In 1933, for example, the *Hanamaulu School World,* reported that 283 students of various races attended the Hanamaulu School. Between 1940 and 1944, however, the school's enrollment declined to 256 students. In addition to managing the school, Stewart also supervised seven classroom teachers, the school librarian, the cafeteria manager, and taught English.[32]

By any standard, Carlotta Stewart's professional career was successful. Even without the support of a large black community, she excelled as both a teacher and an administrator for over four decades and established a network of professional associates throughout Hawaii. She attended conventions of the Hawaii and the Kauai education associations and read the *Hawaii Education Review.* Similarly, she participated actively in the Kauai Historical Society and served on a committee that planned to write a history of Kauai. Her career advancement, as well as the respect she was accorded in the community, were critical factors in her decision to remain in Hawaii permanently.[33]

Because she had been reared in a society that denigrated all black females, irrespective of their education or class standing, Carlotta Stewart was exceedingly conscious of both her public and her professional image. Oral interviews with both surviving family members and teachers who knew her professionally reveal that Carlotta was a refined, cultured, and attractive African-American woman who insisted on decorum and formality. Surviving photographs confirm this description. These characteristics may have been both the manifestation of the positive image that she wished black females to portray and evidence of her strict upbringing. They reflected, too, the culture of black middle-class womanhood to which she had been exposed prior to adulthood.[34] Katherine Stewart Flippin stated that her aunt "liked to dress up and go to dinner in formal style." Carlotta, she continued, "was an elegant lady. She had an air about her. Because she lived in the islands so long most everyone took her for one of those kinky-headed Hawaiians. She didn't do anything to her hair, and it was real crisp and full, and she wore it like they used to wear it, up, so it looked like, not hair, but [a] hat. And then she'd sometimes wear a little circlet of shell or a circlet of brightly colored feathers around the top for decorations."[35]

Similarly, Eleanor Anderson, who had also taught and resided on the island of Kauai, recalled that Carlotta was extremely popular and well respected by everyone who knew her in Kauai, despite the fact that she was a disciplinarian who demanded excellence and respect from her students and colleagues alike. That she had learned some of these qualities from her father T. McCants Stewart, a stern patriarch, there can be no doubt. Yet Anderson also pointed out that Carlotta never shared her private affairs with her or ever discussed her husband. "She was quiet and reserved about these things," Anderson stated.[36]

Carlotta's personal correspondence also reveals a rather reserved woman with only moderate interest in community affairs and no sense of racial identity. Unlike many black professional women who devoted part of their careers to women's groups and benevolent societies, Carlotta Stewart was not a social reformer. She never joined any organization designed to promote the advancement of blacks, Puerto Ricans, Asians, Hawaiians, or women. True, Hawaii during these years did not have chapters of the most prominent black national organizations, such as the National Association for the Advancement of Colored People (NAACP), National Urban League, National Association of Colored Women, or the National Council of Negro Women. Yet Carlotta had been reared in a family of black activists. Her brothers, McCants and Gilchrist, both attorneys, were active in civil rights struggles in Portland and New York, and her father had challenged successfully several Jim Crow laws in the state of New York and won the praise of Booker T. Washington.[37] Her aunt, Verina Morton-Jones, to whom she wrote periodically, had been a charter member of the Brooklyn chapter of the NAACP, a cofounder of the National Urban League, and active in the colored YWCA and settlement house movement.[38] Thus, Carlotta's decision to avoid reform movements was atypical of the Stewarts but may have been predicated on the belief that, relatively speaking, Hawaii did not have a serious racial problem or that she had no sizable ethnic group to align herself with. It also may have been the result of her relative isolation. Here was a black woman who was separated not only from a family of racial activists but also from the culture of the black middle class. In some respects, this gifted African-American woman was permitted to forge a non-race-based identity, something that would have been impossible on the mainland because of the constant and brutal reminders that black people were racially inferior to whites. Thus her life in Hawaii must have been liberating, particularly in light of the constant turmoil that her father and two brothers had experienced as professionals and racial activists. And though Carlotta never denied that she was African-American or tried to pass for another racial or ethnic group, her isolation and her desire to assimilate may also explain why she did not comment on the plethora of racist editorials and cartoons in the Honolulu *Advertiser* that maligned not only blacks, but also Puerto Ricans and Asians.[39]

Hawaii during the early twentieth century offered few opportunities for a black female to meet, date, or marry a black male, and fewer still to interact with black professionals. Thus interracial dating and interracial marriage were both acceptable and realistic, as long as blacks and whites did not intermarry. Indeed, cross-racial relationships were perhaps the only opportunity for a black professional woman like Carlotta Stewart to interact with a male from a comparable social and economic background. So as Carlotta approached her thirty-fifth birthday, she married Yun Tim Lai, a man of Chinese ancestry, at Anahola, Kauai County.[40]

Born in Anahola, Kauai in 1886, Lai was five years younger than Carlotta. When the couple wed in 1916, he was working as sales manager of the Garden Island Motors, Ltd., an automobile dealership in Lihue, Kauai.[41] The circumstances surrounding Carlotta and Yun's courtship are unclear, but she had been a close friend of Lai's sister for many years. The marriage was presumably a happy one, perhaps even a marriage of convenience, and Carlotta and Yun purchased a modest home overlooking Anahola Bay, which was a relatively short drive from Lihue where Lai was employed. The nineteen year marriage ended in 1935, when Lai died suddenly in Hong Kong while visiting his parents. The circumstances surrounding Lai's death were not disclosed, and Carlotta rarely mentioned her husband in her personal correspondence, extending to her personal affairs the formality and reserve that she demanded in her professional career.[42] Carlotta Stewart Lai never remarried but remained in Hawaii for the next seventeen years, serving as principal and English teacher until her retirement in 1945.[43]

Following her retirement from the public schools, Carlotta began arranging her personal affairs with the expectation that she would live in Hawaii during her final years. Apparently fearful that her health might deteriorate with advanced age, she had drawn up her will in 1943 and appointed Ruth Aki Ching, her late husband's sister, as executor and major beneficiary of her estate, a fact that she had kept hidden even from Ching until 1952. Carlotta also gave Ching legal authorization to manage her personal property. "The Trust Company will notify you that I left all my personal property to you as in my will of 1943," Carlotta informed Ching in 1952.[44]

Her decision to appoint Ching as the major beneficiary in her will was the result of a longstanding friendship between the two women and the close personal attachment that developed. The fact that Carlotta had no children and was physically distant from her relatives on the mainland explains, in part, her choice. However, naming Ruth Ching as major beneficiary was a slap in the face to her surviving relatives, particularly to her niece Katherine Stewart Flippin. However, Katherine had made almost no effort to visit Hawaii during the fifty-four years that Carlotta resided there. Responding to an inquiry from Ching concerning why she, rather than a surviving member of the Stewart family, was named so prominently in her will, Carlotta replied straightforwardly: "You were kind to all classes—high or low. You were an outstanding person—not only in my opinion but from many, many higher than I. This is how you got into my will."[45] Carlotta explained that she was also rewarding Ching for her friendship and loyalty. "You have been so fine and good to me and everyone," exclaimed Carlotta, "that you deserve all and more. I made up The Will in 1943 so [I] made up my mind [to] see to things instead of waiting for the end."[46] Thus Carlotta's will was the final testament of how dearly she loved her friend Ruth Ching, who had provided emotional support and helped her to forge a sense of community.

By 1951, Carlotta's health had grown fragile. Unable to care for herself, she entered the Manoa Convalescent Home in 1952. "I feel safe and secure," Carlotta wrote Ruth Ching, "but at home as you know things got beyond my strength."[47] Lai kept a diary of her activities while a patient at the nursing home, one of only several extant diaries by black women, and it serves as an excellent barometer of her declining health and her attempt to remain optimistic in the face of despair. But Carlotta acknowledged frankly that time had finally caught up with her and that she would probably never leave this environment. "If God spares me to return, we will have good times again," she wrote Ruth Ching, although her declining health made this prospect an unlikely one.[48]

In the convalescent home, Lai turned increasingly to religion as a source of strength and inspiration. She had converted to Catholicism decades earlier, probably during the early 1900s, despite the fact that her father was an ordained minister in the African Methodist Episcopal Church. As a young teacher she had often visited the Priory, an Episcopal school, to pray, study, and dine with other females. As early as 1906 she had written McCants that "I frequently sat around the cross and wrote my schoolwork" in the inner court of the Priory.[49] She clung to religion even more firmly in her final year, increasing her financial contribution to the Catholic Church and devoting a portion of her day to prayer and spiritual matters.[50] "Thru God," she recorded on January 27, "I inherit the power to win."[51]

Carlotta had cancer, though she never mentioned her specific ailment, and the disease had spread throughout her body. As a consequence, her legs were in constant pain, and on some days she was completely bedridden.

During March and April, Lai's entries into her diary became less frequent, a signal that her health was feeble. Fearful that death was imminent, she cleared up last minute matters relating to her estate, such as preparing a cemetery plot that had been purchased for the children of T. McCants Stewart.[52] She wrote Ruth Ching regarding her will and was apparently satisfied that she had managed her financial affairs effectively.[53] By early May the manager of the nursing home urged Carlotta to leave the name of her personal physician in the event that her health took a turn for the worst. "The end may be near. Rested much all day," she wrote on May 4.[54] Indeed, within two weeks, her health had declined precipitously. In the final entry in her diary on May 15, Carlotta wrote with her usual brevity and clarity: "Up at 5:45 [a.m.]. Very poor nite. Rest all day. Adjusting my menu. Must prepare for Betty. Bedside prayer. Slept at 8."[55] Carlotta Stewart Lai passed away quietly on July 6, 1952, at the age of seventy-one. A requiem mass was held in her memory at Sacred Hearts Church in Honolulu, and on July 10, 1952, she was buried in the Oahu cemetery in a family plot.[56]

Even though she never achieved national recognition as an educator or civil rights leader, Carlotta Stewart Lai was, nonetheless, a significant figure. Her public career illustrates that Hawaii was a relatively open society for educated middle-class African-Americans during the early twentieth century, despite the fact that the black community represented less than 0.2 percent of the population and that few economic opportunities beyond domestic work and menial labor were available for black women. Few African-American women were employed in teaching or administrative jobs in the western states and territories when Carlotta began teaching at the Normal School in 1902. Fewer still succeeded in moving up the ladder during their careers to become principals or administrators before World War II.[57]

Carlotta's life also reflects the absence of serious racial tension and conflict in Hawaii between blacks and other racial and ethnic groups before World War II. During her five decades in Hawaii, Carlotta did not report one instance of racial discrimination in employment, public accommodations, housing, or in the social arena, although these problems were evident with other racial and ethnic groups on the islands. Yet as Beth Bailey and David Farber argue persuasively in their excellent study of Hawaii during World War II, the first sizable influx of African-American military personnel into Hawaii strained the island's race relations considerably. By the early 1940s the racial attitudes of Hawaiians, in many respects, had come to resemble those of whites on the mainland.[58]

The absence of serious racial conflict in Hawaii also permitted Carlotta to be valued and appreciated as a gifted individual rather than as a gifted African-American, a luxury she would not have been permitted on the mainland. This fact was liberating and explains Carlotta's optimistic outlook as well as her career advancement. Thus Hawaii, which historian John Whitehead called "America's first and last Far West," proved a relatively benign locale from Carlotta's vantage point.[59] True, her education, income, status in the community, and family name may have insulated her from some forms of class or racial proscription. Too, T. McCants Stewart's position as respected attorney and political figure in Hawaii between 1898 and 1905, as well as his reputation and political contacts, may have assisted Carlotta during the early stages of her career.

Yet Carlotta Stewart Lai, like most African-American professional women on the mainland, succeeded in large measure through her own hard work, perseverance, and pioneering spirit, qualities that the entire Stewart family exemplified. The Stewarts had been leaders in their communities, and this fact was not lost on Carlotta. T. McCants Stewart had instilled in each of his children the desire to seek out new vistas and new frontiers, to become leaders, and to contribute to the betterment of the black race.[60] Carlotta heeded her father's call by serving not only the African-American community, but a community composed of many races, ethnic groups, and nationalities. In fact, she attempted to establish a community even broader than that her father had envisioned, one that existed in few American cities at that time. In many respects, her work remains a blueprint for what American society hopes, one day, to become.[61] Carlotta Stewart Lai's legacy, then, was the persistence with which she pursued her career, a career that spanned four decades, her dedication to public education in Hawaii, and her optimistic view that despite America's racist past, a genuinely multiracial society was possible.

9

Robert Flippin and

Katherine Stewart Flippin

❖ ❖ ❖ ❖ ❖ ❖ ❖ ❖ ❖ ❖ ❖ ❖ ❖ ❖ ❖

Robert Browning Flippin and Katherine Stewart Flippin represent the third generation of the Stewart family, and in many respects their lives, ambitions, and careers were typical of their forebears. Robert and Katherine believed that serving the African-American community was a proud and distinguished family tradition, and they felt obligated to carry it on. This obligation included not only obtaining a college education and professional training, but also working in organizations and institutions that would uplift the black community. Thus these values were successfully transmitted from the second to the third generation, and now a woman, Katherine Stewart, a direct descendant of T. McCants Stewart, would be responsible for extending the family's legacy of service to the race. Yet in terms of the success they achieved in their professional careers and in accumulating property, the Flippins diverged sharply from the previous generations. The Flippins' lives also illustrate vividly the difficulties that many black professionals would continue to experience in the Far West and the manner in which racial discrimination impinged upon their lives and restricted their opportunities. Their work illuminates the important role that social organizations continued to play in serving the needs of the African-American community during the twentieth century.

That Katherine Stewart felt duty-bound to improve her community and to uplift the race was no accident. Reared in a loving middle class family, Katherine remembers a very serene, uncomplicated, and idyllic Portland, where racial barriers did not separate either children or adults. But growing up black in Portland during the early decades of the twentieth century was not idyllic, since Portland, like every major West Coast city, retained vestiges of racial discrimination in housing, public accommodations, and employment. However, the State of Oregon prohibited segregation in public schools and in public accommodations. Moreover, there is little evidence of racial violence directed against African-Americans in Portland early in the century, partly because of the small black population, and partly because of the tolerance and civility of white Oregonians.[1]

McCants's inability to support his family in Portland was exacerbated by the fact that his wife, Mary, was not gainfully employed. Like most Oregon women, Mary Delia Stewart was a housewife, despite a degree from the Manning Conservatory of Music in Minneapolis and a teaching certificate from the University of Minnesota. McCants Stewart did not intend to give the appearance that he could not support his family, so he instructed his wife to stay at home, and Mary complied with her husband's wishes. This was a luxury that few African-American families could afford, and certainly one that hindered, rather than helped the Stewart household.

The Stewart household resembled, in most respects, the households of middle-class white Oregonians. The family rented a home in an integrated neighborhood, Katherine attended integrated schools, and her playmates were white as well as black. Mary played an active role in the Portland Parent Teachers Association (PTA), and in 1909 won an award for homemakers when she submitted a recipe to a contest sponsored by the Portland *Oregonian*.[2] Mary Stewart also served as the family's disciplinarian. Perhaps McCants Stewart was rebelling against the strict discipline he had received as a child, but two things are certain. He would not spank Katherine and was much more permissive in raising his daughter than his father had been in rearing him. Katherine Stewart recalled years later, "I can't ever remember his having disciplined me."[3]

Although McCants Stewart's legal practice required that he spend considerable time away from home in order to scratch out a living, he proved to be a warm, loving, and committed father who enjoyed the time he spent with his daughter. Though he was unable to provide adequate financial security for his family, he did provide love and emotional support. He took

Katherine on frequent outings to the country to ride horses and to explore the beauty, texture, and contours of the Oregon countryside. Katherine recalled that "a Portland resident of that area had a big ranch and lots of horses, and it would be an all-day excursion to go out to the ranch."[4] These activities must have been particularly gratifying to McCants, who had been unable to secure even a single dollar from his father to attend a county fair when he attended Tuskegee Institute. He had been urged repeatedly to be industrious, to be frugal, and to avoid frivolous activities. How different things would be for Katherine.[5]

Katherine attended Portland's integrated public schools without incident. Indeed, she never experienced the pernicious effects of racial discrimination as a child. Her world was a sheltered one, perhaps typical of many black middle-class children outside the South. Her father's position as an attorney, despite his financial woes, provided status for the Stewart household. The Stewarts were included among Portland's "black elite," a small group of black professionals, businessmen, racial activists, and pioneer black families. These individuals, however, were not as affluent as Portland's white upper class who composed both a social and an economic elite. Rather, as Kenneth L. Kusmer noted in his study of Cleveland's black community, the black elite was as much a social and ideological grouping within the black community as an economic stratum.[6]

Since Portland had neither a black ghetto nor a sizable concentration of African-Americans between 1902 and 1918, the Stewarts resided in integrated neighborhoods: first at 415 Davis Street; later at 271 Wheeler Street; and then, for several years, at 513 Union Avenue, where Katherine was born. Because of the tenuous economic status of McCants Stewart's legal practice, the family never owned property in Portland.[7]

Katherine's pleasant world was shattered when her father committed suicide in April 1919. Katherine and Mary Stewart had moved to San Francisco from Portland in the summer of 1918 to join McCants and reunite the family. There had been no indication in his letters that his despair had reached this level.[8] This unexpected tragedy also shattered whatever illusions that either Katherine or Mary Stewart had about McCants's ability to cope with adversity. His death was also unsettling for another reason: Mary Stewart had not worked outside of the home during her fourteen-year marriage but was now forced to become the family's breadwinner. If employment opportunities were limited for black male professionals in such

West Coast cities as Portland and San Francisco, they were even more difficult for black women, the majority of whom labored in domestic service or menial labor. Additionally, the majority of San Francisco's labor unions prohibited blacks from membership until World War II, effectively barring them from many skilled, semiskilled, and managerial positions. Although the range of employment opportunities available to Mary Stewart and to most educated black women was exceedingly narrow, Mary found work almost immediately as executive director of the Victory Club, a World War I service agency for black soldiers. Her responsibilities included planning programs and dealing with the multitude of problems that black servicemen and their families encountered. Despite her lack of experience, she executed her job with skill and confidence.[9]

When the Victory Club disbanded during the early 1920s, having fulfilled its function, it not only left Mary Stewart without a job; it left San Francisco's black community without recreational and social facilities for young men and women. With this community need in mind, Mary Stewart and a group of local black leaders approached the War Camp Community Service Center, which maintained the facility, and asked to utilize the remaining funds to create a permanent community service center for black San Franciscans. Officials at the wartime agency agreed, and the new facility became known as the Booker T. Washington Community Service Center (BTWCSC). Under the leadership of Mary Stewart, John Fisher, and the Reverend J. J. Byers, who headed the AME Zion Church, the community center functioned as both a social institution and an agency of protest against racial discrimination, providing a variety of services for an expanding black community. African-American women such as Mary Stewart played a pivotal role in leadership, guidance, and fund-raising during the center's formative years.[10]

The center's work was very demanding, but Mary Stewart guided the organization through some difficult early years in her two terms as president. Within a decade, the BTWCSC had resolved its most serious financial difficulties, moved to a larger facility at 1433 Divisadero Street, expanded its program, and hired a professional social worker to serve as executive director. The organization had also come under the umbrella of the San Francisco Community Chest, the forerunner of the United Way, which provided a significant boost to the center's funding as well as legitimacy within the larger social service community.[11]

Although the BTWCSC's activities were important, Mary Stewart also had the responsibility of raising a child without either the emotional or the financial support of a husband. Mary consciously chose not to remarry, even though she was an educated, attractive, and personable woman and was presented with a tempting marriage proposal by A. P. Alberga, a prominent political leader in San Francisco's black community.[12] Instead of courtship or matrimony, Mary put her energy into work, community service, church, and raising Katherine, which proved to be taxing enough. After several years, she left the BTWCSC to work for the Viavi Company, a local pharmaceutical firm. Though teaching would have seemed the most logical career for Mary Stewart to pursue, considering her excellent qualifications, that choice was out of the question. The San Francisco Unified School District did not hire black teachers or administrators, regardless of their qualifications, until 1943—later than many other far western cities—and then, only after concerted pressure from the city's interracial leadership. Black students were even discouraged from enrolling in teacher training programs at San Francisco State College, which had a "gentleman's agreement" with local school districts not to send African-Americans for job interviews as prospective teachers.[13]

Katherine Stewart's adjustment to her new locale was complicated by her father's death. She had no difficulty adjusting to the San Francisco public schools or making new friends, but she mourned deeply the loss of her father. She particularly missed his warmth, humor, and friendship. McCants Stewart had encouraged inquisitiveness, spontaneity, and informality with his daughter, and the critical role he had played in her life was difficult to fill. Katherine also missed the discussions about her father's clients, the occasional visits to his office, his vivid and exciting descriptions of his travels, and the stern but patient and loving advice that he always gave her. McCants had certainly expected more than mere competence from his daughter, but unlike his own father, he did not demand perfection. The bond between father and daughter had been an extremely close one, and Katherine found it difficult to be without him.[14]

In 1920, the year following McCants Stewart's suicide, Mary's mother, Victoria Frances Weir, moved from Minneapolis to join the family in San Francisco. There Weir, a fair-skinned woman with a commanding presence, lectured on a variety of subjects and demonstrated products at local department stores—an accomplishment of no small measure, since no major department store in San Francisco hired black clerks or salespersons for fear that the white public would object. A firm disciplinarian, Weir brought stability to the Stewart household. "Grandmother Weir had a commanding personality," recalled Katherine Stewart. "As soon as Grandmother Weir opened her mouth, everybody paid attention." Weir's presence in the Stewart household also helped Mary Stewart through the grieving process following the loss of her husband. Unlike Katherine, who had grieved openly about her father's death and the loss it represented, Mary had remained stoic and grieved inwardly. Victoria Weir, though sympathetic to her daughter's feelings and her difficult predicament, tolerated no self-pity and thereby accelerated the healing process so necessary to Mary's future.[15]

Weir also provided the family with an additional income, which they needed desperately. With the help of Weir's pension from her late husband's military service, the Stewarts moved into a larger apartment, and after several years, Mary and Victoria purchased a modest Victorian house on Golden Gate Avenue near Stanyan Street. Katherine recalled that the house was located "in the middle of the cemetery, at least surrounded on two sides by the cemetery."[16] Although the house was modest by the standards of the time, its purchase was a remarkable achievement. It symbolized the kind of middle-class security that the family had always sought. It revealed, too, that the Stewarts had not only persevered despite McCants Stewarts' suicide, but were upwardly mobile.

San Francisco's race relations resembled Portland's. By 1900, the Golden Gate city had abolished segregation in voting, public accommodations, and schools. African-Americans had also won the right to serve on juries and to testify in legal proceedings against whites. Thus young Katherine attended integrated schools and played on her high school tennis team, lived in integrated neighborhoods, and played with children of all races and nationalities. San Francisco's small black community, which numbered 2,414 in 1920, and 3,803 a decade later, was concentrated in the Western Addition, particularly the Fillmore district, where the majority of African-American businesses were located. The city did not contain the blighted urban ghettos that characterized many northern, eastern, and midwestern cities. Perhaps this is why Katherine Stewart's description of San Francisco during her adolescence is extremely benign and makes no reference to either racial discrimination or the difficulties that

Mary and Victoria faced coping with the day-to-day struggles of supporting a household.[17]

San Francisco, as Roger W. Lotchin observed, was a walking city. Many social and recreational events were held outdoors. Katherine and Mary explored the city on foot, taking advantage of San Francisco's mild weather, scenery, and the multitude of outdoor activities. "My mother was a great walker," exclaimed Katherine.[18] Although African-Americans were not always welcome in the city's restaurants, hotels, and night clubs, they were not barred from parks, carnivals, and beaches in San Francisco as they were in some southern cities.[19] So when the Stewarts attended citywide parades, swam at Ocean Beach, strolled through Golden Gate Park, or attended the annual Easter sunrise service on Mount Davidson, they encountered no difficulties because of their race.

This sheltered childhood meant that Katherine had little racial consciousness as a child and almost no awareness of the pernicious effect of segregation on the lives of blacks in San Francisco or elsewhere. Perhaps neither Mary Stewart nor Victoria Weir felt that race was a suitable subject to discuss with a child, so they avoided it. Nor did Mary Stewart permit her daughter to work, Katherine stated, because "there were no jobs for Negro girls that Mama approved [of]."[20] Mary prohibited her daughter from working the menial jobs of domestic labor and personal service, where black women were employed in disproportionate numbers in San Francisco and in cities throughout the nation. In Mary Stewart's mind, unemployment for her daughter was preferable to the indignity of working as a domestic laborer; few black females, however, could afford that luxury. Mary's attitude toward domestic labor also illustrates the importance of class and the behavior associated with it in the Stewart household.[21]

This protective shield around Katherine's world burst in the mid-1920s when she attempted to register for a teachers' training program at San Francisco State College. Although teaching had not been an avenue of employment open to Mary Stewart, she had hoped that conditions would be more favorable for her daughter. Thus she encouraged Katherine to apply to a program that had previously been closed to African-Americans. When Katherine attempted to register for the program, however, she was discouraged by the college registrar because of her race. "I was appalled," she recalled when reflecting upon the episode many years later. "I couldn't speak, I just fled. That had never happened to me before. I dropped out [of high school] then, and I played tennis the rest of the year."[22]

Katherine's reaction reflected the pain and insult of being spurned and rejected because of her race, but it also illustrated her naïveté about racial matters in San Francisco. However, even if she had been well informed about racial discrimination and some of the unspoken limitations on black advancement in San Francisco, it is one thing to be educated about the nuances of racial discrimination, and quite another to personally feel its sting and humiliation. Yet under the circumstances, withdrawing from high school was a drastic reaction. No member of the Stewart family in three generations had ever failed to complete high school, or for that matter, to attend college. The fact that San Francisco State College denied African-Americans an opportunity even to apply to its teachers' training program reveals that Katherine Stewart was as much a victim of discrimination as her father. Little had changed for Bay Area blacks since his suicide in 1919.[23]

Dropping out of high school presented another burden for Katherine: she was then ill-equipped to compete in the labor force except for menial jobs, positions her mother abhorred. She worked briefly at a local cannery before obtaining employment at the Davis Schonwasser Company, an exclusive clothing store and one of only several department stores in San Francisco that employed African-Americans before World War II. There she worked as an elevator operator before moving to the shipping department, where she worked in the stock room. Katherine remembered vividly that the work, though tedious, was satisfying and afforded her a form of independence that she had not known. "The stock work included marking and hanging the stock in the stock rooms, keeping the racks on the floor where the merchandise was shown free of merchandise, hanging it back in the stock room. From that point, as I learned this part of the business, I began to order and reorder and screen lines that would come in for showing from various companies."[24] Eventually Katherine not only learned that she had made a mistake by not completing her education; she also learned that race as well as education made a difference in the workplace, and that both factors had a significant bearing on the occupational mobility of black workers.

Although work and family matters occupied most of Katherine's time, she continued to take part in the social affairs of the BTWCSC and her local church. Katherine took particular interest in the community center's Dramatic Club, a group of amateur performers who staged one-act plays throughout northern California. It was during these years that she met Robert Flippin, her future husband, whom she married in 1932.

Robert Browning Flippin's journey to San Francisco was a circuitous one. Born in Stromsburg, Nebraska, in 1903, he had attended Stromsburg High School (from which he did not graduate), Nebraska Central College, the University of Nebraska, Washington State College, and the University of Chicago before relocating to San Francisco in 1930. Robert had hoped to emulate his father, George Albert Flippin, and pursue a medical career. George Albert had gained acclaim as a football star at the University of Nebraska during the 1890s, where he was touted as one of the best football players in the nation. In 1898, he enrolled in the University of Illinois School of Medicine, which was known commonly as the Illinois College of Physicians and Surgeons. After earning his medical degree in 1900 and serving a brief residency in Chicago, George Albert returned to Stromsburg, where he established a successful medical practice in a predominantly Swedish community.[25]

Following in the footsteps of George Albert was no easy endeavor. Nevertheless, Robert tried. He completed a two-year premedical course at Nebraska Central College but changed his major to sociology when he enrolled at Washington State College. His desire to study medicine, however, returned in the mid 1930s. In 1936, Robert separated briefly from Katherine to study medical technology at the Northwest Institute in Minneapolis. His diary, kept during their separation, reveals his loneliness as well as considerable anxiety about his future.[26]

After completing the program in medical technology, Flippin returned to San Francisco, where he worked not as a medical technician, but as a highly educated delivery boy, janitor, chauffeur, and waiter. But Flippin's underemployment may have been less a function of racial discrimination than the fact that the Great Depression had hit San Francisco and workers of all races were scrambling to find employment. In 1937, however, Flippin was appointed executive director of the BTWCSC, an appointment that was aided by his marriage to Katherine and the fact that despite his limited residence in San Francisco, he had made inroads into important black organizations. In a short period he had become a respected community leader. The polish and ease with which he interacted with whites also marked him as a good choice to run the prestigious community center.[27]

Flippin's early tenure as executive director of the BTWCSC was uneventful and his policies no different from his female predecessors. Flippin did, however, establish the first exhibition of children's art at the California State Fair and started a vacation school for children during the summer.

He also organized a special study group on African-American history long before the demand for black studies swept across college campuses.[28]

The tranquility of Flippin's early years as executive director of the community center was shattered in 1941 with the onset of World War II. The war was a demographic watershed in the history of black San Francisco. Though the city's black population had remained relatively static throughout the nineteenth century, actually declining in some years, it increased by more than 600 percent between 1940 and 1945. By 1950, over 43,460 blacks lived in San Francisco, where less than 5,000 had been reported a decade earlier. The large influx of black migrants, mostly from the southern states, placed enormous strains on housing and social services. Thus their arrival was greeted with ambivalence by black and white residents alike.[29]

As a spokesman for black San Franciscans, Flippin played multiple roles during the war. He attempted, for example, to calm the fears of all San Franciscans that a sizable in-migration of blacks would damage the city's race relations. San Francisco had always demonstrated the capacity and the will to assimilate a variety of white ethnic immigrants and Asians with only a minimum of tension and anxiety, Flippin observed. Could it not do the same for black southern migrants? The black leader was optimistic about the future of San Francisco's race relations, and he urged others to be equally confident.[30]

Flippin, like many black leaders throughout the nation, saw World War II as an opportunity to deal a fatal blow to Jim Crow. After twelve years of economic depression, it appeared as if African-Americans had awakened after a prolonged slumber. San Francisco's black leadership capitalized on the growth of the black community to boost membership in local racial advancement organizations such as the NAACP, and to create new ones, such as chapters of the National Urban League and the National Council of Negro Women. Black leaders also used President Franklin D. Roosevelt's wartime promise of nondiscrimination in federal contracts and defense industries to push vigorously for full integration in housing and employment.[31] This wartime egalitarian fervor, Flippin felt, would increase interracial awareness and serve to eradicate decades of bigotry and racial intolerance.[32]

Flippin's leadership was strengthened by two developments during World War II. In 1942, he was asked to contribute a weekly column to the San Francisco *Chronicle*, the city's largest circulating daily newspaper, on the transformation of the black community. Flippin was expected to serve as both observer and critic and to explain to the *Chronicle*'s large reader-ship how the wartime migration had disrupted the normal pace of life for black San Franciscans. The column, which began publication in November 1942, was called "In the Districts," although Flippin wrote essentially about the Fillmore district.[33]

"In the Districts" revealed the vitality, color, texture, and exuberance of San Francisco's black community during World War II, but it also reported on the difficulties that many wartime migrants faced in San Francisco and the inability of social agencies to provide services for this expanding pop-ulation. Flippin wrote candidly that local social agencies were failing to deal effectively with the "problems of [these] people," and that this failure would "most surely lead to lowered civilian morale, a higher crime rate, increased delinquency, [an] increase in tuberculosis and social diseases, and an aggravation of former amicable race relations."[34]

Flippin was aware that these problems had also surfaced in many other cities. New York, Chicago, Cleveland, and Pittsburgh had all coped poorly with the integration of southern black migrants into their communities between 1915 and 1930. Flippin also was aware that the rapid influx of black migrants into many northern and southern cities during World War I had disrupted race relations and led to race riots and indiscriminate racial violence in some instances. He urged San Franciscans to guard against complacency.[35]

Serving as a weekly columnist for a major San Francisco newspaper solidified Flippin's base of support within the black community, but it also allowed him to make new inroads into the white community as well. In 1943 he was appointed by the San Francisco Housing Authority to manage the Westside Courts project, an integrated public housing project located in the Western Addition. Flippin's appointment to manage the 136-unit housing projects, the only integrated public housing projects in San Fran-cisco, illustrated how far he had come since his arrival in the city in 1930 as well as the political clout that black San Franciscans had gained during the war years. The appointment, which was made with the consent of the mayor of San Francisco, the local housing authority commissioners, and the U.S. Housing Authority's special assistant Frank S. Horne, proved one of the most important political appointments that a black San Franciscan had ever received. By 1944, Robert Flippin was rated as the most important leader in the black community in a survey of African-American families conducted by Charles S. Johnson. Surprisingly, Flippin was even rated more popular than Reverend Frederick Haynes, pastor of Third Baptist Church, the largest African-American church in San Francisco.[36]

But after only one year of managing the Westside Courts housing project, Flippin resigned and returned to the BTWCSC on a full time basis. The center's programs had expanded rapidly during the war, but the center struggled, nevertheless, to keep pace with the demand for social services and recreation in the black community. If the BTWCSC expected to meet this growing demand, funding must be increased, and Flippin had no realistic solution during the war years. He proposed later, however, to reorganize the Center's executive board and to elect more whites to key positions. Additionally, the organization of a local Urban League chapter in 1946 relieved some of the pressure on the BTWCSC to provide support services to African-Americans.[37]

Robert Flippin was also important to the black community as a liaison between the black and white communities and as a nationally recognized expert on race relations. He had served, for example, as a special consultant to the National Youth Administration during the 1930s, as well as an adviser to the eminent sociologist Charles S. Johnson, who conducted a study of black war workers in San Francisco.[38] He served also on the Council for Civic Unity, San Francisco's most prestigious interracial committee, and spoke on the subject of racial tolerance before such diverse organizations as the American Friends Service Committee, the National Conference of Christians and Jews, and the Bahia Fellowship. Regardless of his audience, Flippin's message remained consistent: World War II was a crucial test for American democracy, and blacks and whites should utilize this opportunity to create a more harmonious racial environment. "Today, we are fighting for the creation of a true democracy, a way of life that is honest and based on the concepts of humanity, mercy, truth, and dignity of the individual," Flippin stated in a speech in 1942.[39]

World War II was not only a turning point for blacks in the San Francisco Bay Area, but also throughout the nation. It had been exceedingly difficult for blacks to improve their employment status during the Great Depression, when they competed with unemployed whites for jobs. But when war broke out, several things happened: the demand for labor made discrimination a luxury the society could no longer afford, and the lesson of Hitler's racism against the Jews, Poles, and other Slavs made many white Americans much more sympathetic to the plight of African-Americans. San Franciscos's black leaders, including Flippin, saw this window of opportunity and pressed whites harder than ever before to grant them full equality.

Flippin's racial ideology was consistent with those of most civil rights leaders in San Francisco. Like his mother, Georgia Lelia Flippin, who worked for many years in the San Francisco branch of the NAACP, Flippin was a racial moderate who believed that interracial cooperation was the most effective route to racial progress. (Though the BTWCSC, under his leadershop, served the black community predominantly, it also opened its doors to people of all races and nationalities.) Flippin also believed that social change was a gradual process, especially when it involved changing racial attitudes, and often painfully slow. Therefore, he argued, African-American leaders must work cooperatively with whites in a variety of forums to achieve racial progress.

Although Flippin was a racial moderate, he interacted with people who held a variety of racial and social ideologies. For example, he maintained relationships with two members of the Communist party, William L. Patterson and John Pittman. Flippin never revealed the origins of his friendship with Patterson, a San Francisco attorney who later served as national secretary of the International Labor Defense. The friendship was probably the result of Katherine Flippin's influence, since Patterson had served as executor of her father's will. Thus it is reasonable to assume that Katherine introduced Patterson to her husband following their marriage in 1932.

The two men corresponded periodically after Patterson joined the Communist party and traveled to Russia during the 1930s. Patterson was particularly interested to know if the racially moderate Flippin had been associated with any radical organizations since his arrival in San Francisco. "You must tell me," he wrote, "if your club [the BTWCSC] is affiliated with the National Negro Congress and if not, why not." Patterson went on to explain his ideological shift to the Communist party, insisting that his decision was not made hastily. It was, he wrote "based upon experiences which have irrefutably proven to me that this and only this is the road to the salvation of mankind." Comparing his conversion to communism to a spiritual awakening, Patterson concluded evangelically, "Let me tell you there is new life for every man or woman who finds his or her way to this road."[40]

Robert Flippin's relationship with John Pittman, a young black intellectual and also a member of the Communist party, was more difficult to explain. A native of Atlanta, Georgia, Pittman moved to the Bay Area in the early 1920s to attend the University of California, where he earned a master's degree in economics in 1930. The following year, Pittman started the San Francisco *Spokesman*, a black weekly newspaper, with the financial assistance of the white patron Noel Sullivan, who had assisted such black artists as Roland Hayes and Langston Hughes.

Flippin and Pittman were strange bedfellows. Whereas Flippin always searched for the middle ground, Pittman was radical, abrasive, and welcomed confrontation. Unlike Flippin, who was firmly rooted in the BTWCSC, Pittman never attempted to establish a base of support in the black community. Rather, he criticized San Francisco's black leadership for being apathetic and self-serving.[41] But when Pittman needed access to the African-American community, Flippin, as well as other black leaders, provided that entree. Thus, even though the politics of these two men could not have been further apart, Pittman and Flippin developed a mutual respect. The two men, for example, put their political differences aside to serve together on interracial committees, to work as consultants for Charles S. Johnson's study of black war workers in San Francisco, and to speak against racial discrimination on the same platforms during World War II.[42]

How did Flippin, a racial moderate, reconcile his views with Pittman's radicalism? This question is particularly intriguing in light of the anticommunist hysteria that gripped the nation during the 1940s and the policy of most black organizations, such as the NAACP and the National Urban League, to disassociate themselves from radical organizations for fear of being labeled subversive. Flippin believed that he had an obligation to reach out to all segments of the black community, regardless of their politics—a commitment that proved one of his strengths as a moderate. Thus Flippin could maintain visible and cordial relationships with two members of the Communist party; he could also host Paul Robeson, the controversial black singer, actor, and racial activist who had lived in the Soviet Union and embraced Stalinism, when he visited San Francisco. Moreover, Flippin never felt the need to defend his actions, and his relationship with radicals damaged neither his prestige nor his image in the black or white community.[43]

During the first decade of their marriage, while her husband had forged a reputation as one of San Francisco's most respected African-American leaders and one of the most prominent social workers in the San Francisco Bay Area, Katherine Flippin had been essentially a housewife, working briefly as a stock clerk and occasionally volunteering time to such community organizations as the BTWCSC and the YWCA. Yet during World War II, as San Francisco's large Japanese community was being relocated to detention centers in the western states and black migrants streamed into San Francisco by the thousands each month, Katherine attempted to enroll in an eighteen-week training program for childcare teachers at San Francisco State College, where she had been spurned almost two decades earlier.[44] This time, Katherine was imbued with the egalitarian wartime fervor and the conviction that racial discrimination was not only unjust but also undemocratic. Supported by her husband and her mother, who wished Katherine to further her education, Katherine Flippin enrolled without incident, and excelled in this novel wartime program.

The program, replicated in hundreds of urban communities, illustrated that childcare became a critical concern when more women than ever before entered the workplace.[45] Katherine's ability as an early childhood teacher was recognized nationally when she won a scholarship in 1950 to attend the Vassar Summer Institute for teachers. Katherine's success also motivated her to return to school and earn a bachelor of arts degree in 1952. Two years later she received a master's degree from San Francisco State College. "Apparently I had the flair and had the expertise to work with children," Katherine reflected. "And I climbed the ladder in child care right to the top." She also proved to be a competent administrator, for she coordinated a Head Start Program for the Laguna Salada School District in Pacifica, California, before she retired.[46]

Although working with children brought her tremendous satisfaction, perhaps in part because she never conceived a child of her own, Katherine acknowledged that Robert's career took precedence over her own. Her priorities in this regard reflected the values of working middle-class women of Katherine's generation as much as her own belief that Robert was an important leader. She therefore felt obligated to put his career ahead of her own.[47]

In 1948, Robert Flippin resigned his position as executive director of the BTWCSC to become a parole officer at the California State Prison at San Quentin. Flippin was well qualified to serve as a prison parole officer. As executive director of the BTWCSC, he and his small staff had worked effectively on a shoestring budget to curtail juvenile delinquency in the black community by offering a broad range of social and recreational programs. The BTWCSC had served as a second home for many of these troubled children, particularly for the children of black migrants, whose numbers swelled the community center's rolls by 1945.[48] Flippin's work to curb juvenile delinquency had been recognized by many state leaders, including Clinton T. Duffy, warden of San Quentin, who asked Flippin to apply for the prison job. He became the first black parole officer to be hired in the prison's history.[49]

Flippin's transition from executive director of a community center to parole officer at a maximum security prison was a relatively smooth one. Within a few years, Flippin was one of the most popular officers at the prison—a development that is not surprising, given his twelve years of service at the BTWCSC and his devotion to black youth. Similarly, his relationship with the prison staff was exemplary. Flippin's initial performance evaluation illustrated his rapid adjustment to his new responsibilities. "This Institutional Parole Officer has continued to perform an increasing amount of detailed work in a most proficient manner, and his relationships with the staff and with the inmate body have been most excellent," wrote Flippin's supervisor, who gave him the highest possible ratings in the categories of "Quality of Work" and "Relationship with People." Prison officials were also impressed with his ability to counsel inmates, "particularly those with deep emotional and social problems."[50]

Although counseling emotionally disturbed inmates may well have been his strength as a correctional counselor, Flippin's principal contribution to San Quentin prison was his work with its large population of alcoholics and homosexuals. Though he had shown no interest in either of these populations heretofore, his work with the prison's alcoholic population transformed a relatively modest and unstructured program into one of the leading programs to treat alcoholic prisoners in the nation.[51]

Flippin's work with prison alcoholics absorbed the majority of his energy, but he also found time to counsel homosexuals and to speak periodically before organizations that promoted the rights of homosexuals in California. Although Robert Flippin had no history of working with either gay or lesbian organizations prior to his employment at San Quentin, he expressed no reluctance to counsel this segment of the prison population. In a 1955 speech before the Mattichine Society in San Francisco, a gay rights organization whose work he praised, Flippin attempted to dispel the belief that a sizable segment of the prison was homosexual. He argued that homosexuals formed a relatively low percentage of the men incarcerated at San Quentin. Furthermore, he stated, "Prisons may precipitate latent homosexuality but they do not make homosexuals." Although Flippin could only speculate about the origins of homosexuality, he asserted that "it is life itself that has made them. Prisons cannot effect things that are already in the personality." Moreover, Flippin contended that homosexuality "was not a crime and has nothing whatsoever to do with it," a view that was certainly progressive, if not radical in the 1950s. He also argued that homosexuals were no more apt to break the law than any other segment of the population, attempting to eradicate the common myth that homosexuals were criminally inclined. Flippin insisted, therefore, that prisons like San Quentin "must isolate the sex deviant offender, meaning the rapist, prostitute, [and] exhibitionist from the homosexual." Though Flippin never suggested that homosexuality was merely a matter of sexual preference, he never labeled it a sickness or a sexual malady.[52]

It is doubtful that Flippin's work with the prison's homosexual population was as effective as his work with alcoholics. Gay prisoners were not only maligned and preyed upon by the prison's inmates, a reality that Flippin himself acknowledged, but they were also scorned and despised by the prison's top administration as well. Warden Clinton Duffy had little sympathy for gays, who, he said had been "a nightmare for years." His "enlightened" policy was to separate them from the rest of the prison population. Duffy believed that homosexuals suffered from "some sort of personality disorder," a diagnosis shared by the American Psychiatric Association until 1974, but he was confident that Dr. Alfred Kinsey, the famed researcher of Americans' sexual habits, would ultimately find a cure. Despite Duffy's bias, Flippin's counseling of prison homosexuals was a significant achievement. It represented one of the earliest attempts by a prison official in California to understand the nature of homosexuality and to provide empathy, support, and counseling to gay inmates.[53]

Duffy had been hailed as a reformer in prison circles and considered one of the most progressive wardens in the California State penal system. Under his leadership, San Quentin prison started night classes for inmates and offered a wide spectrum of work programs and recreational facilities. For example, an inmate could take courses in landscape gardening, baking, printing, or learn a trade, for which many received certificates from California labor unions attesting to their expertise in these crafts. The inmates also published a monthly newspaper, *The Insider,* which contained material contributed solely by the prisoners and was regarded as one of the finest prison newspapers in the nation.[54]

Even though Flippin supported Duffy's policies, he did not believe that San Quentin was doing enough to rehabilitate the inmates. "Crime and delinquency prevention measures will remain in their present confused, poorly organized and mis-directed state until revolutionary social reforms are effected, reforms that we are not yet prepared to accept or to bring into being," he wrote in 1950. Flippin was adamant that the criminal was not solely responsible for his crime because "society shares the responsibility for crime." Flippin singled out poverty and its numerous consequences, including the lack of parental supervision, as significant factors leading toward antisocial and criminal behavior. "There is no use repairing the mental health of one generation," he wrote, "if our homes are preparing casualties for the next." An enlightened penal institution, he believed, would not attempt to crush the dignity of the inmates but would create a treatment program "aimed at aiding the offender in readjusting his sense of value—to develope within the nonconformist new appreciations of the importance of living a normal life and assisting him in discovery of reasons for his antisocial behavior patterns."[55]

What, then, was Robert Flippin's contribution to San Quentin prison and the broader reform movement taking place in California prisons? Flippin affected the lives of many inmates of all races. In a letter of gratitude one inmate wrote, "I feel I can and will adjust to adult homosexuality, and it is certainly an improvement over past sexual abnormalities I can assure you."[56] Another inmate, who had taken part in the San Quentin chapter of AA, assured Flippin, "You are in some way responsible for the loss the liquor industry has suffered."[57] These frank testimonies reveal that Robert Flippin was much more than just a role model for black inmates. His popularity with the San Quentin inmate population cut across racial and ethnic lines and across boundaries of sexual orientation. His appointment in 1948 as the prison's first African-American parole officer was symbolically important to many young blacks who were incarcerated, and he always felt a special affinity toward these individuals. Flippin's most significant contributions, however, were his work to reform prison alcoholics and to counsel homosexuals. It was largely under his guidance that the San Quentin AA program became one of the most successful prison AA chapters in the nation. And although Flippin had not fulfilled his lifelong ambition to become a physician, he could take satisfaction from his work in healing some of the emotional wounds that San Quentin's inmates had suffered.

The dedicated African-American leader also set high professional standards in his counseling of gay and alcoholic inmates that would establish a precedent for future parole officers. Not content merely to learn his job on an ad hoc basis, Flippin read numerous publications concerning the rehabilitation of prison drug addicts and alcoholics, attended dozens of

conferences, and spoke before hundreds of organizations about prison reform in general and the San Quentin AA chapter in particular. He attended
the annual conference of the Northern California Council of Alcoholics
Anonymous for many years and was the keynote speaker at the 1963
conference in Eureka, California.[58] But Flippin also made the commitment
to attend the monthly meetings of the San Francisco AA chapter on his own
time and to share his expertise before their members. Thus he never perceived himself as someone who counseled only prison alcoholics or, for
that matter, as someone who counseled only gay prisoners. He saw himself
instead as an active participant in a broader reform movement.[59]

In 1961, after thirteen years of service as a parole officer, Flippin contem-
plated retirement for the first time. A tireless worker throughout his professional life, Flippin found prison work had been both emotionally and
physically demanding. He began to complain about exhaustion. Katherine
had urged her husband, who was fifty-eight years old, to retire and move
to Hawaii. There they planned to build a home on Anahola Bay on the
island of Kauai, where Katherine's aunt Carlotta Stewart Lai had lived and
worked for three decades before her death in 1952.[60]

Flippin, however, could not bring himself to sever his ties with San
Quentin prison just yet. He had work to complete, particularly with the
rapidly growing chapter of AA. It would be a year, he felt, before he could
bring his work to closure and retire in good conscience. Yet, his health
began to deteriorate for the first time in his life, a turn of events that
required him to take a medical leave of absence from the prison in 1961.
He began treatment for a liver ailment that proved to be cancer. Although
he returned to his job briefly in 1962, his weight and stamina declined
rapidly. Even so, he withheld the diagnosis of cancer from Katherine until
the very end. Robert Flippin died quietly on September 1, 1963, at the age
of fifty-nine.[61] He was survived by his wife, Katherine, and a sister, Dorothy
Flippin Jeffers.

Katherine Flippin continued her husband's work after his death. She
attended quarterly meetings of the San Quentin AA chapter for several
years and spoke occasionally at local AA meetings about her husband's
work. In January 1964, the prison's AA chapter was officially renamed the
Robert B. Flippin AA Memorial Fellowship. Perhaps the most fitting tribute
to Flippin was expressed by the inmates themselves, who contributed an
editorial in the *San Quentin News* entitled "The Death of a Friend." The
editorial reported that "the passing of Mr. R. B. Flippin brought sadness

throughout the institution and sorrow to his legion of friends across the nation." It concluded that Flippin "was respected by the inmate body to a degree seldom attained by a free employee."[62]

In the three decades since his arrival in San Francisco, Robert B. Flippin had served others, and he gave much more to the black community than he extracted. This gifted social worker, parole officer, and reformer never lost sight of the fact that African-American leaders like himself had an obligation to lead and contribute to their communities. Black leaders, Flippin believed, were not expected to be martyrs, but to work toward racial tolerance and to leave the black community in better shape as a result of their presence. As Pat Heaton, a family friend, wrote to a bereaved Katherine Stewart Flippin shortly after her husband's death, "Surely he has left his mark."[63]

Robert Flippin left his mark not only on San Francisco's African-American community but also throughout the state of California. Despite the early struggles of Robert and Katherine during the Great Depression, their successful careers and secure financial position would have been envied by the two previous generations of Stewarts. The Flippins had, in the best sense of the word, "triumphed" against difficult odds. Their story is both uplifting and empowering, and it reveals their dedication to racial uplift, community service, and the broader reforms that were taking place in American society. More than a decade after Robert Flippin gained employment at San Quentin prison, black workers collectively had still made only modest inroads into white collar, managerial, and professional jobs in far western states. Thus Robert and Katherine were also the beneficiaries of good timing, particularly of the dramatic changes in American race relations that followed World War II and the civil rights struggle. However, Flippin's tenacity, leadership, and unselfish contribution paved the way for other black parole officers and professionals in California state government.[64]

Conclusion

❖ ❖ ❖ ❖ ❖ ❖ ❖

The Stewarts were a remarkable family, and their achievements are even more impressive when they are viewed against the backdrop of the persistent discrimination and racial inequality that has plagued American society for nearly four centuries.[1] That these men and women excelled, established professional careers, contributed significantly to their communities, educated their children, and passed down their values of racial uplift and community service, reveals the creative approaches that African-Americans developed to foster self-worth and racial pride, and to cope with exclusion and racial prejudice. The Stewarts' lives and contributions, which cover one century of American history, also remind us of the critical role that local institutions such as churches, recreation centers, women's clubs, literary societies, YMCA's and YWCA's, benevolent associations, sororities, and fraternal societies have played in the African-American community.[2]

Community institutions, which often possessed a class component, provided status, fellowship, and many essential services to African-Americans when few others were available. They also trained many generations of African-American leaders, including T. McCants Stewart and his children, Verina Morton-Jones, Mary Delia Weir Stewart, and Robert Flippin. These organizations were not without their shortcomings, and their leaders occasionally were paternalistic and condescending toward the black masses. But they served nonetheless to knit together African-American communities in truly remarkable ways. An effective bulwark against segregation, local institutions helped blacks develop organizational and fund-raising skills and cope with adversity and provided opportunities for blacks to interact with a broader spectrum of people in their communities and to be role models for young African-American males and females. These institutions were critically important during the Jim Crow era, but they were just as significant following the demise of legal segregation. African-American communities were considerably richer and more vibrant because of their presence.

The experiences of the Stewarts also illustrated the manner in which local and national organizations intersected, particularly when volatile racial issues affected a broad spectrum of African-Americans. The careers of T. McCants Stewart and his youngest son, Gilchrist, illuminate this point vividly. Both men, highly respected local leaders, sought to attract a broader constituency and to interact with African-American leaders throughout the nation. The elder Stewart led the Bethel AME Church shortly after arriving in New York in 1880, and this visibility immediately created a base of support in New York's African-American community. Moreover, Stewart's civil rights activism, his important role as an emigrationist and African authority, his legal practice, and his close relationships with Booker T. Washington, T. Thomas Fortune, and Francis J. Grimké, solidified his position as one of the nation's most respected black leaders.

Gilchrist Stewart also contributed significantly to his local community and the nation, though he never gained the acclaim of his father. His excellent work in the New York branch of the NAACP was singled out by *Crisis* magazine in 1911, and Gilchrist was literally thrust into the spotlight when he conducted an investigation for the Constitution League regarding the dismissal of black troops in the wake of the 1906 Brownsville raid. His investigation into this tragedy was balanced and meticulous, and Gilchrist Stewart's principal conclusion—that the soldiers had been punished unfairly—is shared today by most historians.[3]

Carlotta Stewart's career challenges us to rethink the meaning of African-American racial identity and what it meant in Hawaii, perhaps the most multiracial area in the United States during the early 1900s. Physically separated from her family as well as a sizable black community for her entire professional career, Carlotta expressed little of the racial anxiety that marked the lives of her father or two brothers. Yet we can hardly label as passive or apathetic an African-American woman who served as a dedicated educator for over four decades. Carlotta's life and experience teach us, too, that it was liberating for at least one African-American to be appreciated as a dedicated and talented individual rather than as a gifted "black professional." Carlotta's racial identity, although never in question in her own mind, remained a relatively insignificant fact in her life in Hawaii, and her husband as well as her peer group reflected the spectrum of Hawaii's diverse ethnic population.

McCants led the most tragic life of any member of the Stewart family. He was well-educated, articulate, outgoing, and a dedicated attorney, husband,

and father. But McCants lived in an age when employment opportunities for black professionals were restricted by a pernicious and unyielding system of racial discrimination and in an area where black communities were small. Unable to support his family, to live up to the expectations of a demanding father, or to cope with his mounting personal problems, McCants took his own life. This drastic response to the frustrations of racism has been rare among blacks, however. The percentage of African-Americans who have committed suicide during the nineteenth and twentieth centuries, relative to whites, has been exceedingly low. As late as 1940, according to Gunnar Myrdal, the suicide rate for blacks was only 4.0 per 100,000, as compared to 15.5 per 100,000 for whites.[4] His brief professional career also illustrates the problems that African-American professionals would face in two western cities during the early decades of the twentieth century.

Katherine, who represents the third generation of Stewarts, continued the family's proud tradition of service and racial activism while simultaneously attempting to establish their careers. Following the suicide of McCants Stewart in 1919, Katherine and her mother Mary worked for the Booker T. Washington Community Service Center, the most prestigious recreation and social service agency in San Francisco's black community. There they interacted with the city's black elite but also provided inspiration and an array of important services to black children and young adults.

Katherine's childhood and adult life were radically different from her father's. She was reared and grew to maturity in two western cities, Portland and San Francisco, instead of the South, and was raised by two women after the death of her father, instead of receiving the stern parental guidance of T. McCants Stewart. Moreover, Katherine faced neither the anxiety nor the uncertainty about her future that had afflicted many black professionals of her father's generation. McCants Stewart had lived in an age of restricted employment opportunities for black professionals because of a pernicious and unyielding system of racial discrimination and due to the presence of small black communities in Portland and San Francisco.

Katherine, who appeared to possess little of the racial awareness of her forebears during her formative years, seemed to awaken in the early 1930s following her marriage to Robert Flippin, a newcomer to San Francisco and also a descendant of an elite black family. Their marriage, although childless, was fulfilling, and despite some financial difficulties during the early stages of the Great Depression, the Flippins fared remarkably well, achieving financial security as a result not only of their professional employment but also of their real estate holdings, which were unknown to the earlier generations of Stewarts, with the exception of Carlotta. Following the death of her husband, Katherine established a foundation in honor of her mother to provide grants and low-interest loans to underprivileged black students. During the 1970s, she made one of the shrewdest business decisions of her life, converting her modest home on Golden Gate Avenue (the property now faces Turk Boulevard) into a small apartment complex. The rapid escalation of real estate prices in San Francisco during the 1970s and 1980s increased the property's value at an astonishing rate, and in 1988 it was appraised at nearly $1 million. Unfortunately, the devastating San Francisco earthquake of 1989 caused major structural damage to this property.[5]

Katherine and Robert also came to maturity in an era when many of the racial barriers that their elders had faced were either under assault or crumbling. World War II opened the door to a wider range of employment opportunities for African-Americans than ever before in skilled and semi-skilled jobs, and approximately one million African-Americans left the oppressive heat and the stifling racism of the South to work in the wartime defense industries. While African-Americans experienced considerable racial discrimination in defense industry employment, the number of skilled black craftsmen and semiskilled operatives doubled between 1940 and 1944, and black median income rose to 60 percent of white median income in 1950, an increase of nearly 20 percent since 1939. By the conclusion of World War II, African-Americans had also entered the federal civil service in greater numbers than ever before, and these jobs included many technical and white-collar positions where black workers had been only marginally employed heretofore.[6]

World War II also triggered a resurgent militancy in numerous African-American communities, including the Far West, and the Flippins' activism reflected a broad movement to promote racial tolerance, eradicate segregation, gain a greater measure of economic and political power, and demand being treated with dignity.[7] Historian Gerald D. Nash has concluded: "It would be too much to say that World War II ushered in a new era of race relations in the West. But wartime conditions accelerated the breakdown of discrimination patterns and crystallized conditions that generated the civil rights movement just a decade later."[8]

Yet Robert and Katherine also believed intensely that working with strong and committed interracial organizations such as the Council for Civic Unity, Fellowship Church, and the NAACP remained the best hope for achieving racial equality in San Francisco and elsewhere during the postwar era. Thus interracial cooperation became a conspicuous feature of San Francisco's racial landscape after 1945, and numerous western cities adopted a similar philosophy in an attempt to improve race relations. Had Robert Flippin lived beyond 1963, he, like the renowned black diplomat Ralph J. Bunche, would have seemed out of step with the separatism, militancy, and shrill rhetoric that characterized the civil rights struggle of the late 1960s.[9]

There are as many similarities as differences between the three generations of Stewarts, not the least of which was the prevalence of small families. Only T. McCants Stewart, who fathered six children, had anything resembling a large family. To Stewart's regret, neither of his two sons produced a boy to carry on the Stewart family name. His eldest son, McCants, had only a single child (Katherine), and Gilchrist never married. Although Carlotta was married for nineteen years, she never bore a child. Similarly, two of Stewart's daughters from his second marriage, Gladys and Anna, never married and were described by their niece, Beryl E. Kean, as reclusive. Kapulani, the youngest of the daughters, was considerably more outgoing and married Henry Kean in 1930. The Keans were, themselves, members of an elite black family in the Virgin Islands dating back several generations. Kapulani broke the cycle of childless marriages among Stewart's daughters and bore two children, Beryl, born in 1936, and Henry Kean, Jr., born in 1939. However, neither Beryl nor Henry married, and with their deaths and the death of Katherine Stewart Flippin, the Stewart name, though certainly not the Stewart legacy, will die out.[10]

This tendency toward small families was characteristic of black professionals in general, and black westerners in particular during the nineteenth and twentieth centuries. "Concentration in urban areas gave western black women a strikingly lower childbearing rate than those elsewhere, particularly in the South," wrote Lawrence B. de Graaf.[11] Indeed, between 1900 and 1920, the number of black children per 1,000 women in the West, where the majority of women in the Stewart family resided, was less than one-half the rate recorded in the South. This disparity was even greater in large western cities and was evident in spite of the fact that western black women were even more likely to get married than women in other regions of the country. This anomaly does not explain why so many members of the Stewarts chose not to have children, only that they were part of a broader social process that took place in the western states and territories. Nor does it explain why so many Stewarts decided against marriage altogether.

It is admittedly risky to generalize about such delicate and personal issues across three generations. However, evidence seems to indicate that social class and the demands of a professional career were perceived by some Stewarts as impediments to marriage and children. Gladys and Anna Stewart, for example, tried but were unable to attract suitors from the black elite in the Virgin Islands and remained single. The same could be said for Beryl Kean, Kapulani's daughter, who described herself as an "old maid."[12] Career demands were also occasionally perceived as obstacles to raising children. Neither Carlotta nor Katherine, for example, were beyond their childbearing years when they married in 1916 and 1932 respectively. Yet neither woman chose to have children in part because of the demands of their careers. It is ironic that Carlotta and Katherine perceived raising children as obstacles to their careers, for both women worked with children during their entire professional lives.[13]

The Stewarts also personified the common nineteenth century ideals of thrift, frugality, and the accumulation of property. These values were certainly not unique to middle-class black Americans, but the Stewarts were products of the age of Booker T. Washington, and T. McCants Stewart urged each of his children to be frugal, to respect all labor, never to forsake religion, and to attempt to accumulate property. Purchasing property, however, proved exceedingly difficult for many of the Stewarts because property was expensive in large cities outside the South and their professional careers were unstable. Despite a long and distinguished career, T. McCants Stewart never owned a home anywhere except Hawaii, and he defaulted on that mortgage when he left the island abruptly in 1905. Similarly, neither McCants nor Gilchrist owned property; nor were they ever in a financial position to accumulate savings. Quite the contrary, both died deep in debt. Carlotta was an exception, for she owned several homes on the island of Kauai. More than any other member of the second generation of Stewarts, Carlotta typified Booker T. Washington's ideal of the black professional who made her own way, saved diligently, and accumulated property. Her estate was valued at $20,000 at the time of her death in 1952.

Another similarity among the Stewarts was their willingness to take risks, to strike out in new directions, and to continually search for new economic and professional opportunities. In this sense they were pioneers, and the women proved as bold and daring as the men.[14] Similarly, Charlotte Harris attended Wilberforce University in 1870, graduating in 1872, and her daughter, Carlotta, graduated in 1902 from Oahu College in Hawaii, after which she became the first African-American female to teach in the territory of Hawaii. T. McCants's wanderlust represented an extreme case of "trail blazing," for he worked and resided in South Carolina, New Jersey, New York, Liberia, Hawaii, London, and, finally, the Virgin Islands. His two sons were considerably more settled than their father, but they, too, staked out new territory in Portland, the Dakotas, Wisconsin, Canada, New York, and San Francisco in their quest to launch successful careers.

Finally, evaluating the lives of this remarkable family over the course of a century illustrates how the black elite changed over time, and the degree to which this social class in San Francisco either conformed to or deviated from the black elite in other cities between 1930 and 1960. As historian Willard B. Gatewood reminds us, membership in the black elite was never so tightly regulated that outsiders were excluded in perpetuity: "Theirs was a tightly closed society that outsiders found difficult but not impossible to penetrate, provided they possessed a combination of at least several attributes considered essential by the aristocracy of color."[15] Katherine's family name and the fact that she was a direct descendant of T. McCants Stewart secured her elite status in San Francisco's black community in much the same manner that it had for her father in Portland.

But Robert Flippin was an outsider, and his marriage to Katherine alone did not guarantee he would automatically be accepted into this tight-knit social circle. Robert, therefore, earned entry into the black elite by virtue of his position as executive director of the BTWCSC and as a parole officer at San Quentin prison. Moreover, Flippin's membership in numerous interracial organizations and his column in San Francisco's largest daily newspaper made him one of the most respected African-American leaders in the San Francisco Bay area. Thus Robert Flippin's entry into the black elite was consistent with Gatewood's conclusions regarding the changing composition of this social class throughout the nation after 1920. Flippin also represents, however, a new black elite that emerged in far western cities like San Francisco and Oakland as a direct result of the large in-migration of African-Americans during World War II.[16] These men and women, college educated and professionally trained, could not claim pioneer status, family name, or a light complexion as their admission tickets to elite social status. Instead, they earned their status by virtue of their white-collar and professional employment, ties to prestigious community organizations, and their service to the African-American community.

Notes

Introduction

1. Joy Day Buel and Richard Buel, Jr., *The Way of Duty: A Woman and Her Family in Revolutionary America* (New York: W.W. Norton, 1984).

2. Suzanne Lebsock, *The Free Women of Petersburg: Status and Culture in a Southern Town, 1784-1860* (New York: W.W. Norton, 1984).

3. Jacqueline Dowd Hall, James Lelouis, Robert Korstad, et al., *Like a Family: The Making of a Southern Cotton Mill World* (Chapel Hill: University of North Carolina Press, 1987).

4. William H. Chafe, *The American Woman: Her Changing Social, Economic, and Political Roles, 1920-1970* (New York: Oxford University Press, 1972).

5. Carl N. Degler, *At Odds: Women and the Family in America from the Revolution to the Present* (New York: Oxford University Press, 1980).

6. Alex Haley, *Roots: The Saga of an American Family* (Garden City, N.Y.: Doubleday, 1976).

7. Jacqueline Jones, *Labor of Love, Labor of Sorrow: Black Women, Work, and the Family from Slavery to the Present* (New York: Basic Books, 1985); Adele Logan Alexander, *Ambiguous Lives: Free Women of Color in Rural Georgia, 1789-1879* (Fayetteville, Ark: University of Arkansas Press, 1991); Darlene Clark Hine and Kathleen Thompson, *A Shining Thread of Hope: The History of Black Women in America* (New York: Broadway Books, 1998); Glenda E. Gilmore, *Gender and Jim Crow: Women and the Politics of White Supremacy in North Carolina, 1896-1920* (Chapel Hill: University of North Carolina Press, 1996); Carole Ione, *Pride of Family: Four Generations of American Women of Color* (New York: Summit Books, 1991); Sarah Delany and Elizabeth Delany, with Amy Hill Hearth, *Having Our Say: The Delany Sisters' First Hundred Years* (New York: Kodansha America, 1993); James P. Comer, *Maggie's American Dream: The Life and Times of a Black Family* (New York: Plume, 1988).

8. Herbert G. Gutman, *The Black Family in Slavery and Freedom, 1750-1925* (New York: Pantheon Books, 1976), pp. 433, 454-456; E. Franklin Frazier, *The Negro Family in the United States* (Chicago, Ill.: University of Chicago Press, 1939); Gilbert Osofsky, *Harlem: The Making of a Negro Ghetto, 1890-1930* (New York: Harper and Row, 1966); Daniel Patrick Moynihan, "The Negro Family: The Case for National Action," in Lee Rainwater and William L. Yancy, eds.,

The Moynihan Report and the Politics of Controversy (Cambridge, Mass.: M.I.T. Press, 1967).

9. Leon Litwack's monumental study, *Been in Storm So Long: The Aftermath of Slavery* (New York: Alfred A. Knopf, 1979), is an exception and remains the standard work on African-American life in the wake of slavery. See also the fine study by Brenda E. Stevenson, *Life in Black and White: Family and Community in the Slave South* (New York: Oxford University Press, 1996). Stevenson challenges Gutman's conclusion that slave families were stable and headed by two parents.

10. See, for example, Allan H. Spear, *Black Chicago: The Making of a Negro Ghetto, 1890-1920* (Chicago, Ill.: University of Chicago Press, 1967), pp. 51-70; Kenneth L. Kusmer, *A Ghetto Takes Shape: Black Cleveland, 1870-1930* (Urbana: University of Illinois Press, 1976), pp. 91-112.

11. T. McCants Stewart, *Liberia, The Americo-African Republic* (New York: Edward O. Jenkins' Sons, 1886).

CHAPTER 1

Humble Beginnings

1. Walter J. Fraser, Jr., *Charleston! Charleston!: The History of a Southern City* (Columbia: University of South Carolina Press, 1989), pp. 1-13; David R. Goldfield and Blaine A. Brownell, *Urban America: From Downtown to No Town* (Boston, Mass.: Houghton Mifflin, 1979), p. 36; Chapman J. Milling, ed., *Colonial Charleston: Two Contemporary Descriptions* (Columbia: University of South Carolina Press, 1951); Alexander Hewatt, *An Historical Account of the Rise and Progress of the Colonies of South Carolina and Georgia*, vol. 1 (Spartanburg, S.C.: Reprint Company, 1962), pp. 49, 60-64, 96-97.

2. Frederick P. Bowes, *The Culture of Early Charleston* (Chapel Hill: University of North Carolina Press, 1942), pp. 4-8; Louis B. Wright, *South Carolina, A Bicentennial History* (New York: W.W. Norton, 1976), pp. 8-49; David Duncan Wallace, *South Carolina, A Short History, 1520-1948* (Chapel Hill: University of North Carolina Press, 1951), pp. 350-355; Peter H. Wood, *Black Majority: Negroes in Colonial South Carolina from 1670 through the Stono Rebellion* (New York: Alfred A. Knopf, 1975), pp. 35-62; Carl Bridenbaugh, *Cities in the Wilderness: The First Century of Urban Life in America, 1625-1742* (New York: Alfred A. Knopf, 1964), p. 4.

3. Horace E. Fitchett, "The Free Negro in Charleston, South Carolina," Ph.D. dissertation, University of Chicago, 1950, p. 298; Bernard E. Powers, Jr., *Black Charlestonians: A Social History, 1822-1885* (Fayetteville: University of Arkansas Press, 1994), pp. 36-72; Michael P. Johnson and James L. Roark, *Black Masters: A Free Family of Color in the Old South* (New York: Norton, 1984), pp. 206-207.

4. Wood, *Black Majority*, pp. 323-326; William W. Freehling, *Prelude to Civil*

War: The Nullification Controversy in South Carolina, 1816–1836 (New York: Harper and Row, 1965), pp. 53–70; *The Trial Record of Denmark Vesey* (Boston, Mass.: Beacon Books, 1970).

5. Michael P. Johnson and James L. Roark, eds., *No Chariot Let Down: Charleston's Free People of Color on the Eve of the Civil War* (New York: W.W. Norton, 1986), pp. 6, 13; Fitchett, "The Free Negro in Charleston," p. 298.

6. John W. Blassingame, *Black New Orleans, 1860–1880* (Chicago, Ill.: University of Chicago Press, 1973), pp. 10–11.

7. Ira Berlin, *Slaves without Masters: The Free Negro in the Antebellum South* (New York: Random House, 1974), pp. 219–221; Marina Wikramanayake, *A World in Shadow: The Free Black in Antebellum South Carolina* (Columbia: University of South Carolina Press, 1973).

8. Suzanne Lebsock, *The Free Women of Petersburg: Status and Culture in a Southern Town, 1784–1860* (New York: W.W. Norton, 1984), pp. 103–104; Berlin, *Slaves without Masters*, pp. 220–221.

9. Johnson and Roark, eds., *No Chariot Let Down*, pp. 6–7; Fitchett, "The Free Negro in Charleston," 311–312; Robert L. Harris, Jr., "Charleston's Free Afro-American Elite: The Brown Fellowship Society and the Humane Brotherhood," *South Carolina Historical Magazine* 82 (October 1981): 289–310; *Report on the Free Colored Poor of the City of Charleston* (Charleston, S.C.: Burges and James, 1842); Dale Rosengarten, Martha Zierden, Kimberly Grimes, et al., *Between the Tracks: Charleston's East Side During the Nineteenth Century* (Charleston, S.C.: Charleston Museums and Avery Research Center, 1987); Johnson and Roark, *Black Masters*, pp. 158–159, 200–205.

10. Roark and Johnson, eds., *No Chariot Let Down*, pp. 3–7; Berlin, *Slaves without Masters*, pp. 109–110, 151–152, 177–178; Wikramanayake, *A World in Shadow*, pp. 32, 49, 73, 80, 85–87; The best short survey on mulattoes is Joel Williamson's *New People: Miscegenation and Mulattoes in the United States* (New York: New York University Press, 1984).

11. George Tindall, *South Carolina Negroes, 1877–1900* (Baton Rouge: Louisiana State University Press, 1966), pp. 4–5; Joel Williamson, *After Slavery: The Negro in South Carolina, 1861–1877* (New York: W.W. Norton, 1975), pp. 188–189; Powers, *Black Charlestonians*, p. 21; Johnson and Roark, *Black Masters*, p. 38, 231.

12. Harris, "Charleston's Free Afro-American Elite," pp. 289–300; Johnson and Roark, *Black Masters*, p. 212; Berlin, *Slaves without Masters*, p. 58, 73–74.

13. Johnson and Roark, *Black Masters*, p. 213.

14. United States Census, Schedule 1, Free Inhabitants, Schedules for Charleston, South Carolina, 1860, microfilm, Charleston County Library. The details regarding Stewart's birth are conflicting. Stewart, himself, was uncertain about his date of birth, and he wrote at various times during his career that he was born in 1852, 1853, 1854, 1855, and 1857. Stewart's age is listed as six in the 1860 manuscript census for Charleston; however, he was born on December 28 and would turn seven later that year. Thus I have concluded that he was born in

1853, a date that he confirmed when he attended the Princeton Theological Seminary. See also William J. Simmons, *Men of Mark: Eminent, Progressive and Rising* (1887. Chicago, Ill.: Johnson Publishing, 1970), 758–759; T. McCants Stewart, Alumni Record, 1878, Princeton Theological Seminary Archives.

15. State Free Negro Capitation Tax Books, Charleston, South Carolina, 1811–1860, microcopy no. 11, South Carolina Department of Archives and History; Free Colored Book, 1860, H. L. Pinckney, Collector, Charleston, S.C., Carter G. Woodson Collection, Library of Congress; Roark and Johnson, *Black Masters*, pp. 186–187; Population Schedules of the Eighth Census of the United States, 1860, roll 1216, South Carolina, vol. 2, Charleston District, 35; "Thomas McCants Stewart Family Tree," Stewart-Flippin Papers, Moorland-Spingarn Research Center, Howard University.

16. *The Charleston Directory, 1859* (Charleston, S.C.: Walker, Evans., 1859), p. 200.

17. Tax Book, 1863, Free Persons of Color, Charleston, S.C. Charleston Library Society; Population Schedules of the Ninth Census of the United States, roll 1487, South Carolina, 1870 Census of Charleston, S.C., p. 278; *Charleston City Directory, 1872–73* (Charleston, S.C.: Walker, Evans, and Cogswell, 1873).

18. Simmons, *Men of Mark*, p. 758; Leonard P. Curry, *The Free Black in Urban America, 1800–1850: The Shadow of the Dream* (Chicago, Ill.: University of Chicago Press, 1981), pp. 156, 168; Berlin, *Slaves without Masters*, pp. 72–74.

19. Dickson D. Bruce, *Archibald Grimké: Portrait of a Black Independent* (Baton Rouge: Louisiana State University Press, 1993), p. 8; Simmons, *Men of Mark*, p. 758; Curry, *The Free Black in Urban America*, pp. 156, 168; Berlin, *Slaves without Masters*, pp. 72–74.

20. Tindall, *South Carolina Negroes*, p. 4.

21. Curry, *The Free Black in Urban America*, pp. 168–169; Tindall, *South Carolina Negroes*, pp. 5–6.

22. *City Directory, Charleston, S.C., 1869–70*, p. 240; *Jowitt's Illustrated Charleston City Directory and Business Register* (Charleston, S.C.: Walker, Evans, and Cogswell, 1869), p. 175; Rev. R. V. Lawrence, *The Centenary Souvenir. Containing a History of Centenary Church, Charleston, and an Account of the Life and Labors of Rev. R. V. Lawrence, Father and Pastor of Centenary Church* (Philadelphia, Penn.: Collins Printing House, 1885); "The History of Centenary United Methodist Church," April 21, 1991, copy provided to author by the church secretary, June 1993.

23. *American Missionary Society Annual Report, 1878* (New York: American Missionary Association, 1878), p. 68.

24. *AMA Annual Report, 1867*, p. 33; James D. Anderson, *The Education of Blacks in the South, 1865–1930* (Chapel Hill: University of North Carolina Press, 1988), pp. 4, 21–22.

25. *AMA Annual Report, 1878*, p. 68; Henry Allan Bullock, *A History of Negro Education in the South, from 1619 to the Present* (New York: Praeger, 1967), pp. 52–59; Martin Abbott, *The Freedmen's Bureau in South Carolina, 1865–1872* (Chapel

Hill: University of North Carolina Press, 1967), pp. 90, 92; "Catalogue of the Teachers and Pupils," Avery Normal Institute, John L. Dart Branch, Charleston County Library.

26. Willard B. Gatewood, Jr., *Aristocrats of Color: The Black Elite, 1880–1920* (Bloomington: Indiana University Press, 1990), pp. 39–50; William S. McFeely, *Frederick Douglass* (New York: W.W. Norton, 1991), pp. 276–290; Constance M. Green, *The Secret City: A History of Race Relations in the Nation's Capital* (Princeton, N.J.: Princeton University Press, 1967), pp. 91–92, 94–96.

27. William S. McFeely, *General O. O. Howard and the Freedmen* (New York: W.W. Norton, 1968); Oliver Otis Howard, *The Autobiography of Oliver Otis Howard*, vol. 2 (New York: Baker and Taylor, 1908), pp. 452–455, 390–401; Rayford W. Logan, *Howard University, The First Hundred Years: 1867–1967* (New York: New York University Press, 1969), pp. 36–40; Anderson, *The Education of Blacks in the South, 1860–1935*, p. 250.

28. T. McCants Stewart to A. Morris Stewart, December 6, 1873, Stewart-Flippin Papers.

29. John Hope Franklin, *George Washington Williams: A Biography* (Chicago, Ill.: University of Chicago Press, 1985), pp. 8–9, 24, 33; Hugh M. Browne, Alumni Record, Princeton Theological Seminary Archives; Willard B. Gatewood, Jr., "Alonzo Clifton McClennan: Black Midshipman from South Carolina, 1873–1874," *South Carolina Historical Magazine* 89 (January 1988): 30.

30. T. McCants Stewart to A. Morris Stewart, April 8, 1871, Stewart-Flippin Papers.

31. T. McCants Stewart to A. Morris Stewart, December 6, 1873, Stewart-Flippin Papers.

32. Ibid.

33. "Death Record," [Charleston, S.C.], Health Department, George Stewart, January 25, 1879, Charleston County Library.

34. Washington *New National Era*, April 28, 1870.

35. Ibid.

36. Ibid.

37. Drago, *Initiative, Paternalism, and Race Relations*, pp. 44–46; Maximilian M. Ladorde, *History of the South Carolina College* (Charleston, S.C.: Walker, Evans, and Cogswell, 1874); John F. Potts, Sr., *A History of South Carolina State College, 1896–1978* (Orangeburg: South Carolina State College, 1978), pp. 8–9; Eric Foner, *Reconstruction*, p. 368.

38. David Walker Hollis, *University of South Carolina*, vol. II, *College to University* (Columbia: University of South Carolina Press, 1956), pp. 76–77; Willard B. Gatewood, Jr., "William D. Crum: A Negro in Politics," *Journal of Negro History* 53 (October 1968): 301–320; Louis R. Harlan, *Booker T. Washington: The Wizard of Tuskegee, 1901–1915* (New York: Oxford University Press, 1983), pp. 19–20, 20–23, 339–340.

39. "University of South Carolina Junior Exhibition," Class of 1875, March

12, 1874, Stewart-Flippin Papers; Hollis, *History of South Carolina*, p. 72; Williamson, *After Slavery: The Negro in South Carolina During Reconstruction, 1861-1877*, p. 236.

40. G. F. Richings, *Evidence of Progress among the Colored People* (Philadelphia, Penn.: Ferguson, 1899), pp. 291-296; T. McCants Stewart, Alumni Record, 1878, Princeton Theological Seminary, Princeton Theological Seminary Archives. Stewart placed the date of his graduation from the University of South Carolina on December 21, 1875. This date was confirmed in a letter from the reference librarian at the University of South Carolina to the author. See also I. A. Newby, *Black Carolinians, A History of Blacks in South Carolina from 1895 to 1968* (Columbia: University of South Carolina Press, 1973), p. 196.

41. On Bishop C. R. Harris, consult W. F. Fonvielle, *Reminiscences of College Days* (Goldsboro, N.C.: Edwards and Broughton, 1904), p. 118; "A Brief History of the Noble Negro Ancestry and Institutions of Salisbury and Rowan County, North Carolina," Carolina Price High School, Salisbury, N.C., 1957; David Henry Bradley, Sr., *A History of the AME Zion Church*, pt. 1, 1796-1872 (Nashville, Tenn.: Parthenon Press, 1956), p. 176; and Bradley, Sr., *A History of the AME Zion Church*, pt. 2, 1872-1968 (Nashville, Tenn.: Parthenon Press, 1970, pp. 62, 150, 178-179, 407; James Abajian, *Blacks in Selected Newspapers, Censuses and Other Sources: An Index to Names and Subjects*, vol. 3 (Boston, Mass.: G. K. Hall and Company, 1977), p. 412. T. McCants Stewart listed the date of his marriage to Charlotte Harris in his 1878 Princeton Theological Seminary Alumni Record, Princeton Theological Seminary Archives.

42. "Wilberforce University, A Short Historical Sketch," Wilberforce University, Archives and Special Collections; *The Reporter* (Wilberforce), August 23-30, 1986; Richard Robert Wright, Jr., ed., *The Encyclopaedia of the African Methodist Episcopal Church*, 2d ed. (Philadelphia, Penn.: Book Concern of the AME Church, n.d.), p. 533; Frederick A. McGinnis, *A History and an Interpretation of Wilberforce University* (Wilberforce, Ohio: Brown Publishing, 1941).

43. *New National Era*, May 5, 1870; Daniel A. Payne, *History of the African Methodist Episcopal Church* (Nashville, Tenn.: Publishing House of the A.M.E. Sunday-School Union, 1891), pp. 423-440; William Cheek and Aimes Lee Cheek, *John Mercer Langston and the Fight for Black Freedom, 1829-65* (Urbana: University of Illinois Press, 1989), p. 326; Carter G. Woodson, *The Education of the Negro Prior to 1861* (New York: Arno Press and the New York Times, 1968), pp. 272-274; Daniel Alexander Payne, *Recollection of Seventy Years*, pp. 149-157.

44. Paul R. Griffin, *Black Theology As the Foundation of Three Methodist Colleges: The Educational Views and Labors of Daniel Payne, Joseph Price, Isaac Lane* (Lanham, Md.: University Press of America), pp. 99-100; Charles S. Smith, *The Life of Daniel Alexander Payne* (Nashville, Tenn.: A.M.E. Publishing House, 1894); Payne, *History of the African Methodist Episcopal Church*, pp. 430, 431, 433; [Charlotte] Lottie P. Harris, "Academic Transcript," 1870-1872, Wilberforce University, Archives and Special Collections; Charlotte P. Harris, "Diploma," Wilberforce University,

1872, Stewart-Flippin Papers, Moorland-Spingarn Research Center; *Triennial Catalogue of Wilberforce University for the Academic Year, 1872-73* (Xenia, Ohio: Torchlight Steam Printing House, 1873), copy in Archives and Special Collections, Wilberforce University; Hattie Q. Brown, *Pen Pictures of Pioneers of Wilberforce* (Xenia, Ohio: Aldine Publishing, 1937).

45. *Catalogue of Claflin University and South Carolina Agricultural College and Mechanics Institute, Orangeburg, South Carolina, 1877-78* (Middletown, Conn.: Felton and King Steam Printers, 1878), p. 8.

46. Willard B. Gatewood, *Aristocrats of Color: The Black Elite, 1880-1920* (Bloomington: Indiana University Press, 1990), pp. 41, 80-82; Charlotte P. Harris, "Diploma," Wilberforce University, 1872, Stewart-Flippin Papers; [Charlotte] Lottie P. Harris, "Academic Transcript," 1870-1872, Wilberforce University, Archives and Special Collections.

47. "Verina Morton Harris Jones," in Darlene Clark Hine, ed., *Black Women in America: An Historical Encyclopedia*, vol 2 (Brooklyn, N.Y.: Carlson Publishing, 1993), pp. 656-657; "Application for Charter, August 18, 1920, Brooklyn Branch, National Association for the Advancement of Colored People, Branch Files, NAACP Papers, Library of Congress; "Minutes of the First Meeting of the Executive Board of the National League on Urban Conditions among Negroes, Inc.," May 2, 1913, National Urban League Papers, Library of Congress.

48. Charlotte Stewart to McCants Stewart, May 27, 1906, Stewart-Flippin Papers.

49. Ibid.; Albert S. Broussard, "Carlotta Stewart Lai, A Black Teacher in the Territory of Hawai'i," *Hawaiian Journal of History* 24 (1990): 129-154; Albert S. Broussard, "McCants Stewart: The Struggles of a Black Attorney in the Urban West," *Oregon Historical Quarterly* 89 (Summer 1988): 157-179.

50. Tindall, *South Carolina Negroes*, p. 7; Litwack, *Been in the Storm So Long*, pp. 263-264, 280; John Hope Franklin, *Reconstruction after the Civil War* (Chicago, Ill.: University of Chicago Press, 1961), pp. 35, 119-120, 157, 162; Robert Cruden, *The Negro in Reconstruction* (Englewood Cliffs, N.J.: Prentice-Hall, 1969), pp. 20-23; William C. Hine, "Black Organized Labor in Reconstruction Charleston," *Labor History 25 (Fall 1984): 504-517.*

51. Litwack, *Been in the Storm So Long*, pp. 366-367; Johnson and Roark, *Black Masters*, pp. 195-232.

52. Tindall, *South Carolina Negroes*, p. 8; The literature on the role and treatment of African-Americans during Reconstruction and the meaning of freedom in the black community is voluminous. See Ira Berlin, ed., *Freedom, A Documentary History of Emancipation, 1861-1867:* Series 2, *The Black Military Experience* (Cambridge: Cambridge University Press, 1982).

53. *Catalogue of Claflin University and South Carolina Agricultural College and Mechanical Institute, 1877-78, Orangeburg, S.C.* (Middleton, Conn.: Felton and King, 1878), p. 8; T. McCants Stewart, Alumni Record, 1878, Princeton Theological Seminary Archives; Fitzhugh Lee Styles, *Negroes and the Law* (Boston, Mass.:

Christopher Publishing House, 1937), pp. 128-131; Peggy Lamson, *The Glorious Failure: Black Congressman Robert Brown Elliott and the Reconstruction in South Carolina* (New York: W.W. Norton, 1973), pp. 25, 75, 271; Franklin, *Reconstruction after the Civil War*, pp. 209, 216-217, 231; William C. Hine, "Black Politicians in Reconstruction Charleston, South Carolina: A Collective Study," *Journal of Southern History* 49 (November 1983): 555-584; William C. Hine, "South Carolina State College: A Legacy of Education and Public Service," *Agricultural History* 65 (Spring 1991): 149-167.

54. Lamson, *The Glorious Failure*, p. 205; Dorothy Drinkard-Hawkshawe, "David Augustus Straker: Black Lawyer and Reconstruction Politician, 1842-1908," Ph.D. dissertation, Catholic University of America, 1974; Logan, *Howard University, The First Hundred Years*, p. 49.

55. Cleveland *Gazette*, May 29, 1886.

56. T. McCants Stewart, Alumni Record, 1878 and 1908, Princeton Theological Seminary Archives; Alexander W. Wayman, *Cyclopaedia of American Methodism* (Baltimore, Md.: Methodist Episcopal Book Depository, 1882), p. 156; Richings, *Evidence of Progress*, pp. 291-294: Tindall, *South Carolina Negroes, 1877-1900*, pp. 233-259.

57. Theodore Sedgwick Wright, Alumni File, Princeton Theological Seminary Archives; Jonathan Greenleaf, *History of the Churches, of All Denominations in the City of New York* (New York: Hyde, Lord and Duren, 1846), pp. 153-154. "Minutes of Faculty," May 8, 1826, vol. 1, p. 116, Princeton Theological Seminary Archives; Benjamin Quarles, *Black Abolitionists* (New York: Oxford University Press, 1969), pp. 38, 45-46, 68, 79-80, 87, 95; August Meier and Elliott Rudwick, *From Plantation to Ghetto*, rev. ed. (New York: Hill and Wang, 1970), pp. 115-116, 118, 120, 127-128.

58. On Browne's backround and early education, consult the *African Repository* 59 (1883): 26-27; Logan, *Howard University, The First Hundred Years*, p. 94; Hugh H. Browne, Alumni File, Princeton Theological Seminary Archives; Hugh Mason Browne, Princeton Seminary Necrological Report, n.d., Princeton Theological Seminary Archives.

59. Francis James Grimké, Alumni File, Princeton Theological Seminary Archives; *Princeton Theological Seminary Catalogue, 1877-78* (Philadelphia, Penn.: Caxton Press of Sherman and Company, [1878], p. 7; Bruce, *Archibald Grimké: Portrait of a Black Independent*, pp. 1-17, 66-77; A. A. Hodge, *The Life of Charles Hodge* (New York: Charles Scribner's Sons, 1880); Henry Justice Ferry, "Francis James Grimké: Portrait of a Black Puritan," Ph.D. dissertation, Yale University, 1970.

60. T. McCants Stewart, Alumni File, 1878 and 1908, Princeton Theological Seminary Archives; James McCosh, *The Life of James McCosh, A Record Chiefly Autobiographical* (New York, 1896); John Hageman, *History of Princeton and Its Institutions*, vol. 2 (Philadelphia, Penn.: J.B. Lippincott, 1879), p. 439; Interview with Henry MacAdam, associate archivist, May 28, 1992, Princeton Theological Seminary Archives, Princeton, N.J.; *Princeton Theological Seminary Catalogue, 1878-79*, p. 9.

61. Willard B. Gatewood, Jr., "Aristocrats of Color: South and North, The Black Elite, 1880–1920," *Journal of Southern History* 54 (February 1988): 3–20.

CHAPTER 2

A National Leader Emerges

1. Alexander W. Wayman, *Cyclopaedia of African Methodism* (Baltimore, Md.: Methodist Episcopal Church Book Depository, 1882), p. 156; Nell Painter, *Exodusters: Black Migration to Kansas after Reconstruction* (New York: W.W. Norton, 1976); Leon Litwack, *Been in the Storm So Long: The Aftermath of Slavery* (New York: Alfred A. Knopf, 1979), pp. 274–280, 547.

2. *Trow's New York City Directory, 1880–81* (New York: Trow's City Directory, 1881), p. 1496; *Trow's New York City Directory, 1881–82*, p. 1565; *Trow's New York City Directory, 1883*, p. 1580; *Compendium of the Tenth Census, 1880*, Part I (Washington, D.C.: Government Printing Office, 1883), pp. 230, 364; *Twelfth Census of the United States, 1900, Population*, Part l (Washington, D.C.: Government Printing Office, 1901), pp. 550, 594.

3. *First Annual Report of the New York Committee of Vigilance for the Year 1837* (New York: Piercy and Reed, 1837); Dorothy B. Porter, "The Organized Educational Activities of Negro Literary Societies, 1826–1846," August Meier and Elliott Rudwick, eds., *The Making of Black America*, vol. 1 (New York: Atheneum, 1969), pp. 276–288; Rhoda Freeman, "The Free Negro in New York City in the Era before the Civil War," Ph.D. dissertation, Columbia University, 1966; Leo H. Hirsch, "The Negro and New York, 1783–1865," *Journal of Negro History* 16 (October 1931): 383–473; Gilbert Osofsky, *Harlem: The Making of a Ghetto, Negro New York, 1890–1930* (New York: Harper and Row, 1966), pp. 3–16; Howard H. Bell, ed., *Minutes and Proceedings of the National Negro Conventions, 1830–1864* (New York: Arno Press and the New York Times, 1969); Martin Delany, *The Condition, Elevation, and Destiny of the Colored People of the United States* (New York: Arno Press and the New York Times, 1969); F. T. Ray, *Sketch of the Life of Reverend Charles B. Ray* (New York: J.J. Little, 1887); Herman D. Bloch, "New York Negro's Battle for Political Rights, 1777–1865," *International Review of Social History* (1964): 65–80.

4. Osofsky, *Harlem: The Making of a Ghetto*, pp. 5, 8–10.

5. Ibid., p. 11; New York *Freeman*, February 19, 1887.

6. New York *Sun*, April 10, 1882; New York *Times*, November 6, 1882; New York *Globe*, January 6, 1883, August 4, 1883; Osofsky, *Harlem: The Making of a Ghetto*, p. 10; Roi Ottley and William J. Weatherly, *The Negro in New York: An Informal Social History* (New York: Oceana Publications, 1967), p. 55; Joseph R. Washington, *Black Religion: The Negro and Christianity in the United States* (Boston, Mass.: Beacon Press, 1964), pp. 199–200; Caroline F. Ware, *Greenwich Village, 1920–1930* (Boston, Mass.: Houghton Mifflin, 1935), pp. 11–12, 16, 51, 130–133, 153, 312; *Catalogue of Wilberforce University, 1883–84 and 1884–85* (Xenia, Ohio:

Gazette Office, 1885), p. 3; R. R. Wright, Jr., ed., *The Centennial Encyclopaedia of the African Methodist Episcopal Church*, vol. 1 (Philadelphia, Penn.: Book Concern of the A.M.E. Church, 1916), pp. 15, 83–84.

7. T. McCants Stewart, *In Memory of Rev. James Morris Williams, D.D., A Sermon Preached in Sullivan Street A.M.E. Church, New York City* (Philadelphia: A.M.E. Book Room), [1880]; Benjamin Quarles, *Black Abolitionists* (New York: Oxford University Press, 1969), pp. 46–47; David E. Swift, *Black Prophets of Justice: Activist Clergy before the Civil War* (Baton Rouge: Louisiana State University Press, 1989); Martin Kilson, "Adam Clayton Powell, Jr.: The Militant as Politician," in John Hope Franklin and August Meier, eds., *Black Leaders of the Twentieth Century* (Urbana: University of Illinois Press, 1982), p. 263.

8. New York *Sun*, April 10, 1882; New York *Globe*, January 6, 1883; Robert J. Swan, "Thomas McCants Stewart and the Failure of the Mission of the Talented Tenth in Black America, 1880–1923," Ph.D. dissertation, New York University, 1990, pp. 53–54; Nina Mjagkij, *Light in the Darkness: African Americans and the YMCA, 1852–1946* (Lexington: University of Kentucky Press, 1994), p. 68.

9. New York *Sun*, April 10, 1882; John Hope Franklin, *George Washington Williams, A Biography* (Chicago: University of Chicago Press, 1985), p. 15.

10. Swan, "T. McCants Stewart," pp. 54–55.

11. Swift, *Black Prophets of Justice*, pp. 113–145; Sterling Stuckey, *The Ideological Origins of Black Nationalism* (Boston, Mass.: Beacon Press, 1972), pp. 165–173; "Henry Highland Garnet," in Rayford Logan and Michael Winston, eds., *Dictionary of American Negro Biography* (New York: Norton, 1982), pp. 252–253; Joel Schor, *Henry Highland Garnet, A Voice of Black Radicalism in the Nineteenth Century* (Westport, Conn.: Greenwood Press, 1977); William Brewer, "Henry Highland Garnet," *Journal of Negro History* 13 (January 1928): 36–52; Howard H. Bell, *A Survey of the Negro Convention Movement, 1830–1861* (New York: Arno Press and the New York Times, 1969), pp. 72–79; Allan Peskin, *Garfield: A Biography* (Kent, Ohio: Kent State University Press, 1978).

12. Washington, D.C., *Exodus*, July 24, 1880; New York *Times*, June 29, 1879, July 26, 1879.

13. Daniel A. Payne, *Recollections of Seventy Years* (Nashville, Tenn.: Publishing House of the A.M.E. Sunday School Union, 1888), pp. 286–289.

14. Payne, *Recollections of Seventy Years*, p. 289; Swan, "T. McCants Stewart," pp. 57–58; Edward L. Ayers, *The Promise of the New South: Life after Reconstruction* (New York: Oxford University Press, 1992), pp. 137–146; For an excellent discussion of terrorism and racial violence, consult George C. Wright, *Racial Violence in Kentucky, 1865–1940: Lynching, Mob Rule, and "Legal Lynchings"* (Baton Rouge: Louisiana State University Press, 1990).

15. *African Repository* 59 (January 1883): 26–27; New York *Times*, November 6, 1882.

16. Peter J. Staudenraus, *The African Colonization Movement, 1816–1865* (New York: Columbia University Press, 1961); Christopher Fyfe, ed., *'Our Children Free and Happy': Letters from Black Settlers in Africa in the 1790's* (Edinburgh,

Scotland: Edinburgh University Press, 1991); Christopher Fyfe, *A History of Sierra Leone* (London, Oxford University Press, 1962), p. 112; Edwin S. Redkey, *Black Exodus: Black Nationalist and Back-to-Africa Movements, 1890-1910* (New Haven, Conn.: Yale University Press, 1969), pp. 16–22; John Hope Franklin and Alfred A. Moss, Jr., *From Slavery to Freedom: A History of African Americans*, 7th ed. (New York: McGraw-Hill, 1994), pp. 168–170; Tom W. Shick, *Behold the Promised Land: A History of Afro-American Settler Society in Nineteenth-Century Liberia* (Baltimore, Md.: Johns Hopkins University Press, 1977).

17. *African Repository* 59 (January 1883): 26–27; *African Repository* 59 (April 1883): 43; "Hugh H. Browne," in Logan and Winston, eds., *Dictionary of American Negro Biography*, pp. 73–74; "Hugh H. Browne," Alumni File, Princeton Theological Seminary, Archives and Special Collections; Rayford W. Logan, *Howard University: The First Hundred Years: 1867-1967* (New York: New York University Press, 1969), p. 94.

18. *African Repository* 59 (January 1883): 12–14.

19. Hollis Lynch, *Edward Wilmot Blyden: Pan-Negro Patriot, 1832-1912* (New York: Oxford University Press, 1967), pp. 147–150, 152.

20. New York *Globe*, January 6, 1883, January 13, 1883.

21. New York *Globe*, January 6, 1883; Dorothy Drinkard Hawkshawe, "David Augustus Straker: Black Lawyer and Reconstruction Politician, 1842-1908," Ph.D. dissertation, Catholic University of America, 1974, pp. 48–56.

22. *African Repository* 59 (January 1883): 27; William Milligan Sloane, ed., *The Life of James McCosh, A Record Chiefly Autobiographical* (New York: Charles Scribners Sons, 1896).

23. New York *Globe*, August 4, 1883.

24. The black Presbyterian minister Alexander Crummell had similar views of Africa. Consult Wilson Moses, *Alexander Crummell, A Study of Civilization and Discontent* (New York: Oxford University Press, 1989), and Wilson Moses, *The Golden Age of Black Nationalism, 1850-1925* (Hamden, Conn.: Archon Books, 1978).

25. New York *Globe*, January 13, 1883, August 4, 1883.

26. New York *Globe*, August 4, 1883; Jacqueline Jones, *Labor of Love, Labor of Sorrow: Black Women, Work, and the Family from Slavery to the Present* (New York: Basic Books, 1985).

27. Gardner W. Allen, *The Trustees of Donations for Education in Liberia: A Story of Philanthropic Endeavor, 1850-1923* (Boston, Mass. Thomas Todd, 1923).

28. Edward Blyden to John C. Braman, September 13, 1883, quoted in Hollis R. Lynch, ed., *Selected Letters of Edward Wilmot Blyden* (Millwood, N.Y.: KTO Press, 1978), p. 314; Lynch, *Edward Wilmot Blyden*, p. 147; Swan, "T. McCants Stewart," p. 69.

29. Lynch, *Edward Wilmot Blyden*, pp. 147–148.

30. Ibid., p. 153.

31. Holden, *Blyden of Liberia*, p. 967.

32. Lynch, *Edward Wilmot Blyden*, pp. 152–153, 159–160.

33. Edward Blyden to William Coppinger, *African Repository* 59 (October 25, 1883), quoted in Edith Holden, *Blyden of Liberia: An Account of the Life and Letters of Edward Wilmot Blyden* (New York: Vantage Press, 1966), p. 513.

34. Edward Blyden to Thomas Davenport, October 25, 1883, quoted in Holden, *Blyden of Liberia,* p. 513.

35. Ibid., pp. 513-514; Blyden to John C. Braman, September 13, 1883, in Hollis R. Lynch, ed., *Selected Letters of Edward Wilmot Blyden* (Millwood, N.Y.: KTO Press, 1978), p. 314.

36. Lynch, *Edward Wilmot Blyden,* pp. 150-152; Louis R. Harlan, *Booker T. Washington: The Making of a Black Leader, 1856-1901* (New York: Oxford University Press, 1972); Edith Armstrong Talbot, *Samuel Chapman Armstrong: A Biographical Study* (New York: Doubleday, Page, 1904); Suzanne Carson, "Samuel Chapman Armstrong: Missionary to the South," Ph.D. dissertation, Johns Hopkins University, 1952.

37. Broussard, "McCants Stewart," pp. 158-159; Lynch, *Edward Wilmot Blyden,* pp. 161-164.

38. William Coppinger to Blyden, November 3, 1883, quoted in Holden, *Blyden of Liberia,* p. 515.

39. Blyden to Coppinger, November 3, 1883, quoted in Holden, *Blyden of Liberia,* p. 510.

40. Blyden to J. C. Braman, January 16, 1884, quoted in Holden, *Blyden of Liberia,* p. 520; New York *Freeman,* October 24, 1885; Lynch, *Edward Wilmot Blyden,* p. 160.

41. H. R. W. Johnson to Trustees of Donations for Education in Liberia, n.d., quoted in Holden, *Blyden of Liberia,* pp. 523-524.

42. Lynch, *Edward Wilmot Blyden,* pp. 154, 160-161.

43. New York *Freeman,* January 10, 1885, April 25, 1885; *African Repository* 60 (July 1884): 85-86; Broussard, "McCants Stewart," pp. 157-179.

44. T. McCants Stewart, *Liberia, The Americo-African Republic* (New York: Edward O. Jenkins' Sons, 1886).

45. Lamont D. Thomas, *Rise to Be a People: A Biography of Paul Cuffe* (Urbana: University of Illinois Press, 1986); Sheldon H. Harris, *Paul Cuffe, Black America and the African Return* (New York: Simon and Schuster, 1972), pp. 59-60; Cleveland *Gazette,* January 3, 1885, December 26, 1885, February 2, 1886, March 27, 1886.

46. Stewart, *Liberia,* pp. 103, 105; August Meier, *Negro Thought in America: Racial Ideologies in the Age of Booker T. Washington, 1880-1915* (Ann Arbor: University of Michigan Press, 1963), pp. 66-67. Stewart's impressions of Liberia can also be found in the introduction to Charles S. Smith's, *Liberia in the Light of Living Testimony* (Nashville, Tenn.: Publishing House of the A.M.E. Church Sunday School Union, 1895), pp. 6-15.

47. New York *Globe,* January 13, 1883; Charlotte Stewart to McCants Stewart, May 27, 1906, Stewart-Flippin Papers.

48. Ibid.

CHAPTER 3

Years of Triumph and Frustration

1. New York *Freeman,* October 24, 1885.

2. Emma Lou Thornbrough, *T. Thomas Fortune, Militant Journalist* (Chicago, Ill.: University of Chicago Press, 1972).

3. J. Clay Smith, Jr., *Emancipation: The Making of the Black Lawyer, 1844–1944* (Philadelphia: University of Pennsylvania Press, 1993), p. 4.

4. New York *Freeman,* January 9, 1886; Smith, Jr., *Emancipation,* p. 395.

5. New York *Freeman,* February 5, 1887.

6. Ibid.

7. Ibid.

8. Smith, Jr., *Emancipation,* pp. 394–395.

9. Huntsville, Alabama, *Gazette,* February 16, 1887.

10. Smith, Jr., *Emancipation,* p. 395.

11. Ibid.

12. Thornbrough, *T. Thomas Fortune,* pp. 117–119; Emma Lou Thornbrough, "The National Afro-American League, 1887–1908," *Journal of Southern History* 27 (November 1961): 494–512.

13. Carleton Mabee, *Black Education in New York State, from Colonial to Modern Times* (Syracuse, N.Y.: Syracuse University Press, 1979), pp. 200–201.

14. Smith, Jr., *Emancipation,* p. 396.

15. Thornbrough, *T. Thomas Fortune,* p. 119; Smith, Jr., *Emancipation,* p. 396; Louis R. Harlan, *Booker T. Washington: The Making of a Black Leader, 1856–1901* (New York: Oxford University Press, 1972), p. 192.

16. Booker T. Washington to T. McCants Stewart, April 14, 1891, February 26, 1892, April 2, 1892, Stewart-Flippin Papers; *Programme of the Twelfth Anniversary Exercises of the Tuskegee Normal and Industrial Institute,* May 18, 1893, Stewart-Flippin Papers.

17. Mabee, *Black Education in New York State,* pp. 155, 220; Mary White Ovington, *Half a Man: The Status of the Negro in New York* (New York: Longmans, Green, 1911), p. 18; New York *Freeman,* April 18, 1885, April 25, 1885.

18. New York *Age,* April 19, 1890; Smith, Jr., *Emancipation,* p. 396.

19. New York *Freeman,* January 9, 1886, copy in Grover Cleveland Papers, series 2, reel 38, Library of Congress; Smith, Jr., *Emancipation,* pp. 396, 438.

20. Mabee, *Black Education in New York State,* pp. 152, 155; Brooklyn Board of Education, *Proceedings,* May 3, May 5, May 19, August 4, 1891, Columbia University, Archives and Special Collections.

21. Brooklyn Board of Education, *Proceedings,* August 4, 1891.

22. G. F. Richings, *Evidence of Progress among Colored People* (Philadelphia: Ferguson and Company, 1899), pp. 291–296.

23. Mabee, *Black Education in New York State,* pp. 155, 196–205, 221–225; Harold X. Connolly, *A Ghetto Grows in Brooklyn* (New York: New York University Press, 1977), pp. 27–28.

24. David M. Ment, "Racial Segregation in the Public Schools of New England and New York, 1840-1940," Ph.D. dissertation, Columbia University, 1975, pp. 179, 184; Mabee, *Black Education in New York State,* pp. 222-223.

25. Mabee, *Black Education in New York State,* p. 223.

26. Ment, "Racial Segregation in the Public Schools," pp. 184-185; Brooklyn Board of Education, *Proceedings, 1893,* pp. 183-187; Mabee, *Black Education in New York State,* pp. 223, 225.

27. It is unclear when Stewart divorced Lottie Harris, his first wife. Since he seldom mentioned her in his personal correspondence between 1886 and 1893, and never affectionately, it is apparent that the two were estranged long before a formal divorce was decreed.

28. Cleveland *Gazette,* April 15, 1893; T. McCants Stewart, Alumni Record, 1878, Princeton Theological Seminary Archives.

29. Cleveland *Gazette,* April 15, 1893; Interview with Ms. Beryl E. Kean, December 14, 1990, St. Thomas, Virgin Islands.

30. New York *Freeman,* August 8, October 3, October 31, 1885.

31. New York *Freeman,* October 31, 1885, November 14, 1885, July 10, 1886, January 15, 1887; New York *Age,* January 7, 1888.

32. August Meier, *Negro Thought in America, 1880-1915: Racial Ideologies in the Age of Booker T. Washington* (Ann Arbor: University of Michigan Press, 1963), p. 33.

33. Stanley P. Hirshon, *Farewell to the Bloody Shirt: Northern Republicans and the Southern Negro, 1877-1893* (Bloomington: Indiana University Press, 1962).

34. C. Vann Woodward, *The Origins of the New South, 1877-1913* (Baton Rouge: Louisiana State University Press, 1971), pp. 42-45, 209; Meier, *Negro Thought in America,* p. 30; Lawrence Grossman, *The Democratic Party and the Negro: Northern and National Politics, 1868-92* (Urbana: University of Illinois Press, 1976).

35. Meier, *Negro Thought in America,* p. 30.

36. T. McCants Stewart to Grover Cleveland, August 10, 1886, series 2, reel 38, Grover Cleveland Papers, Library of Congress (Hereafter cited as Cleveland Papers).

37. Stewart to Cleveland, August 10, 1886, series 2, reel 38, Cleveland Papers.

38. John A. Garraty, *The New Commonwealth, 1877-1890* (New York: Harper and Row, 1968), pp. 252-254.

39. New York *Freeman,* January 9, 1886.

40. New York *Herald,* August 21, 1886.

41. Stewart to Cleveland, August 18, 1886, series 2, reel 38, Cleveland Papers.

42. New York *Herald,* August 21, 1886, p.3.

43. Stewart to Cleveland, March 1, 1887, series 2, reel 46, Cleveland Papers; Grossman, *The Democratic Party and the Negro,* pp. 134-136, 138-139.

44. Stewart to Cleveland, December 31, 1887, series 2, reel 56, Cleveland Papers; Grossman, *The Democratic Party and the Negro,* p. 144.

45. Stewart to Col. Lamont, December 31, 1887, series 2, reel 56, Cleveland Papers.

46. Grossman, *The Democratic Party and the Negro,* pp. 115-120, 121, 149-150,

158; Carl R. Osthaus, *Freedmen, Philanthrophy, and Fraud: A History of the Freedmen's Savings Bank* (Urbana: University of Illinois Press, 1976); Woodward, *Origins of the New South*, pp. 205–243; Allen J. Going, "The South and the Blair Bill," *Mississippi Valley Historical Review* 44 (September 1957): 466–489; Daniel W. Crofts, "The Black Response to the Blair Education Bill," *Journal of Southern History* 37 (February 1971): 41–65.

47. Stewart to Cleveland, May 17, 1888, series 2, reel 59, Cleveland Papers.

48. William S. McFeely, *Frederick Douglass* (New York: W.W. Norton, 1991), pp. 334–358; Blanche K. Bruce to Elijah W. Halford, July 28, 1891, series 2, reel 77; August 13, 1891, series 2, reel 77; August 15, 1891, series 2, reel 77; September 2, 1891, series 2, reel 77, Benjamin Harrison Papers, Library of Congress.

49. Gilbert Ware, *William Hastie: Grace under Pressure* (New York: Oxford University Press, 1984), pp. 233–241; John Hope Franklin and Alfred A. Moss, Jr., *From Slavery to Freedom, A History of African-Americans*, 7th ed. (New York: McGraw-Hill, 1994), p. 466; Meier, *Negro Thought in America*, pp. 31–32; Grossman, *The Democratic Party and the Negro*, pp. 149–150; Bess Beatty, *A Revolution Gone Backward: The Black Response to National Politics, 1876–1896* (Westport, Conn.: Greenwood Press, 1987), pp. 113, 136.

50. Stewart to Cleveland, September 15, 1892, series 2, reel 71, Cleveland Papers.

51. Stewart to Cleveland, Telegram, March 6, 1893, series 2, reel 73, Cleveland Papers.

52. Stewart to Cleveland, September 19, 1894, series 2, reel 87, Cleveland Papers.

53. Ibid.

54. Stewart to Cleveland, September 15, 1894, series 2, reel 87, Cleveland Papers.

55. Ibid.

56. Edward L. Ayers, *The Promise of the New South: Life after Reconstruction* (New York: Oxford University Press, 1992), pp. 132–159; McFeely, *Frederick Douglass*, p. 364.

57. On the limitations of politics as an instrument of change, see Leslie H. Fishel, Jr., "The Negro in Northern Politics, 1870–1900," *Mississippi Valley Historical Review* 42 (December 1955): 466–489.

58. John Porter to T. McCants Stewart, December 9, 1898, series 2, reel 23; Porter to Stewart, March 23, 1898, series 2, reel 27; Porter to Stewart, May 13, 1898, series 2, reel 29; Porter to Stewart, May 23, 1898, series 2, reel 29, William McKinley Papers, Library of Congress.

CHAPTER 4

The Talented Tenth

1. Alfred A. Moss, Jr., *The American Negro Academy: Voice of the Talented Tenth* (Baton Rouge: Louisiana State University Press, 1981), pp. 23–34. The best biography of Crummell is Wilson J. Moses, *Alexander Crummell: A Study of Civilization and Discontent* (New York: Oxford University Press, 1989).

2. W. E. B. Du Bois, "The Talented Tenth," in Booker T. Washington et al., *The Negro Problem* (rpt., New York: Arno Press and the New York Times, 1969), pp. 33-75.

3. Moss, Jr., *The American Negro Academy*, pp. 1, 3.

4. *American Negro Academy Occasional Papers, 1-22* (rpt., New York: Arno Press and the New York Times, 1969): Moss, Jr., *The American Negro Academy*, p. 2.

5. Moss, Jr., *The American Negro Academy*, pp. 27-28, 37-38.

6. August Meier, *Negro Thought in America: Racial Ideologies in the Age of Booker T. Washington, 1880-1915* (Ann Arbor: University of Michigan Press, 1963), pp. 46-47; Emma Lou Thornbrough, *T. Thomas Fortune, Militant Journalist* (Chicago, Ill.: University of Chicago Press, 1972), pp. 42, 55; Henry George, *Progress and Poverty* (New York: Doubleday, Page, 1891).

7. AME *Church Review* 5 (October 1888): 83-95.

8. T. McCants Stewart to Grover Cleveland, September 19, 1894, Grover Cleveland Papers, series 2, reel 87, Library of Congress.

9. AME *Church Review* 15 (July 1898): 529-546.

10. On the role of an American industrialist as philanthropist, see Harold C. Livesay, *Andrew Carnegie and the Rise of Big Business* (Boston, Mass.: Little Brown, 1975).

11. AME *Church Review* 15 (July 1898): 533.

12. Louis R. Harlan, *Booker T. Washington: The Wizard of Tuskegee, 1901-15* (New York: Oxford University Press, 1983), pp. 133-138, 181-182; Livesay, *Andrew Carnegie and the Rise of Big Business,* passim; Allan Nevins, *John D. Rockefeller: The Heroic Age of American Enterprise* (New York: C. Scribner's Sons, 1940).

13. There are no extant copies of the New York *Globe* for 1884 that mention Stewart's visit to Hampton Institute. Stewart did correspond with General Samuel Armstrong on at least one occasion in 1884 regarding Hampton's program of industrial education. See T. McCants Stewart to General Samuel Chapman Armstrong, May 1, 1884, Hampton University Archives and Special Collections, Hampton University; T. Thomas Fortune, *Black and White: Land, Labor and Politics in the South* (New York: Fords, Howard, and Hulbert, 1884), pp. 51-54. Stewart also mentions his survey of industrial education at Hampton in a letter to the *African Repository.* See "Letter from T. McCants Stewart," *African Repository* 60 (July 1884): 85-86.

14. Fortune, *Black and White*, p. 52; Donal F. Lindsey, *Indians at Hampton Institute, 1877-1923* (Urbana: University of Illinois Press, 1995).

15. Fortune, *Black and White*, p. 53; Robert Francis Engs, *Freedom's First Generation: Black Hampton, Virginia, 1861-1890* (Philadelphia, Penn.: University of Pennsylvania Press, 1979).

16. Louis R. Harlan, *Booker T. Washington: The Making of a Black Leader, 1856-1901* (New York: Oxford University Press, 1972), pp. 109-133; Meier, *Negro Thought in America*, pp. 36, 94; Thornbrough, *T. Thomas Fortune*, p. 75; Dorothy Drinkard Hawkshawe, "David Augustus Straker: Black Leader and Reconstruc-

tion Politician, 1842–1908," Ph.D. dissertation, Catholic University of America, 1974.

17. T. McCants Stewart, "Popular Discontent," AME *Church Review* 7 (April 1891): 363–364; The most comprehensive account of the status of African-Americans following slavery remains Leon Litwack, *Been in the Storm So Long: The Aftermath of Slavery* (New York: Alfred A. Knopf, 1979).

18. U. B. Phillips, *American Negro Slavery* (New York: D. Appleton, 1918).

19. T. McCants Stewart, "Discontent—The Forerunner of Reform," commencement address, College of West Africa, Monrovia, Liberia, November 14, 1912, microfilm, pp. 19–25, Library of Congress.

20. Ibid. pp. 15–17; Rayford W. Logan, *The Betrayal of the Negro, from Rutherford B. Hayes to Woodrow Wilson* (New York: Collier Books, 1965).

21. T. McCants Stewart, "The Afro-American as a Factor in the Labor Problem," AME *Church Review* 6 (1889): 30.

22. Albert S. Broussard, "McCants Stewart: The Struggles of a Black Attorney in the Urban West," *Oregon Historical Quarterly* 89 (Summer 1988):158–160.

23. T. McCants Stewart, "Heredity in Character," AME *Church Review* 7 (July 1890): 33.

24. Ibid. p. 32.

25. T. McCants Stewart, "Whittier," AME *Church Review* 10 (January 1894): 364–384; Invitation, "Commeoration of George Washington's Inauguration," May 1, 1889, Stewart-Flippin Papers; Charles H. Freeman to T. McCants Stewart, April 14, 1891, Invitation to attend the ground breaking ceremony for a monument to U. S. Grant, Stewart-Flippin Papers; Waldo E. Martin, *The Mind of Frederick Douglass* (Chapel Hill: Univerity of North Carolina Press, 1984); William S. McFeely, *Frederick Douglass* (New York: Norton, 1991).

26. T. McCants Stewart, "The Life and Character of Frederick Douglass," AME *Church Review* 12 (July 1895): 144.

27. Edwin S. Redkey, *Black Exodus: Black Nationalist and Back-to-Africa Movements, 1890–1910* (New Haven, Conn.: Yale University Press, 1969).

28. David L. Lewis, *W. E. B. Du Bois, Biography of a Race, 1868–1919* (New York: Henry Holt, 1993), p. 162; Wilson J. Moses, *The Golden Age of Black Nationalism, 1850–1925* (Hamden, Conn.: Archon Books, 1978), pp. 197–219.

29. Lewis, *W. E. B. Du Bois*, p. 102.

30. Rufus L. Perry, *The Cushite or the Descendants of Ham* (Springfield, Mass.: Wiley, 1893), pp. 3–6.

31. Ibid., p. 3.

32. Ibid., p. 1.

33. Frank M. Snowden, *Blacks in Antiquity: Ethiopians in the Greco-Roman Experience* (Cambridge, Mass.: Belknap Press of Harvard University Press, 1970); Perry, *The Cushite*, pp. iv–v, x, 11–18.

34. T. McCants Stewart, "The Condition—The Measure of Power," 1884, Princeton Theological Seminary Archives and Special Collections.

35. Stewart, "The Condition—The Measure of Power," pp. 3–4; John Hope

Franklin, *George Washington Williams, A Biography* (Chicago, Ill.: University of Chicago Press, 1985). The term "Nigrition" probably refers to "Nigritia." The *African Repository* wrote that this included "all the region of West Central Africa embraced between Lake Tchad on the east and Sierra Leone on the west, and between Timbuktu on the north and the Bight of Benin on the south, including the Niger from its source to its mouth." See *African Repository* 62 (July 1886): 97.

36. T. McCants Stewart to Theodore Roosevelt, October 26, 1911, series 1, reel 115, Theodore Roosevelt Papers, Library of Congress.

37. Theodore Roosevelt to T. McCants Stewart, October 31, 1911, series 3A, reel 369, Theodore Roosevelt Papers, Library of Congress.

38. James T. Haley, *Sparkling Gems of Race Knowledge Worth Reading* (Nashville, Tenn.: J.T. Haley, 1897), pp. 169-172; Emma Lou Thornbrough, "T. Thomas Fortune: Militant Editor in the Age of Accommodation," in John Hope Franklin and August Meier, eds., *Black Leaders of the Twentieth Century* (Urbana: University of Illinois Press, 1982), p. 24; On the image of blacks in the late nineteenth century, see George Fredrickson, *The Black Image in the White Mind: The Debate on Afro-American Character and Destiny, 1817-1914* (New York: Harper and Row, 1971).

39. New York *Age*, n.d. [January 1923].

40. New York *Freeman*, September 25, 1886; October 9, 1886; Carleton Mabee, *Black Education in New York State, from Colonial to Modern Times* (Syracuse. N.Y.: Syracuse University Press, 1979), pp. 111-113, 154-155; City of Brooklyn, *Board of Education Proceedings*, January 6, 1891, Columbia University Archives and Special Collections.

41. New York *Freeman*, December 18, 1886; May 19, 1888.

42. Harlan, *Booker T. Washington: The Wizard of Tuskegee*, pp. 376-377.

43. New York *Freeman*, April 18, 1885; April 25, 1885; May 2, 1885; C. Vann Woodward, *The Stange Career of Jim Crow*, 3rd ed. (New York: Oxford University Press, 1974), pp. 38-41. Woodward writes incorrectly that Stewart began his "Southern Rambles" in Boston. In fact, as the New York *Freeman* indicated in the April 18, 1885, issue, Stewart began his journey from New York.

44. New York *Freeman*, April 25, 1885; Woodward, *The Strange Career of Jim Crow*, p. 39.

45. New York *Freeman*, April 25, 1885; June 19, 1886.

46. Woodward, *The Strange Career of Jim Crow*, p. 40.

47. New York *Freeman*, April 25, 1885; Woodward, *The Strange Career of Jim Crow*, p. 40. On race relations in South Carolina after Reconstruction, see George B. Tindall, *South Carolina Negroes, 1877-1900* (Baton Rouge: Louisiana State University Press, 1966).

48. Woodward, *The Strange Career of Jim Crow*, p. 34.

49. Ibid. For an insightful discussion of Woodward's critics, consult C. Vann Woodward, *American Counterpoint: Slavery and Racism in The North-South Dialogue* (Boston: Little, Brown, 1971), pp. 234-260.

50. Broussard, *Black San Francisco*, pp. 14-20; David Gerber, *Black Ohio and the Color Line, 1865-1900* (Urbana: University of Illinois Press, 1976), pp. 44-59;

David M. Katzman, *Before the Ghetto: Black Detroit in the Nineteenth Century* (Urbana: University of Illinois Press, 1973).

51. Charles A. Lofgren, *The Plessy Case: A Legal-Historical Approach* (New York: Oxford University Press, 1987), p. 11.

52. Lofgren, *The Plessy Case*, p. 11; Woodward, *The Strange Career of Jim Crow*, p. 53; Edward L. Ayers, *The Promise of the New South: Life after Reconstruction* (New York: Oxford University Press, 1992), pp. 136-137, 141-146.

53. Woodward, *The Strange Career of Jim Crow*, p. 40.

54. T. McCants Stewart, *Liberia, The Americo-African Republic* (New York: Edward O. Jenkins' Sons, 1886).

CHAPTER 5

New Challenges, New Frustrations

1. Honolulu *Pacific Commercial Advertiser*, November 29, 1898, May 2, 1900. For information on Alice Stewart see the *Cleveland Gazette*, January 29, 1887, April 15, 1893. On Stewart's daughter Carlotta, see Albert S. Broussard, "Carlotta Stewart Lai, A Black Teacher in the Territory of Hawai'i," *Hawaiian Journal of History* 23 (1990): 129-154; T. McCants Stewart to McCants Stewart, September 18, 1898, Stewart-Flippin Papers.

2. *Sixty-fifth Annual Report for the Year 1956*, Hawaiian Historical Society (Honolulu, 1957), p. 26; Ralph S. Kuykendall and A. Grove Day, *Hawaii: A History*, rev. ed. (Englewood Cliffs, N.J.: Prentice-Hall, 1976), p. 37; R. A. Greer, "Blacks in Old Hawaii," *Honolulu* 21 (November 1986): 120-121; Eleanor C. Nordyke, "Blacks in Hawaii: A Demographic and Historical Perspective," *Hawaiian Journal of History* 22 (1988): 241-255.

3. Nell I. Painter, *Exodusters: Black Migration to Kansas After Reconstruction* (New York: Norton, 1976); Robert G. Athearn, *In Search of Canaan: Black Migration to Kansas, 1879-80* (Lawrence: The Regents Press of Kansas, 1978).

4. *Report of the Commissioner of Labor on Hawaii, 1901*, Senate Document 169 (Washington, D.C.: Government Printing Office, 1902), pp. 147, 152, 166, 174, 212; *Hawaiian Almanac and Annual for 1902* (Honolulu, 1901), p. 164; *Advertiser*, April 4, 1901; Ronald Takaki, *Pau Hana: Plantation Life and Labor in Hawaii, 1835-1920* (Honolulu: University of Hawaii Press, 1983), pp. 25-26; Eleanor C. Nordyke, *The Peopling of Hawaii*, 2d ed. (Honolulu: University of Hawaii Press, 1989), pp. 71-73.

5. Edwin S. Redkey, *Black Exodus: Black Nationalist and Back-to-Africa Movements, 1890-1910* (New Haven, Conn.: Yale University Press, 1969); Philip J. Staudenraus, *The African Colonization Movement, 1816-1861* (New York: Columbia University Press, 1961); William H. Pease and Jane Pease, *Black Utopia: Negro Communal Experiments in America* (Madison: State Historical Society of Wisconsin, 1963); Nordyke, "Blacks in Hawaii," p. 242.

6. T. McCants Stewart to McCants Stewart, June 2, 1905, Stewart-Flippin Papers; *Advertiser*, November 29, 1898.

7. *Advertiser,* November 29, 1898, May 4, 1900; Theophilus Gould Steward, *Fifty Years in the Gospel Minstry* (Philadelphia, Penn.: AME Book Concern, n.d.), pp. 308-309; James Serale, *Theophilus Gould Steward* (New York: Carlson Publishers, 1992); Emma Lou Thornbrough, *T. Thomas Fortune, Militant Black Journalist* (Chicago: University of Chicago Press, 1972), pp. 235-236.

8. New York *Freeman,* February 5, 1887; J. Clay Smith, Jr., *Emancipation: The Making of the Black Lawyer, 1844-1944* (Philadelphia, Penn.: University of Pennsylvania Press, 1993), pp. 492-493.

9. 11 *Hawaii Reports* 812 (1899).

10. 12 *Hawaii Reports* 138 (1899); 12 *Hawaii Reports* 435 (1900); Smith, Jr., *Emancipation,* pp. 492-493.

11. 12 *Hawaii Reports* 142 (1899); 12 *Hawaii Reports* 329 (1900); 13 *Hawaii Reports* 459 (1901).

12. 13 *Hawaii Reports* 637 (1901); 14 *Hawaii Reports* 15 (1902); 14 *Hawaii Reports* 145 (1902); 14 *Hawaii Reports* 232 (1902).

13. Smith, Jr., *Emancipation,* p. 493.

14. T. McCants Stewart, "The Afro-American as a Factor in the Labor Problem," AME *Church Review* 6 (1889): 30-38.

15. *Advertiser,* May 2, May 3, 1900.

16. *Advertiser,* May 3, May 4, May 5, 1900; Helen G. Chapin, "Newspapers of Hawaii 1884 to 1903: From He Liona to the Pacific Cable," *Hawaiian Journal of History* 18 (1984): 55-56.

17. T. McCants Stewart to McCants Stewart, May 16, 1905, Stewart-Flippin Papers.

18. T. McCants Stewart to McCants Stewart, June 6, 1905, Stewart-Flippin Papers.

19. *Advertiser,* July 25, July 26, 1905; Broussard, "Carlotta Stewart Lai," pp. 129-148; T. McCants Stewart to McCants Stewart, October 14, 1905, Stewart-Flippin Papers; *Supplemental Report of the Superintendent of Public Instruction, June 30 to December 31, 1902,* p. 76, Hawaii State Archives, Honolulu; *Report of the Superintendent of Public Instruction from December 31, 1908 to December 31, 1910,* p. 95, Hawaii State Archives, Honolulu.

20. Carlotta Stewart to McCants Stewart, August 12, 1906, Stewart-Flippin Papers.

21. *Advertiser,* January 7, April 3, April 4, 1901; March 5, 1903.

22. T. McCants Stewart to McCants Stewart, May 16, 1905, Stewart-Flippin Papers.

23. T. McCants Stewart to McCants Stewart, September 18, 1898, Stewart-Flippin Papers.

24. T. McCants Stewart to McCants Stewart, October 14, 1905, Stewart-Flippin Papers.

25. T. McCants Stewart to Francis J. Grimké, July 18, 1920, in Carter G. Woodson, ed., *The Works of Francis J. Grimké, vol. 4, Letters* (Washington, D.C.: Associated Publishers, 1942), p. 283; Jeffrey P. Green, *Edmund Thornton Jenkins: The*

Life and Times of an American Black Composer, 1894-1926 (Westport, Conn.: Greenwood Press, 1987).

26. T. McCants Stewart to McCants Stewart, December 15, 1908, Stewart-Flippin Papers.

27. James Walvin, *Black and White: The Negro and English Society, 1555-1945* (London: Allen Lane, Penguin Press, 1973), pp. 202-203.

28. Folaria Shyllon, "Blacks in Britain: A Historical and Analytical Overview," in Joseph E. Harris, ed., *Global Dimensions of the African Diaspora* (Washington, D.C.: Howard University Press, 1982), pp. 178-186.

29. W. E. B. Du Bois, *The Souls of Black Folk* (1903. New York: Penguin, 1989), p. 13; Nordyke, *The Peopling of Hawaii*, pp. 28-98.

30. T. McCants Stewart to McCants Stewart, April 2, 1906, Stewart-Flippin Papers; Interview with Ms. Beryl E. Kean, the surviving daughter of Kapulani Stewart, 14 December 1990, St. Thomas, Virgin Islands; T. McCants Stewart to Francis J. Grimké, August 14, 1920, in Woodson, ed., *The Works of Francis J. Grimké*, vol. 4, p. 285.

31. T. McCants Stewart to McCants Stewart, October 14, 1905, Stewart-Flippin Papers.

32. *Liberia. Laws and Regulations with Instructions to Customs Officers, 1906. Republic of Liberia, Custom's Service* (London: Henry Good and Sons, 1906); *Revised Statutes of the Republic of Liberia, 1910-11. Made under the Authority of the Government of Liberia by T. McCants Stewart* (Paris: Establissements Russon, 1928).

33. T. McCants Stewart to McCants Stewart, October 1, 1910, Stewart-Flippin Papers; *Liberia. Code for Justices of the Peace, 1907. Codified by Order of the Government of the Republic of Liberia by T. McCants Stewart* (Monrovia, Liberia: College of West Africa Press, 1907).

34. *Inaugural Meeting of the Liberian National Bar Association, January 2, 1907* (Monrovia, Liberia: College of West Africa Press, 1907); *Liberia National Bar Association. Second Annual Meeting of the Liberian National Bar Association in the Executive Mansion, Monrovia, February 5, 1908* (Monrovia, Liberia: College of West Africa Press, 1908).

35. *Liberia* (November 1906): 82; *Liberia* (November 1907): 30-32.

36. *Alexander's Magazine* (July 1907): 173-175; *Alexander's Magazine* (February 1908): 80-86.

37. Hollis R. Lynch, *Edward Wilmot Blyden: Pan-Negro Patriot, 1832-1912* (New York: Oxford University Press, 1967), p. 169.

38. T. McCants Stewart to McCants Stewart, July 14, 1908, Stewart-Flippin Papers.

39. T. McCants Stewart to McCants Stewart, December 15, 1908, Stewart-Flippin Papers.

40. *Liberian Law Reports*, vol. 2, Cases Adjudged in the Supreme Court of the Republic of Liberia, Jan. term, 1908-Nov. term 1926 (Ithaca, N.Y.: Cornell University Press, 1960).

41. T. McCants Stewart to McCants Stewart, September 26, 1910, Stewart-Flippin Papers.

42. T. McCants Stewart's investments and his tenuous financial status were topics of lively discusion among family members after his death. See Mrs. McCants Stewart and daughters to Francis J. Grimké, January 8, 1923, in Carter G. Woodson, ed., *The Works of Francis James Grimké*, vol. 4, p. 361; Verina Morton-Jones to Carlotta Stewart, January 23, 1927; Alice Stewart to Carlotta Stewart, March 24, 1927, Stewart-Flippin Papers; Interview with Ms. Beryl E. Kean, 14 December 1990, St. Thomas, Virgin Islands.

43. William D. Crum to P. G. Knox, August 16, 1911; D. C. Howard to P. G. Knox, August 16, 1911; T. McCants Stewart to Hon. P. G. Knox, October 30, 1911, Records of the Department of State Relating to Internal Affairs of Liberia, Record Group 59, reel 16, National Archives.

44. Crum to Knox, August 16, 1911; Kuhn, Loeb, and Company to Alvery A. Ades, Acting Secretary of State, November 9, 1911, Records of the Department of State Relating to Internal Affairs of Liberia, Record Group 59, reel 16, National Archives; T. McCants Stewart to President Theodore Roosevelt, October 26, 1911, series 1, reel 115, Theodore Roosevelt Papers, Library of Congress; see also Gilchrist Stewart to McCants Stewart, November 9-11, 1911, Stewart-Flippin Papers.

45. *Liberian Law Reports*, vol. 2, 1908-1926, pp. 175-183; "The Liberian Judiciary," n.d. [1914-15]," typescript, Stewart-Flippin Papers.

46. T. McCants Stewart to McCants Stewart, April 27, 1915, Stewart-Flippin Papers.

47. T. McCants Stewart to McCants Stewart, November 4, 1914, June 8, 1915; T. McCants Stewart to Gilchrist Stewart, December 10, 1914, Stewart-Flippin Papers.

48. Gilchrist Stewart to McCants Stewart, December 10, 1914, August 27, 1915, Stewart-Flippin Papers.

49. Gilchrist Stewart to McCants Stewart, August 27, 1915, Stewart-Flippin Papers.

50. T. McCants Stewart to Gilchrist Stewart, December 10, 1914; T. McCants Stewart to McCants Stewart, April 27, 1915, Stewart-Flippin Papers.

51. Edward Scobie, *Black Britannia: A History of Blacks in Britain* (Chicago, Ill.: Johnson Publishing, 1972), pp. 253-255; Walvin, *Black and White*, pp. 204-205.

52. W. E. B. Du Bois to T. McCants Stewart, February 25, 1921, W. E. B. Du Bois Papers, microfilm, reel 10, Library of Congress; T. McCants Stewart to Carlotta Stewart, December 26, 1920, Stewart-Flippin Papers; On the Pan-African conferences, see Elliott M. Rudwick, *W. E. B. Du Bois, Propagandist of the Negro Protest* (New York: Atheneum, 1968), pp. 208-235; David L. Lewis, *W. E. B. Du Bois: Biography of a Race, 1868-1919* (New York: Henry Holt, 1993), pp. 551-562, 567-569.

53. T. McCants Stewart to Carlotta Stewart, July 31, [1922], Stewart-Flippin Papers.

54. Broussard, "Carlotta Stewart Lai," pp. 129–148.

55. St. Thomas *Mail Notes,* March 18, March 19, March 23, April 2, April 4, July 2, 1921; *Lightbourn's Annual and Commercial Directory of the Virgin Islands, 1923* (St. Thomas: A.G. Lightbourn, 1923); St. Thomas *Bulletin,* March 17, 1921, April 11, 1921, April 15, 1921, April 19, 1921; *Methodist Quarterly Review* 62 (1880): 200; Governor of West Virginia to Whom It May Concern, October 31, 1905, Christopher Harris Payne Folder, Enid Baa Library, St. Thomas, Virgin Islands; William J. Simmons, *Men of Mark, Eminent, Progressive, and Rising* (Cleveland, Ohio: George E. Rewell, 1887), pp. 241–243.

56. T. McCants Stewart to Carlotta Stewart, October 21, 1922, Stewart-Flippin Papers.

57. *Mail Notes,* July 2, 1921; St. Thomas *Bulletin,* March 17, 1921, April 11, 1921, April 15, 1921, April 19, 1921.

58. *Mail Notes,* July 11, August 9, August 12, 1921.

59. *Mail Notes,* March 3, 1922.

60. *Mail Notes,* August 27, 1921, October 27, 1921.

61. *Mail Notes,* November 10, 1921.

62. *Mail Notes,* January 18, 1922.

63. St. Thomas *Bulletin,* September 9, 1921, September 14, 1921; St. Croix *Emancipator,* November 9, 1921, March 1, 1922; St. Croix *Avis,* November 6, 1922.

64. *Mail Notes,* June 1, 1922.

65. *Mail Notes,* March 24, 1922,

66. *Mail Notes,* May 15, May 16, October 9, 1922; For information on the UNIA in the Virgin Islands, see the St. Croix *Emancipator,* July 30, 1921, August 26, 1921, October 14, 1921.

67. *Mail Notes,* August 1, August 5, August 12, August 15, August 16, 1922.

68. *Mail Notes,* June 27, 1922, August 1, 1922; St. Thomas *Bulletin,* July 20, 1922; Rothschild Francis, "Social, Political, and Economic Conditions in the Virgin Islands," [1923], Administrative Files, NAACP Papers, Library of Congress.

69. *Mail Notes,* August 15, August 16, August 19, 1922; *Profiles of Outstanding Virgin Islanders* (St. Thomas: Government of the Virgin Islands, 1976), pp. 204–207; *Lightbourn's Annual and Commercial Directory of the Virgin Islands,1923,* pp. 104, 146.

70. New York *Negro World,* January 20, March 31, May 5, 1923; St. Thomas *Bulletin,* July 20, 1922; *Emancipator,* October 14, 1922; Isaac Dockhan, *A History of the Virgin Islands of the United States* (St. Thomas: Caribbean University Press, 1974), p. 278;

71. *Mail Notes,* October 30, 1922.

72. St. Croix *Avis,* November 6, 1922.

73. Gilbert Ware, *William Hastie: Grace under Pressure* (New York: Oxford University Press, 1984), p. 83.

74. Ware, *William Hastie,* pp. 84–85; Gordon K. Lewis, *The Virgin Islands* (Evanston, Ill.: Northwestern University Press, 1972), pp. 42–67.

75. Carter G. Woodson, ed., *The Works of Francis James Grimké,* vol. 3 (Washington, D.C.: Associated publishers, 1942), pp. 112–113.

76. Carter G. Woodson, ed., *The Works of Francis James Grimké,* vol. 3, p. 113.

77. Stewart to Grimké, July 18, 1920, Francis J. Grimké Papers, Box 40-5, Moorland-Spingarn Research Center, Howard University.

78. Stewart to Grimké, July 10, 1922, Box 40-5, Francis J. Grimké Papers, Moorland-Spingarn Research Center, Howard University.

79. *Mail Notes,* January 3, January 8, 1923; St. Thomas *Bulletin,* January 8, 1923.

80. *Mail Notes,* January 8, 1923; St. Thomas *Times,* January 13, February 10, 1923.

81. St. Thomas *Times,* January 13, 1923. Neither the London *Times* nor the *New York Times* published an obituary of Stewart.

82. New York *Negro World,* January 27, 1923; *Crisis* 26 (June 1923): 71–72; Chicago *Defender,* January 25, 1923; *Negro Year Book, 1925-26* (Tuskegee, Ala.: Negro Year Book Publishing, 1925), p. 421.

83. William S. McFeely, *Frederick Douglass* (New York: W.W. Norton, 1991); Thornbrough, *T. Thomas Fortune, Militant Journalist,* passim.

CHAPTER 6

McCants Stewart

1. See, for example, Albert S. Broussard, "McCants Stewart: The Struggles of a Black Attorney in the Urban West," *Oregon Historical Quarterly* 89 (Summer 1989): 157–179; Albert S. Broussard, "Carlotta Stewart-Lai, a Black Teacher in the Territory of Hawai'i," *Hawaiian Journal of History* 24 (1990): 129–154; Willard B. Gatewood explores the role of the African-American elite and their descendants in *Aristocrats of Color: The Black Elite, 1880–1920* (Bloomington: Indiana University Press, 1990).

2. McCants Stewart's place of birth has heretofore been listed as Brooklyn, New York. My research reveals, however, that T. McCants and Charlotte Harris Stewart did not live in New York prior to 1880, and both were employed in 1877 at Claflin University, a black college located in Orangeburg, South Carolina. I conclude, therefore, that Orangeburg is the most probable birthplace for McCants Stewart. See *Catalogue of Claflin University and South Carolina Agricultural College and Mechanics Institute, Orangeburg, S.C., 1877-78* (Middletown, Conn.: Felton and King Steam Printers, 1878), p. 8; On the role of black professional women in the South, see Stephanie J. Shaw, *What a Woman Ought to Be and to Do: Black Professional Women During the Jim Crow Era* (Chicago, Ill.: University of Chicago Press, 1996).

3. T. McCants Stewart to "My very dear young ones" [McCants and Gilchrist], September 6, 1885, Stewart-Flippin Papers.

4. Ibid.

5. T. McCants Stewart to McCants and Gilchrist (Stewart), June 11, 1892,

Stewart-Flippin Papers; T. McCants Stewart to McCants Stewart, January 1, 1887, October 10, 1890, August 8, 1891, July 8, 1893, July 21, 1893, August 26, 1893, Stewart-Flippin Papers.

6. Williamson, *After Slavery,* p. 231.

7. *Catalogue of Claflin University and South Carolina Agricultural College and Mechanics Institute, Orangeburg, S.C., 1877–78* (Middletown, Conn.: Felton and King, Steam Printers, 1878).

8. *Catalogue of Claflin University, 1890–91* (New York: Hunt and Eaton, 1891), p. 20.

9. T. McCants Stewart to "Dear Boys" [McCants and Gilchrist], June 11, 1892, Stewart-Flippin Papers.

10. T. McCants Stewart to McCants and Gilchrist [Stewart], February 14, 1893, Box 119, Booker T. Washington Papers, Library of Congress (hereinafter cited as Washington Papers); T. McCants Stewart to Booker T. Washington, May 18, 1894, Box 119, Washington Papers.

11. T. McCants Stewart to "Dear Boys" [McCants and Gilchrist], January 24, 1893, Stewart-Flippin Papers.

12. Ibid; T. McCants Stewart to Booker T. Washington, May 23, 1894, September 24, 1894, Box 119, Washington Papers.

13. Louis R. Harlan, *Booker T. Washington: The Making of a Black Leader, 1856–1901* (New York: Oxford University Press, 1972), pp. 61–66; Louis R. Harlan, *Booker T. Washington: The Wizard of Tuskegee, 1901–1915* (New York: Oxford University Press, 1983), pp. 143–173; August Meier, *Negro Thought in America, 1880–1915: Racial Ideologies in the Age of Booker T. Washington* (Ann Arbor: University of Michigan Press, 1963), pp. 95–106.

14. Booker T. Washington to McCants Stewart, May 10, 1894, July 14, 1894, October 11, 1894, October 31, 1894, Stewart-Flippin Papers; McCants Stewart to Washington, May, 1894, May 23, 1894, May 30, 1894, Box 119, Washington Papers; T. McCants Stewart to Washington, May 18, 1894, September 27, 1894, Box 119, Washington Papers; Mrs. Booker T. Washington to McCants Stewart, October 31, 1894, July 20, 1895, Stewart-Flippin Papers; T. McCants Stewart to McCants [Stewart] May 22, 1896, June 3, 1896, June 8, 1896, June 18, 1896, Stewart-Flippin Papers.

15. T. McCants Stewart to McCants [Stewart], June 3, 1896, June 18, 1896, June 8, 1896, May 22, 1896, Stewart-Flippin Papers; See also McCants Stewart's New York University "Law Student Certificate," May 28, 1896, Stewart-Flippin Papers.

16. Minneapolis *Afro-American Advance,* May 27, 1899, June 3, 1899, June 10, 1899, June 24, 1899, July 1, 1899, September 2, 1899, October 21, 1899, February 17, 1900, November 3, 1900; "Scrapbook of McCants Stewart," n.d., Stewart-Flippin Papers; Portland *Illustrated Weekly,* June 25, 1910; Interview with Katherine Stewart Flippin, McCants Stewart's surviving daughter, February 17, 1976, San Francisco; Taylor, "A History of Blacks in the Pacific Northwest," p. 164. Taylor errs in giving the date of Stewart's graduation from the University of Minnesota

Law School as 1901; Smith, Jr., "In the Shadow of Plessy," pp.502-503; For general information on the Minneapolis black community, consult Abram L. Harris, *The Negro Population in Minneapolis: A Study in Race Relations* (Minneapolis, Minn.: Minneapolis Urban League and Phyllis Wheatley Settlement House, 1926).

17. Smith, Jr.,"In the Shadow of Plessy," p. 502.

18. Harris, *The Negro Population in Minneapolis*, pp. 6-8, 18; *Afro-American Advance*, May 27, 1899, June 10, 1899, June 24, 1899, August 26, 1899; David V. Taylor, "Pilgrim's Progress: Black St. Paul and the Making of an Urban Ghetto, 1870-1930," Ph.D. dissertation, University of Minnesota, 1977, p. 58.

19. Taylor, "Pilgrim's Progress," pp. 63, 71; Harris, *The Negro Population in Minneapolis*, pp. 6-8; Seattle *Republican*, June 29, 1900; *History of Bench and Bar of Oregon* (Portland, Ore.: Historical Publishing, 1910), pp. 229-230.

20. Portland *New Age*, August 3, 1901, March 8, 1902, July 9, 1904, July 23, 1904, August 13, 1904, December 24, 1904, April 8, 1905, April 28, 1906.

21. T. McCants Stewart to McCants Stewart, January 10, 1905, Stewart-Flippin Papers; "Wedding Invitation," Mary Delia Weir and McCants Stewart, August 22, 1905, Minneapolis, Minnesota, Stewart-Flippin Papers; *History of Bench and Bar of Oregon*, pp. 229-230.

22. Taylor, "A History of Blacks in the Pacific Northwest," pp. 128-130; Hogg, "Negroes and Their Institutions in Oregon," pp. 272-285; Hill, "The Negro in Oregon," pp. 52-62; *Thirteenth Census of the United States, 1910, vol. 2, Population Reports by States* (Washington, D.C.: Government Printing Office, 1910), pp. 94-96, 450-451, 550; Oznathylee A. Hopkins, "Black Life in Oregon, 1899-1907: A Study of the Portland *New Age*," B.A. thesis, Reed College, 1974; Interview with May Hill, conducted by the Black Women's Oral history project, 1978, copy at Bancroft Library, University of California, Berkeley; *History of Bench and Bar of Oregon*, pp. 229-230; Elizabeth McLagan, *A Peculiar Paradise: A History of Blacks in Oregon, 1788-1940* (Portland, Ore.: Georgian Press, 1980), pp. 110-116; Portland *Oregonian*, March 21, 1908; For background material on early black settlers in Oregon, consult Fred Lockley, "Some Documentary Records of Slavery in Oregon," *Oregon Historical Quarterly* 17 (June 1916): 107-115; Lockley, "The Case of Robin Holmes vs. Nathaniel Ford," *Oregon Historical Quarterly* 23 (June 1922): 111-137; Franz M. Schneider, "The 'Black Laws' of Oregon," M.A. thesis, University of Santa Clara, 1970; Quintard Taylor, "Blacks in the American West: An Overview" *Western Journal of Black Studies* 1 (March 1977): 4-10; Taylor, "Slaves and Free Men: Blacks in the Oregon Country, 1840-1860," *Oregon Historical Quarterly* 83 (Summer 1982): 153-170; K. Keith Richards, "Unwelcome Settlers: Black and Mulatto Oregon Pioneers" (Part 1), *Oregon Historical Quarterly* 84 (Spring 1983): 29-55; (Part 2), (Summer 1983): 173-205. Two bibliographies compiled by Lenwood G. Davis were also useful: *Blacks in the State of Oregon, 1788-1971*, Exchange Bibliography No. 229 (Monticello, Ill., 1971), and Davis, *Blacks in the State of Oregon, 1788-1974*, 2d ed. (Monticello, Ill., 1974); See also Davis, "Sources for History of Blacks in Oregon," *Oregon Historical Quarterly* 73 (September 1972): 197-211.

23. Portland *New Age*, April 5, 1902, September 8, 1900, December 21, 1901.

24. Hill, "The Negro in Oregon," pp. 56-60, 95-96, 110-111; Portland *New Age*, December 2, 1899; "Cancelled Checks, 1914," Stewart-Flippin Papers; The plight of black attorneys in both the North and the South is examined in Johnson, *The Negro College Graduate*, pp. 331-337; Regarding the struggles of black attorneys in northern cities, see W. E. B. Du Bois, *The Philadelphia Negro* (Philadelphia: University of Pennsylvania Press, 1899), pp. 114-115; David M. Katzman, *Before the Ghetto: Black Detroit in the Nineteenth Century* (Urbana: University of Illinois Press, 1973), p. 128; Geraldine R. Segal, *Blacks in the Law: Philadelphia and the Nation* (Phildelphia: University of Pennsylvania Press, 1983).

25. "Mary Delia Weir Stewart," Biographical sketch compiled by her daughter, Katherine Stewart Flippin, n.d., Stewart-Flippin Papers; "Manning College of Music, Oratory and Language Graduate Recitals," June 3, 1895; June 8, 1896, Stewart-Flippin Papers; "Mary Delia Weir, University of Minnesota Literary Course," n.d., Stewart-Flippin Papers; "Certificate of Mary Delia Weir," for Physical Culture, Freshman English, Rhetoric, Mathematics, Psychology, German, Latin," 1892-1893, Stewart-Flippin Papers; Mary Delia Weir, University of Minnesota Teacher's Certificate, August 5, 1901, Stewart-Flippin Papers.

26. *Advocate*, September 1, 1923; Portland *Oregonian*, September 20, 1916; *Notable Pioneers in the History of Oregon* (Portland: Oregon Lung Association, 1983).

27. Letter of recommendation from Henry L. Benson, October 10, 1917; Letter of recommendation from the firm of Bernstein and Cohen, October 22, 1917; Letter of recommendation from John H. Jones, September 27, 1917; Letter of recommendation from John P. Kavanaugh, October 11, 1917, all in Stewart-Flippin Papers.

28. Smith, Jr., "In the Shadow of Plessy," pp. 504-505.

29. Appellant brief, *Taylor vs. Cohn* (March 1905), Stewart-Flippin Papers; Portland *New Age*, July 28, 1900, August 4, 1900, August 18, 1900, September 15, 1900, February 23, 1901; Charles [ ] to McCants Stewart, March 5, 1906, Stewart-Flippin Papers; Pauli Murray, *States' Laws on Race and Color* (Cincinnati, Ohio: Methodist Church, 1950), pp. 8, 12-13, 18; *Taylor vs. Cohn, Pacific Reporter* 84 (1906): 388-389; *Oregonian*, May 19, 1905, May 20, 1905.

30. *Oregonian*, May 19, 1905, May 20, 1905.

31. T. McCants Stewart to McCants [Stewart], April 2, 1906; Charlotte Stewart to McCants Stewart, October 8, 1906, December 18, 1906; Stock certificates, American Telephone Company, July 12, 1907, May 7, 1910; Beavis Oil Company, April 26, 1910; Portland Coal and Development Company, June 28, 1908; Bonanza Queen Mining Company, n.d.; United States Cashier Company, October 1910, all in Stewart-Flippin Papers; Regarding the dissolution of these companies, see Dorothy B. Porter to commissioner of incorporation, Washington, D.C., April 6, 1972, Stewart-Flippin Papers; Boutell Bros. to McCants Stewart, July 10, 1916, Stewart-Flippin Papers.

32. McCants Stewart to Booker T. Washington, January 4, 1910, Washington Papers; Mrs. Booker T. Washington to McCants Stewart, February 13, 1916;

Emmett Scott to McCants Stewart, November 22, 1915, Stewart-Flippin Papers; Seattle *Republican,* July 6, 1900. Regarding critics of Booker T. Washington and more militant black racial ideologies, consult Stephen R. Fox, *The Guardian of Boston, William Monroe Trotter* (New York: Atheneum, 1970); Harlan, *Booker T. Washington: The Wizard of Tuskegee,* pp. 32–62, 84–106; David L. Lewis, *W. E. B. Du Bois: Biography of a Race, 1868–1919* (New York: Henry Holt, 1993); Broussard, "McCants Stewart," p. 165.

33. Portland *Oregonian,* September 20, 1916, p. 10; *Notable Pioneers in the History of Oregon* (Portland: Oregon Lung Association, 1983).

34. *Oregonian,* December 14, 1914.

35. John B. Cleland to Stewart, October 24, 1910; Letter of Introduction and recommendation from attorneys Bernstein and Cohen for McCants Stewart, October 11, 1917; Letter of introduction and recommendation from Associate Justice Lawrence T. Harris, Oregon Supreme Court, October 10, 1917; Letter of introduction from C. E. Field, manager, Abstract Title Company, August 16, 1917; Letter of recommendation from Circuit Court Judge John P. Kavanaugh, October 11, 1917; Letter of recommendation from Joseph H. Jones, judge of the Portland District Court, September 27, 1917; Letter of recommendation from Samuel White, president of the Oregon Bar Association, September 18, 1917; Letter of introduction from Oregon governor William D. Stephens, October 10, 1917, all in Stewart-Flippin Papers. See also C. B. Moore and Edward D. Baldwin to McCants Stewart, September 19, 1912; Letter of recommendation, Archbishop of Portland, October 10, 1917; Letter of recommendation, Henry L. Benson, associate justice, Oregon Supreme Court, October 10, 1917, all in Stewart-Flippin Papers.

36. *New Age,* November 25, 1899, December 2, 1899, February 10, 1900, March 17, 1900, April 17, 1900, May 19, 1900; McCants Stewart to Victoria Weir, March 10, 1918; Stewart to Harry Jones, October 5, 1914; William N. Gatens to Mayor H. R. Albee, December 20, 1914, Stewart-Flippin Papers.

37. Oglesby Young to Mrs. McCants Stewart, April 26, 1909; T. McCants Stewart to McCants Stewart, June 13, 1910; P. L. Mingo to McCants Stewart, May 17, 1909, Stewart-Flippin Papers; Portland *Advocate,* May 1, 1909; Oregon *Daily News,* April 21, 1909.

38. McCants Stewart to Victoria Weir, March 10, 1918; McCants Stewart to Katherine Stewart, November 29, 1917, March 24, 1918, Stewart-Flippin Papers; Law firm of Dolph, Malley, Simon, and Gearin to McCants Stewart, December 6, 1917, Stewart-Flippin Papers; McCants Stewart to Theodore Green, May 26, 1916, Stewart-Flippin Papers; *Pacific Coast Appeal,* January 5, 1918; McLagan, *A Peculiar Paradise,* p. 115.

39. Telegram, McCants Stewart to Oscar Hudson, January 5, 1918, Stewart-Flippin Papers; Biographical information on Oscar Hudson was obtained in an interview with Mr. A. P. Alberga, November 8, 1976, Oakland, California. See also Frank Lincoln Mather, ed., *Who's Who of the Colored Race,* vol. 1 (Chicago, Ill.: n.p. 1915), pp. xxvii, 146; Oakland *Sunshine,* December 27, 1913; Segal, *Blacks in the Law,* p. 192.

40. McCants Stewart to Katherine Stewart, November 29, 1917, Stewart-Flippin Papers.

41. McCants Stewart to Katherine Stewart, March 24, 1918, Stewart-Flippin Papers.

42. McCants Stewart to Katherine Stewart, November 29, 1917, Stewart-Flippin Papers.

43. Ibid.

44. McCants Stewart to Katherine Stewart, December 11, 1917, Stewart-Flippin Papers.

45. McCants Stewart to Katherine Flippin, March 15, 1918, Stewart-Flippin Papers.

46. McCants Stewart to Katherine Stewart, March 10, 1918, Stewart-Flippin Papers.

47. McCants Stewart to Katherine Stewart, March 31, 1918, Stewart-Flippin Papers.

48. McCants Stewart to Katherine Stewart, June 23, 1918, Stewart-Flippin Papers.

49. Broussard, *Black San Francisco: The Struggle for Racial Equality in the West, 1900–1954* (Lawrence: University Press of Kansas, 1993), pp. 94–95; Smith, Jr., "In the Shadow of Plessy," p. 513.

50. Broussard, *Black San Francisco*, pp. 38–58; Interview with Josephine Cole, December 9, 1976, San Francisco. Mrs. Cole, in 1944, was the first black teacher hired by the San Francisco Unified School District. Interview with Naomi Johnson, September 30, 1976, San Francisco. Johnson's sister, Tabytha Anderson, was the first black female attorney in San Francisco; "William Byron Rumford, Legislator for Fair Employment, Fair Housing, and Public Health," interview conducted by the Bancroft Regional Oral History Office, 1973, University of California, Berkeley, pp. 5–9.

51. William L. Patterson, *The Man Who Cried Genocide: An Autobiography* (New York: International Publishers, 1971), pp. 40–41; Johnson, *The Negro College Graduate*, p. 336; On the career of Charles Houston, consult Genna Rae McNeil, *Groundwork: Charles Hamilton Houston and the Struggle for Civil Rights* (Philadelphia: University of Pennsylvania Press, 1983).

52. Oscar Hudson to McCants Stewart, January 29, 1918, Stewart-Flippin Papers.

53. Interview with Katherine Stewart Flippin, February 17, 1976, San Francisco; Patterson, *The Man Who Cried Genocide*, pp. 40–41; See "Attorney Going Blind, Ends Life," [1919], Stewart-Flippin Papers; San Francisco *Call and Post*, April 15, 1919; San Francisco *Chronicle*, April 19, 1919; San Francisco *Bulletin*, April 15, 1919.

54. See Quintard Taylor, *The Forging of a Black Community: Seattle's Central District from 1870 through the Civil Rights Era* (Seattle: University of Washington Press, 1994), pp. 71–78.

55. T. McCants Stewart to McCants Stewart, July 14, 1908, Stewart-Flippin Papers.

56. W. Sherman Savage, *Blacks in the West* (Westport, Conn.: Greenwood Publishing, 1976), p. 199; Kenneth L. Kusmer, *A Ghetto Takes Shape: Black Cleveland, 1870-1930* (Urbana: University of Illinois Press, 1976), pp. 80-81, 191-192; James Grossman, *Land of Hope: Chicago, Black Southerners, and the Great Migration* (Chicago, Ill.: University of Chicago Press, 1989); Allan H. Spear, *Black Chicago: The Making of a Negro Ghetto, 1890-1920* (Chicago, Ill.: University of Chicago Press, 1967), pp. 51-90; Joe William Trotter, *Black Milwaukee: The Making of an Industrial Proletariat, 1915-45* (Urbana: University of Illinois Press, 1985), pp. 20, 93, 96.

57. On the growth and decline of labor unions in San Francisco, consult William Issel and Robert W. Cherny, *San Francisco, 1865-1932: Politics, Power, and Urban Development* (Berkeley: University of California Press, 1986), pp. 80-100; Taylor, *Forging a Black Community,* pp. 13-45; Taylor, "Black Urban Development—Another View: Seattle's Central District, 1910-1940," *Pacific Historical Review* 58 (November 1989): 429-448; Richard White, *"It's Your Misfortune and None of My Own": A New History of the American West* (Norman: University of Oklahoma Press, 1991), pp. 322-325, 508-510; Richard White, "Race Relations in the American West," *American Quarterly* 38 (1986): 394-416; Ronald G. Coleman, "A History of Blacks in Utah," pp. 199-217; Cox, *Blacks in Topeka,* pp. 166-196; Rudolph M. Lapp, *Blacks in Gold Rush California* (New Haven, Conn.: Yale University Press, 1977), pp. 170-173; Daniels, *Pioneer Urbanites,* pp. 37-43; de Graaf, "The City of Black Angels," pp. 326-330; McLagan, *A Peculiar Paradise,* pp. 115, 129, 144-145.

CHAPTER 7

Gilchrist Stewart

1. Biographical information on Gilchrist Stewart's career is scattered in numerous sources. See Ann J. Lane, *The Brownsville Affair: National Crisis and Black Reaction* (Port Washington, N.Y.: Kennikat Press, 1971), pp. 27-28, 97-98; *Crisis* 1 (August 1911): 146-147; Mary Church Terrell, *A Colored Woman in a White World* (Washington, D.C.: Ransdell, 1940); Louis R. Harlan and Raymond W. Smock, eds., *The Booker T. Washington Papers,* vol. 12, 1912-1914 (Urbana: University of Illinois Press, 1982), pp. 31, 49, 89-91; Emma Lou Thornbrough, *T. Thomas Fortune, Militant Journalist* (Chicago, Ill.: University of Chicago Press, 1971), pp. 276-277, 284, 315; John D. Weaver, *The Brownsville Raid* (New York: W.W. Norton, 1970), pp. 104, 108; Louis R. Harlan, ed., *The Booker T. Washington Papers,* vol. 3, 1889-95 (Urbana: University of Illinois Press, 1974), pp. 444, 447, 453, 455-456; J. Clay Smith, Jr., *Emancipation: The Making of the Black Lawyer, 1844-1944* (Philadelphia: University of Pennsylvania Press, 1993), pp. 295, 400, 441.

2. Like his brother McCants, Gilchrist Stewart also misreported his place of birth throughout his life. I have concluded that he was born in Orangeburg, South Carolina.

3. Charlotte Harris Stewart to McCants Stewart, May 16, 1906, Stewart-

Flippin Papers, Moorland-Spingarn Research Center, Howard University (hereinafter cited as Stewart-Flippin Papers); Rayford W. Logan and Michael R. Winston, eds., *Dictionary of American Negro Biography* (New York: W.W. Norton, 1982), pp. 73–74, 571–573.

4. T. McCants Stewart to McCants and Gilchrist Stewart, February 14, 1893, Stewart-Flippin Papers; Louis R. Harlan, *Booker T. Washington: The Wizard of Tuskegee, 1901–1915* (New York: Oxford University Press, 1983), p. 144; Harlan, ed., *The Booker T. Washington Papers,* vol 3, pp. 455–456.

5. *Tuskegee Alumni Bulletin* 8 (October 1926): 8; Harlan, *Booker T. Washington: The Wizard of Tuskegee,* p. 156; Harlan, *Booker T. Washington: The Making of a Black Leader, 1856–1901* (New York: Oxford University Press, 1972), pp. 272–287; T. McCants Stewart to McCants Stewart, April 11, 1894, Stewart-Flippin Papers.

6. T. McCants Stewart to Booker T. Washington, May 18, 1894, Box 119, Booker T. Washington Papers, Library of Congress (hereinafter cited as Washington Papers); T. McCants Stewart to McCants Stewart, April 11, 1894, Stewart-Flippin Papers.

7. *Catalogue of the Tuskegee Normal and Industrial Institute, 1893–94* (Tuskegee, Ala.: Normal School Press, 1894), p. 33; Harlan, *Booker T. Washington: The Wizard of Tuskegee,* pp. 144–146.

8. *Catalogue of the Tuskegee Normal and Industrial Institute, 1898–99* (Tuskegee, Ala.: Normal School Press, 1899), pp. 43, 77–79.

9. "Biographical sketch of Gilchrist Stewart," n.d., Stewart-Flippin Papers; "Undated newspaper clipping of Gilchrist Stewart," Stewart-Flippin Papers; Thornbrough, *T. Thomas Fortune,* p. 176.

10. "Biographical sketch of Gilchrist Stewart," n.d., Stewart-Flippin Papers; T. McCants Stewart to McCants [Stewart], June 3, June 18, June 8, May 22, 1896, Stewart-Flippin Papers; Clark Smith to Carlotta Stewart-Lai, September 8, 1926, Stewart-Flippin Papers.

11. Gilchrist Stewart to Booker T. Washington, [1900], reel 16, Washington Papers.

12. Gilchrist Stewart to Emmett Scott, April 11, May 9, 1914, reel 16, Washington Papers.

13. Verina Morton-Jones to McCants Stewart, May 13, 1907, May 8, 1910, Stewart-Flippin Papers; "In Relation to the Estate of Gilchrist Stewart," [1926–1927], Stewart-Flippin Papers. Dr. Daniel T. Williams, Tuskegee University archivist, also provided information on Gilchrist Stewart's employment.

14. T. McCants Stewart to McCants Stewart, January 10, 1905, June 6, 1905, Stewart-Flippin Papers.

15. T. McCants Stewart to McCants Stewart, December 15, 1908, Stewart-Flippin Papers.

16. T. McCants Stewart to McCants Stewart, June 13, 1910, September 26, 1910, Stewart-Flippin Papers.

17. T. McCants Stewart to McCants Stewart, June 6, 1905, Stewart-Flippin Papers.

18. Gilchrist Stewart to Mary Church Terrell, September 23, 1909, reel 23, Mary Church Terrell Papers, Library of Congress.

19. Harlan, *Booker T. Washington: The Wizard of Tuskegee,* pp. 311-313, 375; Lane, *The Brownsville Affair,* pp. 25-31; *Crisis* l (August 1911): 146-147; Thornbrough, *T. Thomas Fortune,* pp. 276-277; Gilchrist Stewart to Emmett Scott, February 7, 1905; Gilchrist Stewart to Booker T. Washington, reel 16, Washington Papers.

20. Lane, *The Brownsville Affair,* pp. 25-31, 41, 78-79; Terrell, *A Colored Woman in a White World,* pp. 177, 211-212, 269-273; Weaver, *The Brownsville Raid,* p. 104; Stewart to Booker T. Washington, June 10, 1900, reel 16, Washington Papers; For background information on the Philippine Insurrection, consult Henry F. Graff, ed., *American Imperialism and the Philippine Insurrection* (Boston, Mass.: Little, Brown, 1969); Brian M. Linn, *Guardians of Empire: The U.S. Army and the Pacific, 1902-1940* (Chapel Hill: University of North Carolina Press, 1997), pp. 23-77.

21. Lane, *The Brownsville Affair,* pp. 25-31; Weaver, *The Brownsville Raid,* pp. 145-181; Emma Lou Thornbrough, "The Brownsville Episode and the Negro Vote," *Mississippi Valley Historical Review* 44 (December 1957): 469-492; Harlan, *Booker T. Washington: The Wizard of Tuskegee,* pp. 323-337; Telegram, Gilchrist Stewart to President Theodore Roosevelt, December 8, 1906, series 1, reel 70, Theodore Roosevelt Papers, Library of Congress (hereinafter cited as Roosevelt Papers).

22. *Summary Discharge or Mustering Out of Regiments or Companies* (Washington, D.C.: Government Printing Office, 1906); Weaver, *The Brownsville Raid,* pp. 15-42.

23. William S. McFeely, *Grant: A Biography* (New York: W.W. Norton, 1981).

24. *Inquiry Relative to Certain Companies of the Twenty-fifth United States Infantry, Preliminary Report of the Commission of the Constitution League of the United States,* December 10, 1906, Senate Document No. 107, 59th Cong., 2nd session; Thornbrough, "The Brownsville Episode and the Negro Vote," 469-492; Thornbrough, *T. Thomas Fortune,* p. 284; Lane, *The Brownsville Affair,* pp. 27-28; Weaver, *The Brownsville Raid,* p. 108; James A. Tinsley, "Roosevelt, Foraker, and the Brownsville Affray," *Journal of Negro History* 41 (January 1956): 43-65.

25. W. Carpenter, U.S. War Department, December 1, 1906, Memo regarding Gilchrist Stewart, Records of the Adjutant General's Office, Record Group 94, National Archives; Telegrams, Gilchrist Stewart to William Howard Taft, November 23, 1906, November 29, 1906, Records of the Adjutant General's Office, Record Group 94, National Archives; Booker T. Washington to Military Secretary, War Department, November 26, 1906, Records of the Adjutant General's Office, Record Group 94, National Archives; William Howard Taft, "Preliminary Statement By the Secretary of War to the Arrangement of the Evidence," [1906], Records of the Adjutant General's Office, Record Group 94, National Archives; Joseph Benson Foraker, *Notes of a Busy Life,* vol. 2 (Cincinnati, Ohio: Stewart and Kidd, 1917), p. 325; Francis J. Grimké to Senator Joseph B. Foraker, April 15, 1908, Box 18, Joseph B. Foraker Papers, Cincinnati Historical Society.

26. Weaver, *The Brownsville Raid,* pp. 145–182; Lane, *The Brownsville Affair,* pp. 33–52; Harlan, *Booker T. Washington: The Wizard of Tuskegee,* p. 323; Harlan, ed., *The Booker T. Washington Papers,* vol. 3, p. 455; *Inquiry Relative to Certain Companies of the Twenty-fifth United States Infantry,* pp. 1–32.

27. Gilchrist Stewart to Senator Joseph B. Foraker, September 10, 1909, Box 125, Joseph B. Foraker Papers, Cincinnati Historical Society.

28. Stewart to Washington, April 11, 1906, reel 16, Washington Papers; Stewart to Washington, December 16, 1912, quoted in Harlan and Smock, eds., *The Booker T. Washington Papers,* vol. 12, pp. 90–91; Booker T. Washington also took an interest in the plight of Jack Johnson, but never spoke out publicly on this matter. See Charles W. Anderson to Emmett Scott, December 26, 1908, Anderson to Scott, July 12, 1910, reel 21, Washington Papers; Anderson to Scott, November 5, 1913, reel 22, Washington Papers.

29. Thornbrough, *T. Thomas Fortune,* pp. 276–277.

30. Stewart to Emmett Scott, January 20, 1904, reel 16, Washington Papers; Stewart to Booker T. Washington, February 13, 1906, reel 16, Washington Papers.

31. Stewart to Scott, January 20, 1904, reel 16, Washington Papers; Harlan and Smock, eds., *The Booker T. Washington Papers,* vol. 12, pp. 31, 49, 195.

32. Harlan, *Booker T. Washington: The Wizard of Tuskegee,* pp. 311–313, 375; On the origins and philosophy of the Niagara Movement, see Elliott Rudwick, "The Niagara Movement," *Journal of Negro History* 42 (July 1957): 177–200; David L. Lewis, *W. E. B. Du Bois: Biography of a Race, 1868–1919* (New York: Henry Holt, 1993), pp. 321–332, 339–340, 439; Charles W. Anderson to Emmett Scott, February 15, 1908; Anderson to Booker T. Washington, April 1, 1908, April 19, 1910, January 16, 1911, January 23, 1911, reel 21, Washington Papers.

33. Stewart to Washington, April 11, 1906, reel 16, Washington Papers.

34. Stewart to Washington, February 13, 1906, reel 16, Washington Papers.

35. *Crisis* 1 (August 1911): 146–147; "Gilchrist Stewart, Chairman of New York Vigilance Committee," New York NAACP, [1910–1911], Stewart-Flippin Papers; Stewart to J. E. Spingarn, September 10, 1911, July 11, 1914, July 31, 1916, Box 95-2, J. E. Spingarn Papers, Moorland-Spingarn Research Center (hereinafter cited as Spingarn Papers); W. E. B. Du Bois to J. E. Spingarn, n.d., [1911], Box 95-2, Spingarn Papers; Stewart to Spingarn, September 11, 1911, December 16, 1912, December 1, 1913, Box 95-5, Spingarn Papers; Charles Flint Kellogg, *NAACP: A History of the National Association for the Advancement of Colored People* (Baltimore, Md.: Johns Hopkins University Press, 1967), pp. 121–123.

36. Anderson to Washington, November 10, 1906, December 26, 1905, reel 20, Washington Papers.

37. Anderson to Washington, January 19, 1906, January 4, January 8, January 14, January 19, January 21, 1907, reel 20, Washington Papers; Stewart to Washington, December 16, 1912; Washington to Stewart, December 19, 1912, quoted in Harlan and Smock, eds., *The Booker T. Washington Papers,* vol. 12, pp. 90–91; Washington to Anderson, December 6, 1907, reel 20, Washington Papers; Harlan, *Booker T. Washington: The Wizard of Tuskegee,* pp. 374–376; August Meier,

Negro Thought in America, 1880–1915: Racial Ideologies in the Age of Booker T. Washington (Ann Arbor: University of Michigan Press, 1963), pp. 180–181.

38. Stewart to Scott, January 20, 1904; Scott to Stewart, February 7, 1904, reel 16, Washington Papers.

39. Stewart to J. E. Spingarn, March 10, 1917, Box 95–2, Spingarn Papers; Ross, *J. E. Spingarn and the Rise of the NAACP, 1911–1939* (New York: Atheneum, 1972), p. 90; Kellogg, *NAACP*, pp. 250–256.

40. Interview with Judge Franklin W. Morton, Jr., October 29–30, 1990. Sarasota, Florida; Katherine Stewart Flippin, "Notes on the Collection," n.d. [1976], Stewart-Flippin Papers.

41. Alice Franklin Stewart to Carlotta Stewart-Lai, February 25, 1927, April 24, 1927, Stewart-Flippin Papers; Cecilia Cianci to Carlotta Stewart-Lai, September 28, 1926, Stewart-Flippin Papers.

42. Albert S. Broussard, "Carlotta Stewart-Lai: A Black Teacher in the Territory of Hawai'i," *Hawaiian Journal of History* 24 (1990): 129–154; Eleanor C. Nordyke, *The Peopling of Hawai'i*, 2d ed. (Honolulu: University of Hawaii Press, 1989).

43. Verina Morton-Jones to Carlotta Stewart-Lai, August 29, 1926, Stewart-Flippin Papers; Morton-Jones to Stewart-Lai, September 2, 1926, Stewart-Flippin Papers; "In the Matter of the Application for Letters of Administration on the Estate of Gilchrist Stewart Deceased," February 24, 1927, Surrogate Court, County of New York, Stewart-Flippin Papers; William L. Patterson to Catherine [*sic*] Stewart, August 31, 1926, Stewart-Flippin Papers; P. E. Godridge to Bankers Trust Company, September 2, 1926, Stewart-Flippin Papers; "In Relation to the Estate of Gilchrist Stewart," [1926], Stewart-Flippin Papers; New York *Age*, August 28, 1926; Cleveland *Gazette*, August 28, 1926.

44. Some representative studies of black leadership on the local level include Theodore Rosengarten, *All God's Dangers: The Life of Nate Shaw* (New York: Alfred A. Knopf, 1974); Raymond Gavins, *The Perils and Prospects of Southern Black Leadership: Gordon Blaine Hancock, 1884–1970* (Durham, N.C.: Duke University Press, 1977); John Hope Franklin, *George Washington Williams: A Biography* (Chicago, Ill.: University of Chicago Press, 1985); George C. Wright, "William Henry Steward: Moderate Approach to Black Leadership," in Leon Litwack and August Meier, eds., *Black Leaders of the Nineteenth Century* (Urbana: University of Illinois Press, 1988), pp. 275–289; Darlene Clark Hine, *When the Truth Is Told: A History of Black Women's Culture and Community in Indiana, 1875–1950* (Indianapolis, Ind.: National Council of Negro Women Indianapolis Section, 1981); Eric Foner, "Black Reconstruction Leaders at the Grass Roots," in Leon Litwack and August Meier, eds., *Black Leaders of the Nineteenth Century* (Urbana: University of Illinois Press, 1988), pp. 219–234.

45. Weaver, *The Brownsville Raid* (1970. College Station, Tex.: Texas A & M University Press, 1992), pp. 321–323; On the NAACP's legal strategy, consult Richard Kluger, *Simple Justice: The History of Brown v. Board of Education and Black America's Struggle for Equality*, 2 vols. (New York: Alfred A. Knopf, 1975); Ross, *J. E. Spingarn and the Rise of the NAACP, 1911–1939*, pp. 106–115.

CHAPTER 8
Carlotta Stewart Lai

1. Albert S. Broussard, "Carlotta Stewart-Lai, A Black Teacher in the Territory of Hawai'i," *Hawaiian Journal of History* 24 (1990): 129–154; Stephanie J. Shaw, *What a Woman Ought To Be and To Do: Black Professional Women Workers during the Jim Crow Era* (Chicago, Ill., and London: University of Chicago Press, 1996).

2. William Atherton Du Puy, *Hawaii and Its Race Problem* (Washington, D.C.: Government Printing Office, 1923), pp. 122–123; Sidney L. Gulick, *Mixing the Races in Hawaii: A Study of the Coming Neo-Hawaiian American Race* (Honolulu: Hawaiian Board Book Rooms, 1937), pp. 189–191; Ruth Tabrah, *Hawaii, A Bicentennial History* (New York: Norton, 1980), pp. 69–70, 120, 136; Interview with Judge Franklin M. Morton, Jr., October 29–30, 1990, Sarasota, Florida. Judge Morton, a relative of Carlotta's, recalled that she visited the family on several occasions during his childhood in Brooklyn. Interview with Katherine Stewart Flippin, July 19, 1986, San Francisco. Flippin, Carlotta's niece, recalled that Carlotta made frequent trips back to the mainland to visit her family in both Portland and San Francisco. Carlotta also made at least one trip to Brooklyn after she settled in Hawaii. See Verina Morton-Jones to Carlotta Stewart, January 23, 1927, Stewart-Flippin Papers.

3. Honolulu *Advertiser*, July 8, July 10, 1952.

4. *Pacific Commercial Advertiser*, November 29, 1898; Takara, "Who Is the Black Woman in Hawaii?," in Nancy Foon Young and Judy R. Parrish, eds., *Montage* (Honolulu, Hawaii: General Assistance Center for the Pacific), pp. 86–87; R. A. Greer, "Blacks in Old Hawaii," *Honolulu* 21 (November 1986): 120–121, 183–184.

5. Ralph S. Kuykendall and A. Grove Day, *Hawaii, A History: From Polynesian Kingdom to American Statehood*, rev. ed. (Englewood Cliffs. N.J.: Prentice-Hall, 1961), pp. 178, 184, 306.

6. Ralph S. Kuykendall, *The Hawaiian Kingdom*, vol. 3, 1874–1893, *The Kalakaua Dynasty* (Honolulu: University of Hawaii Press, 1967), pp. 46–78, 94–96, 112–117.

7. Kuykendall, *The Hawaiian Kingdom*, vol. 3, pp. 53–62; Ralph S. Kuykendall, *The Hawaiian Kingdom*, vol. 2, 1854–1874, *Twenty Critical Years* (Honolulu: University of Hawaii Press, 1966), pp. 135–176.

8. Albert S. Broussard, "McCants Stewart: The Struggles of a Black Attorney in the Urban West," *Oregon Historical Quarterly* 89 (Summer 1988): 156–179.

9. "Commencement Invitation," Oahu College, June 1902, Stewart-Flippin Papers; "Oahu College Commencement," June 27, 1902, Stewart-Flippin Papers; C. T. Rogers, secretary, Department of Public Instruction, Territory of Hawaii to Carlotta Stewart, July 23, 1902, Stewart-Flippin Papers; Interviews with Katherine Stewart Flippin, July 19, 1986, June 4, 1987, San Francisco; *Report of the Superintendent of Public Instruction to the Governor of the Territory of Hawaii, 1902–1904* (Honolulu, 1904); Telephone interview with Mrs. Mary Judd, archivist,

Punahou School, June 27, l989; Mary S. Judd to Albert S. Broussard, June 27, 1989; *The Oahuan*, Commencement (1902).

10. Rogers to Stewart, July 23, 1902, Stewart-Flippin Papers.

11. M. Bobbitt to Carlotta Stewart, November 13, 1906, Stewart-Flippin Papers.

12. Carlotta Stewart to McCants Stewart, March 4, August 12, 1906, January 17, September 4, September 27, 1907, Stewart-Flippin Papers; On the economic status of black female wage-earners, consult David M. Katzman, *Seven Days a Week: Women and Domestic Service in Industrializing America* (New York: Oxford University Press, 1978), pp. 184–222; Jacqueline Jones, *Labor of Love, Labor of Sorrow, Black Women, Work, and the Family from Slavery to the Present* (New York: Basic Books, 1985); William H. Harris, *The Harder We Run: Black Workers since the Civil War* (New York: Oxford University Press, 1985), pp. 65, 121–122, 135, 183; Darlene Clark Hine, *Black Women in White: Racial Conflict and Cooperation in the Nursing Profession, 1890–1950* (Bloomington: Indiana University Press, 1989), pp. 93–94; Elizabeth Clark-Lewis, *Living In, Living Out: African American Domestics in Washington, D.C., 1910–1940* (Washington, D.C.: Smithsonian Institution Press, 1994).

13. Carlotta Stewart to McCants Stewart, March 4, 1906, Stewart-Flippin Papers.

14. Carlotta Stewart to McCants Stewart, August 12, 1906, January 17, 1907, Stewart-Flippin Papers.

15. Carlotta Stewart to McCants Stewart, March 4, 1906, February 11, 1907, September 4, 1907, Stewart-Flippin Papers; Steward, *Fifty Years in the Gospel Ministry*, pp. 308–309.

16. Nordyke, "Blacks in Hawaii: A Demographic and Historical Perspective," *Hawaiian Journal of History* 22 (1988): 242; Bobette Gugliotta, *Nolle Smith: Cowboy, Engineer, Statesman* (New York: Dodd, Mead, 1971), pp. 70, 96–104, 119, 139; Hubert H. White, "Negroes in Hawaii," *Ebony* (July 1959): 25–34.

17. Carlotta Stewart to McCants Stewart, September 4, 1907, Stewart-Flippin Papers.

18. Export Manager, Madam C. J. Walker Manufacturing Company to Mrs. [Carlotta Stewart] Lai, 15 July 1926, Stewart-Flippin Papers. Brief biographical sketches of Madam C. J. Walker and her business enterprise are contained in Rayford W. Logan and Michael P. Winston, eds., *Dictionary of American Negro Biography* (New York: Norton, 1982), p. 621, and Darlene Clark Hine, ed., *Black Women in America: An Historical Encylopedia* (Brooklyn, N.Y.: Carlson Publishing, 1993), pp. 1209–1214; New York *Times Magazine*, November 4, 1917.

19. Carlotta Stewart to McCants Stewart, January 17, 1907, Stewart-Flippin Papers.

20. Ibid.; Alice Stewart to Carlotta Stewart, March 24, 1927, Stewart-Flippin Papers.

21. Carlotta Stewart to McCants Stewart, January 17, 1907, Stewart-Flippin Papers.

22. Broussard, "McCants Stewart," pp. 157–159.

23. Carlotta Stewart to McCants Stewart, August 12, 1906, Stewart-Flippin Papers.

24. Carlotta Stewart to McCants Stewart, January 17, 1907, Stewart-Flippin Papers.

25. Ibid.

26. Carlotta Stewart to McCants Stewart, October 22, 1907, Stewart-Flippin Papers.

27. Carlotta Stewart to McCants Stewart, September 27, 1907, Stewart-Flippin Papers.

28. Carlotta Stewart to McCants Stewart, February 11, 1907, Stewart-Flippin Papers.

29. County Clerk to Carlotta Stewart, Principal, Koolau Public School, September 7, 1909, Stewart-Flippin Papers; Kauai *Garden Island*, September 19, 1911, March 12, 1912, January 14, 1913, all in Stewart-Flippin Papers; Koolau School Principals, n.d., Department of Education, Kauai School District Administrative Office.

30. Lawrence B. de Graaf, "The City of Black Angels: Emergence of the Los Angeles Ghetto, 1890-1930," *Pacific Historical Review* 39 (August 1970): 323-352; de Graaf, "Race, Sex, and Region: Black Women in the American West, 1850-1920," *Pacific Historical Review* 49 (May 1980): 285-313; Broussard, "McCants Stewart," pp. 157-179; Ronald G. Coleman, "A History of Blacks in Utah, 1825-1910," Ph.D. dissertation, University of Utah, 1980; Brian R. Werner, "Colorado's Pioneer Blacks: Migration, Occupations and Race Relations in the Centennial State," Senior honors thesis, University of Northern Colorado, 1979; Quintard Taylor, Jr., "A History of Blacks in the Pacific Northwest, 1788-1970," Ph.D. dissertation, University of Minnesota, 1977; Douglas Henry Daniels, *Pioneer Urbanites: A Social and Cultural History of Black San Francisco* (Philadelphia, Penn.: Temple University Press, 1980).

31. *Hanamaulu School World*, June 2, 1933; "Hanamaulu School Grand Reunion," July 28-29, 1989, Kauai Historical Society; *Kauai Garden Island*, June 11, 1944, June 19, 1945; Nordyke, "Blacks in Hawaii," p. 242.

32. Honolulu *Star Bulletin*, August 26, 1926; *Hanamaulo School World*, June 2, 1933; "Schools of Kauai, 1940-1944," Stewart-Flippin Papers; "Kauai High School Commencement Exercises," June 7, 1926, Stewart-Flippin Papers.

33. Program, "8th Annual Convention of the Hawaii Education Association," Honolulu, December 28-30, 1927, copy in Stewart-Flippin Papers; "Annual Convention of the Kauai Education Association," October 28, 1927, Parish House, Lihue, Kauai, copy in Stewart-Flippin Papers; Hawaii *Educational Review* 16 (June 1928); "Report of the Committee of the Kauai Historical Society Appointed to Report on the Preparing a History of Kauai," June 14, 1948, Kauai Historical Society.

34. See, for example, Paula Giddings, *When and Where I Enter: The Impact of Black Women on Race and Sex in America* (New York: William Morrow, 1984); Darlene Clark Hine, *When the Truth Is Told: A History of Black Women's Culture and Community in Indiana, 1875-1950* (Indianapolis, Ind.: The National Council of Negro Women Indianapolis Section, 1981).

35. Interview with Katherine Flippin, conducted by Diana Lachatanere, March

1977–June 1978, Black Women Oral History Project, Schlesinger Library, Radcliffe College (hereinafter cited as Flippin Interview); Telephone interview with Franklin W. Morton, Jr., June 12, 1990.

36. Telephone Interview with Eleanor Anderson, March 9, 1990; Letter, Eleanor Anderson to Albert S. Broussard, January 19, 1990; Flippin interview, March 1977–June 28, 1978; Interview with Eleanor Anderson, May 20, 1987, conducted by the Center for Oral History, University of Hawaii.

37. On the role of black women in benevolent and reform societies see Cynthia Neverdon-Morton, *Afro-American Women of the South and the Advancement of the Race, 1895–1925* (Knoxville: University of Tennessee Press, 1989); Dorothy Sterling, ed., *We Are Your Sisters: Black Women in the Nineteenth Century* (New York: Norton, 1984), pp. 418–450; Gerda Lerner, "Community Work of Black Club Women," *Journal of Negro History* 59 (April 1974): 158–167; Darlene Clark Hine, "To Be Gifted, Female, and Black," *Southwest Review* 67 (Autumn 1982): 357–369.

38. Verina Morton-Jones to Carlotta Stewart Lai, November 19, 1926, October 31, 1926, Stewart-Flippin Papers; Nancy J. Weiss, *The National Urban League, 1910–1940* (New York: Oxford University Press, 1974), p. 320; Chicago *Defender,* February 8, 1919; "Lincoln Settlement Follies, 1929," benefit for Lincoln Settlement House, Brooklyn Urban League, 1929, original copy in the possession of Judge Franklin W. Morton, Jr.

39. *Advertiser,* January 7, April 3, April 4, 1901; March 5, 1903; January 22, 1924; Katherine F. Gerould, "Honolulu: The Melting Pot," *Scribner's Magazine* 59 (May 1916): 517–537. Gerould's article is typical of the racism that many American writers expressed toward the Hawaiian people. For an analysis of Hawaiian newspapers, including the racist views of the Honolulu *Advertiser,* consult Helen G. Chapin "Newspapers of Hawaii 1834 to 1903: From He Liona to the Pacific Cable," *Hawaiian Journal of History* 18 (1984): 47–86.

40. Dr. Thomas A. Burch, Hawaii Department of Health, to Dorothy Porter, Curator Moorland-Spingarn Research Center, March 7, 1973, Stewart-Flippin Papers. For a broad survey of interracial marriage in Hawaii, see Romanzo C. Adams, *Interracial Marriage in Hawaii: A Study of the Mutually Conditioned Processes of Acculturation and Amalgamation* (New York, 1937).

41. Verina Morton-Jones to Carlotta Stewart Lai, March 27, 1927, Stewart-Flippin Papers.

42. "Obituary of Yun Tim Lai," [1935], Stewart-Flippin Papers.

43. Lihue *Garden Island,* June 15, 1944, August 29, 1944.

44. Carlotta Stewart to Ruth A. Ching, n.d. [1952], Stewart-Flippin Papers.

45. Stewart to Ching, n.d. [1952], Stewart-Flippin Papers; Anthony Yun Seto to Dr. Sau Yee Chang, December 28, 1952, Stewart-Flippin Papers.

46. Carlotta Stewart to Ruth A. Ching, n.d. [1951–1952], Stewart-Flippin Papers.

47. Stewart to Ching, n.d. [1952], Stewart-Flippin Papers.

48. Carlotta Stewart to Ruth A. Ching, n.d. [1951–1952], Stewart-Flippin Papers.

49. Carlotta Stewart to McCants Stewart, March 4, 1906, Stewart-Flippin Papers; Carlotta Stewart, Diary, January 6, January 13, 1952, Stewart-Flippin Papers.

50. Carlotta Stewart, Diary, January 13, January 16, 1952, Stewart-Flippin Papers.

51. Carlotta Stewart, Diary, January 27, January 28, 1952, Stewart-Flippin Papers.

52. Carlotta Stewart, Diary, March 18, 1952, Stewart-Flippin Papers; "Burial Records and Plot of T. McCants Stewart," lot 18, section 5, Oahu cemetery, Honolulu, Hawaii.

53. Carlotta Stewart, Diary, March 27, April 5, April 16, April 17, 1952, Stewart-Flippin Papers.

54. Carlotta Stewart, Diary, May 4, 1952, Stewart-Flippin Papers.

55. Carlotta Stewart, Diary, May 15, 1952, Stewart-Flippin Papers.

56. Thomas A. Burch to Dorothy Porter, March 7, 1973, Stewart-Flippin Papers. My request for an official death certificate from the Hawaii Department of Public Health was denied, since birth and death records are provided only for members of the immediately family. Under Hawaii law, seventy-five years must pass before these documents can be provided to researchers. An obituary of Lai appeared in the Honolulu *Advertiser* on July 8, 1952. Mrs. Eleanor Anderson, whose mother was also in the Manoa nursing home during Carlotta's illness, informed me that Carlotta died of cancer. Telephone interview with Mrs. Eleanor Anderson, March 9, 1990; "Burial Records and Plot of T. McCants Stewart," lot 18, section 5, Oahu cemetery.

57. de Graaf, "Race, Sex and Region," pp. 285–313; On the merits of placing Hawaii in the broader context of western history, consult John Whitehead, "Hawai'i: The First and Last Far West?" *Western Historical Quarterly* 23 (May 1992): 153–177.

58. Beth Bailey and David Farber, *The First Strange Place: The Alchemy of Race and Sex in World War II Hawaii* (New York: Free Press, 1992), pp. 133–142; Beth Bailey and David Farber, "The Double V Campaign in World War II Hawaii: African Americans, Racial Ideology, and Federal Power," *Journal of Social History* 26 (Spring 1993): 817–843.

59. Whitehead, "Hawai'i: The First and Last Far West?" p. 156.

60. Broussard, "McCants Stewart," pp. 157–160.

61. Patricia Nelson Limerick, "The Multicultural Islands," *American Historical Review* 97 (February 1992): 121–135; Eleanor C. Nordyke, *The Peopling of Hawaii*, 2d ed. (Honolulu: University of Hawaii Press, 1989).

CHAPTER 9

Robert Flippin and Katherine Stewart Flippin

1. Elizabeth McLagan, *A Peculiar Paradise: A History of Blacks in Oregon, 1788–1940* (Portland, Ore.: Georgian Press, 1980), pp. 129–146.

2. "Early-day black Portlanders," undated clipping, Portland *Oregonian*, courtesy of Oregon Historical Society; Portland *Observer*, February 23, 1983, p. 8.

3. Interview with Katherine Stewart Flippin, March 1977-June 1978, pp. 2, 35-36, Black Women Oral History Project, Schlesinger Library, Radcliffe College (hereafter cited as Flippin interview).

4. Flippin interview, p. 35.

5. T. McCants Stewart to McCants and Gilchrist Stewart, August 7, 1893, Stewart-Flippin Papers.

6. Kenneth L. Kusmer, *A Ghetto Takes Shape: Black Cleveland, 1870-1930* (Urbana: University of Illinois Press, 1976), p. 115.

7. Albert S. Broussard, "McCants Stewart: The Struggles of a Black Attorney in the Urban West," *Oregon Historical Quarterly* 89 (Summer 1988): 167.

8. Broussard, "McCants Stewart," pp. 171-172.

9. Interview with Katherine Stewart Flippin, February 17, 1976, San Francisco.

10. Albert S. Broussard, "Organizing the Black Community in the San Francisco Bay Area, 1915-30," *Arizona and the West* 23 (Winter 1981): 353-354.

11. *History of the Booker T. Washington Community Center, 1920-1970* (San Francisco, Calif., n.d.).

12. Interview with Katherine Stewart Flippin, June 5, 1987, San Francisco; On A. P. Alberga's life, see the oral interview conducted by Albert S. Broussard, December 1, 1976, San Francisco Public Library, Special Collections.

13. Mary D. Weir, University of Minnesota Teacher's Certificate, August 5, 1901, Stewart-Flippin Papers; Fourth Annual Program of the Manning College of Music, Oratory, and Language, June 10, 1895, Stewart-Flippin Papers; Manning College Graduation Recital, Mary D. Weir, June 12, 1896, Stewart-Flippin Papers; Mayme Delia Weir, "Notebook of Holograph Writings and Clippings, n.d, Stewart-Flippin Papers; Interview with Mrs. Josephine Cole, December 9, 1976, San Francisco. Cole was the first black teacher hired by the San Francisco Unified School District. She had a distinguished career as a teacher and administrator before her retirement.

14. McCants Stewart to Katherine Stewart, November 29, 1917, Stewart-Flippin Papers.

15. Flippin interview, March 1977-June 28, 1978, p. 16.

16. Pension Certificate, James S. Weir, Private, 54th Regiment, Massachusetts Volunteer Infantry, June 27, 1890; Flippin interview, p. 67.

17. Albert S. Broussard, *Black San Francisco: The Struggle for Racial Equality in the West, 1900-1954* (Lawrence: University Press of Kansas, 1993), pp. 21-37.

18. Flippin interview, p. 14.

19. On segregation in southern parks, see George C. Wright, *Life behind a Veil: Blacks in Louisville, Kentucky, 1865-1930* (Baton Rouge: Louisiana State University Press, 1985), pp. 5, 207, 244, 274-280.

20. Flippin interview, p. 15.

21. For a broad discussion of domestic service employment, see David M. Katzman, *Seven Days a Week: Women and Domestic Service in Industrializing America* (New York: Oxford University Press, 1978); Elizabeth Clark-Lewis, *Living In, Living Out: African American Domestics in Washington, D.C., 1910-1940* (Washington, D.C.: Smithsonian Institution Press, 1994).

22. Flippin interview, pp. 15–16, 20.

23. On racial discrimination in San Francisco during the early 1900s, see Broussard, *Black San Francisco*, pp. 75–112.

24. Interviews with Katherine Stewart Flippin, February 17, 1976, July 19, 1986, San Francisco; Flippin interview, p. 78.

25. Albert S. Broussard, "George Albert Flippin and Race Relations in a Western Rural Community," *MidWest Review* 12 (1900): 1–15.

26. "Admissions application," Robert B. Flippin, April 7, 1936, Stewart-Flippin Papers. On Flippin's years in Nebraska, consult "Stromsburg High School Academic Transcript," Robert B. Flippin, 1916, Stromsburg Public Schools; Ron Cornwell, Principal, Stromsburg High School to Albert S. Broussard, June 3, 1988, author's files.

27. Interview with Katherine Stewart Flippin, July 19, 1986, San Francisco.

28. *History of the Booker T. Washington Community Center, 1920–1970.*

29. *Special Census of San Francisco, California, Population by Age, Color, and Sex, for Census Tracts: August 1, 1945* (Washington, D.C.: Government Printing Office, 1945); *1950 Census of Population*, vol. 2, pt. 5, *Characteristics of the Population* (Washington, D.C.: Government Printing Office, 1952), pp. 5–207; Broussard, *Black San Francisco*, pp. 133–142.

30. Robert B. Flippin, "The Negro in San Francisco, [1943]," Stewart-Flippin Papers.

31. "In the Districts," San Francisco *Chronicle*, November 29, 1942, January 3, January 17, March 14, April 18, May 2, 1943.

32. See, for example, Rayford W. Logan, ed., *What the Negro Wants* (Chapel Hill: University of North Carolina Press, 1944).

33. Bill Simons to Robert Flippin, January 14, November 18, 1942, Stewart-Flippin Papers.

34. "Districts Reports," San Francisco *Chronicle*, March 16, 1943.

35. Allan H. Spear, *Black Chicago: The Making of a Negro Ghetto, 1890–1920* (Chicago, Ill.: University of Chicago Press, 1967); Gilbert Osofsky, *Harlem: The Making of a Ghetto, 1890–1930* (New York: Harper and Row, 1966); Kenneth L. Kusmer, *A Ghetto Takes Shape: Black Cleveland, 1870–1930* (Urbana: University of Illinois Press, 1976); Peter Gottlieb, *Making Their Own Way: Southern Blacks' Migration to Pittsburgh, 1916–1930* (Urbana: University of Illinois Press, 1987); Elliott Rudwick, *Race Riot at East St. Louis: July 2, 1917* (New York: Atheneum, 1972).

36. Broussard, *Black San Francisco*, pp. 176–178; Charles S. Johnson, *The Negro War Worker in San Francisco* (San Francisco, Calif.: n.p., 1944), p. 90.

37. John W. Beard to Robert Flippin, April 27, 1945; Sidney S. Clark to Robert Flippin, April 9, 1943, Stewart-Flippin Papers; Robert E. Brown to Robert Flippin, September 30, 1941, Stewart-Flippin Papers; Broussard, *Black San Francisco*, pp. 189–192.

38. Charles S. Johnson to Robert Flippin, October 6, 1944, Stewart-Flippin Papers; Charles S. Johnson, *The Negro War Worker in San Francisco*, passim.

39. Robert B. Flippin, "The Negro in San Francisco," [1943], Stewart-Flippin Papers.

40. William L. Patterson to Flippin family, n.d. [1936], Stewart-Flippin Papers. For information on Patterson's career with the International Labor Defense, see Charles H. Martin, *The Angelo Herndon Case and Southern Justice* (Baton Rouge: Louisiana State University Press, 1976), pp. 11–13.

41. Broussard, *Black San Francisco*, pp. 97–104; Arnold Rampersad, *The Life of Langston Hughes*, vol. 1: 1902–1941, *I, Too, Sing America* (New York: Oxford University Press, 1986), pp. 123, 212, 238–240, 276–277.

42. John Pittman to Robert Flippin, April 2, 1941, Stewart-Flippin Papers; Al Richmond, *A Long View from the Left: Memoirs of an American Revolutionary* (New York: Dell, 1972), p. 289.

43. Wilson Record, *Race and Radicalism: The NAACP and the Communist Party in Conflict* (Ithaca, N.Y.: Cornell University Press, 1964); Martin Bauml Duberman, *Paul Robeson* (New York: Alfred A. Knopf, 1988).

44. Roger Daniels, *America's Concentration Camps: A Documentary History of the Relocation and Incarceration of Japanese Americans, 1942–1945* (New York: Garland, 1989); Peter Irons, *Justice at War: The Story of the Japanese American Internment Cases* (New York: Oxford University Press, 1983).

45. William H. Chafe, *The American Woman: Her Changing Social, Economic, and Political Role, 1920–1970* (New York: Oxford University Press, 1972), pp. 135–150; Karen Anderson, *Wartime Women: Sex Roles, Family Relations, and the Status of Women During World War II* (Westport, Conn.: Greenwood, 1981); Susan M. Hartmann, *The Home Front and Beyond: American Women in the 1940s* (Boston, Mass.: Twayne, 1982); Flippin interview, p. 79.

46. Interview with Katherine Stewart Flippin, February 17, 1976, San Francisco.

47. Interviews with Katherine Stewart Flippin, February 17, 1976, July 7, 1986, San Francisco; San Francisco *Tribune*, December 29, 1950; Ann Gillette to Katherine Flippin, n.d., [1951], Stewart-Flippin Papers.

48. Interviews with Katherine Stewart Flippin, July 19, 1986, June 5, 1987, San Francisco.

49. *San Quentin News*, August 6, 1948; Business card, Robert B. Flippin, Institutional Parole Officer, Department of Corrections, California State Prison at San Quentin, in the possession of Judge Franklin W. Morton, Jr.

50. "San Quentin Employee Register," August 5, 1948, California State Archives, Sacramento; "Report on Performance for Permanent Employee," February 28, 1949, Stewart-Flippin Papers (hereinafter cited as Performance Evaluation); "1948 Performance Evaluation"; "1954 Performance Evaluation," Stewart-Flippin Papers; Warden Clinton Duffy to Robert Flippin, August 2, 1949, August 4, 1949, August 11, 1949, Stewart-Flippin Papers. There is only one indication in his entire personnel file which reveals that Flippin may not have been performing at a satisfactory level. Approximately one year after Flippin began working at San Quentin, he was suspended by warden Duffy without pay for fifteen days for an unspecified infraction of prison rules and Flippin's admission of guilt. This problem was apparently corrected to Duffy's satisfaction, for it never resurfaced.

51. Interview with Katherine Stewart Flippin, June 1986, San Francisco.

52. Robert Flippin, "The Homophile in State Prisons," n.d., [1950s], Stewart-Flippin Papers; Interview with Katherine Stewart Flippin, July 19, 1986, San Francisco; Harry Hay, *The Trouble with Harry Hay: The Founder of the Modern Gay Movement* (Boston, Mass.: Alyson Publications, 1990). See also Martin B. Duberman, *Stonewall* (New York: Dutton, 1993).

53. Duffy, *The San Quentin Story*, pp. 150–151; On the changing perception of homosexuality by the American Psychiatric Association, see *Time Magazine* 142 (July 26, 1993), p. 36.

54. Duffy, *The San Quentin Story*, passim; *San Quentin News*, September 20, 1951; May 29, 1956, August 9, 1951, September 15, 1955, *California State Employee*, March 1962; San Francisco *Chronicle*, April 20, 1951; *The Insider*, June–July 1967. The *San Quentin News* was named the best printed newspaper in the U.S. penal system in 1967 and 1968. See *San Quentin News*, January 22, February 23, 1968.

55. Robert B. Flippin, "Delinquency—Prison and After," Sociology e160, Crime and Delinquency, January 24, 1950, Stewart-Flippin Papers.

56. Inmate to Robert Flippin, May 14, 1963, Stewart-Flippin Papers.

57. Inmate to Robert Flippin, May 6, 1963, Stewart-Flippin Papers.

58. San Francisco *Good News*, January 1952, March, 1960, June 1962, May 1963; See also *Mimico Mirror* (April 1957), a monthly publication by the patients at the Drug Addiction Clinic of the Ontario Department of Reform Institution, Mimico, Ontario, Canada.

59. San Francisco *Good News*, February 1952.

60. Albert S. Broussard, "Carlotta Stewart Lai, A Black Teacher in the Territory of Hawai'i," *Hawaiian Journal of History* 24 (1990): 129–154.

61. I wish to thank Katherine Stewart Flippin for sharing the events of her husband's death with me in a lenthy (three hour) interview, July 19, 1986, San Francisco; *San Quentin News*, September 12, 1963, May 21, 1964; San Francisco *Sun-Reporter*, September 14, 1963; San Francisco *News-Call Bulletin*, September 3, 1963; Los Angeles, California *Eagle*, September 12, 1963.

62. *San Quention News*, September 12, 1963; May 21, 1964; *The Insider*, April, 1966.

63. Pat Heaton to Mrs. Robert B. Flippin, n.d. [September, 1963], Stewart-Flippin Papers.

64. Irving Babow and Edward Howden, *A Civil Rights Inventory of San Francisco*, Part 1, *Employment* (San Francisco, 1958); Harvard Sitkoff, *The Struggle for Black Equality, 1954–1980* (New York: Hill and Wang, 1981).

Conclusion

1. John Hope Franklin, *The Color Line: Legacy for the Twenty-First Century* (Columbia: University of Missouri Press, 1993).

2. Paula Giddings, *In Search of Sisterhood: Delta Sigma Theta and the Challenge of the Black Sorority Movement* (New York: William Morrow, 1988); Nina Mjagkij,

Light in the Darkness: African Americans and the YMCA, 1852-1946 (Lexington: University of Kentucky Press, 1994).

3. Ann Lane, *The Browsville Affair: National Crisis and Black Reaction* (Port Washington, N.Y.: Kennikat Press, 1971); John D. Weaver, *The Brownsville Raid* (New York: W.W. Norton, 1970).

4. Gunnar Myrdal, *An American Dilemma: The Negro Problem and Democracy* (New York: Harper and Row, 1994), p. 982.

5. Interviews with Katherine Stewart Flippin, July 7, 1986, June 5, 1987, San Francisco; Interviews with Judge Franklin W. Morton, Jr., October 27-30, 1990, Sarasota, Florida; Katherine Stewart Flippin to Judge Franklin W. Morton, Jr., March 13, 1987, letter in the Morton family papers.

6. William H. Harris, *The Harder We Run: Black Workers since the Civil War* (New York: Oxford University Press, 1982), pp. 121-122; Harvard Sitkoff, *The Struggle for Black Equality, 1954-1980* (New York: Hill and Wang, 1981), pp. 11-12.

7. Richard Dalifiume, "The Forgotten Years of the Negro Revolution," *Journal of American History* 55 (June 1968): 90-106.

8. Gerald D. Nash, *The American West Transformed: The Impact of the Second World War* (Bloomington: Indiana University Press, 1985), p.106.

9. On Ralph Bunche, see Charles P. Henry, ed., *Ralph J. Bunche: Selected Speeches and Writings* (Ann Arbor: University of Michigan Press, 1995); William L. Van Deberg, *New Day in Babylon: The Black Power Movement and American Culture, 1965-1975* (Chicago, Ill.: University of Chicago Press, 1992).

10. Interview with Beryl E. Kean, December 14, 15, 1990, St. Thomas, Virgin Islands.

11. Lawrence B. de Graaf, "Race, Sex, and Region: Black Women in the American West, 1850-1920," *Pacific Historical Review* 49 (May 1980): 285-313.

12. Interviews with Beryl E. Kean, December 14, 15, 1990, St. Thomas, Virgin Islands.

13. Interview with Katherine Stewart Flippin, June 1986, San Francisco.

14. Darlene Clark Hine, "Co-Laborers in the Work of the Lord: Nineteenth-Century Black Women Physicians," in Darlene Clark Hine, *Hine Sight: Black Women and the Re-Construction of American History* (Brooklyn, N.Y.: Carlson, 1994).

15. Willard B. Gatewood, *Aristocrats of Color: The Black Elite, 1880-1920* (Bloomington: Indiana University Press, 1990), p. 345.

16. Albert S. Broussard, *Black San Francisco: The Struggle for Racial Equality in the West, 1900-1954* (Lawrence: University Press of Kansas, 1993), pp. 180-192.

Index

❖ ❖ ❖ ❖ ❖ ❖ ❖